THE CHILDREN OF NATURE

OTHER LOTUS TITLES

Adi B. Hakim, Rustom B. Bhumgara & Jal P. Bapasola	*With Cyclists Around The World*
Ajit Bhattacharjea	*Sheikh Mohammad Abdullah: Tragic Hero of Kashmir*
Anil Dharker	*Icons: Men & Women Who Shaped Today's India*
Aitzaz Ahsan	*The Indus Saga: The Making of Pakistan*
Ajay Mansingh	*Firaq Gorakhpuri: The Poet of Pain & Ecstasy*
Alam Srinivas & TR Vivek	*IPL: The Inside Story*
Amarinder Singh	*The Last Sunset: The Rise & Fall of the Lahore Durbar*
Amjad Ali Khan	*My Father Our Fraternity: The Story of Haafiz Ali Khan*
B.K. Trehan & Indu Trehan	*Retired But Not Tired: Retirement Made Easy*
Indira Menon	*The Madras Quartet: Women in Karnatak Music*
Jaiwant Paul	*The Greased Cartridge: The Heroes and Villains of 1857-58*
John Lal	*Begam Samru: Fading Portrait in a Gilded Frame*
Lakshmi Vishwanathan	*Women of Pride: The Devdasi Heritage*
Lucy Peck	*Agra: The Architectural Heritage*
Lucy Peck	*Delhi a Thousand Years of Building: An INTACH-Roli Guide*
Madan Gopal	*My Life and Times: Munshi Premchand*
M.J. Akbar	*Byline*
M.J. Akbar	*Blood Brothers: A Family Saga*
Maj. Gen. Ian Cardozo	*Param Vir: Our Heroes in Battle*
Maj. Gen. Ian Cardozo	*The Sinking of INS Khukri: What Happened in 1971*
Madhu Trehan	*Tehelka as Metaphor*
Monisha Rajesh	*Around India in 80 Trains*
Noorul Hasan	*Meena Kumari: The Poet*
Rachel Dwyer	*Yash Chopra: Fifty Years in India Cinema*
Rajika Bhandari	*The Raj on the Move: Story of the Dak Bungalow*
R.V. Smith	*Delhi: Unknown Tales of a City*
Salman Akthar	*The Book of Emotions*
Sharmishta Gooptu	*Bengali Cinema: An Other Nation*
Shovana Narayan	*Kathak*
Shrabani Basu	*Spy Princess: The Life of Noor Inayat Khan*
S. Hussain Zaidi	*Dongri to Dubai*
Sunil Raman & Rohit Aggarwal	*Delhi Durbar: 1911 The Complete Story*
Swapan K. Bandyopadhyay	*An Unheard Melody: Annapurna Devi an Authorised Biography*
Thomas Weber	*Going Native: Gandhi's Relationship with Western Women*
Thomas Weber	*Gandhi at First Sight*
Zubin Mehta	*Zubin Mehta: The Score of My Life*

FORTHCOMING TITLES

Ralph Russell	*The Famous Ghalib: The Sound of my Moving Pen*
Kunal Purandare	*Ramakant Achrekar: A Biography*

THE CHILDREN OF NATURE

The Life and Legacy of Ramana Maharshi

SUSAN VISVANATHAN

LOTUS COLLECTION
ROLI BOOKS

Lotus Collection

First published in 2010
Second impression, 2015
The Lotus Collection
An imprint of
Roli Books Pvt. Ltd.
M-75, Greater Kailash II Market, New Delhi 110 048
Phone: ++91 (011) 4068 2000
Fax: ++91 (011) 2921 7185
E-mail: info@rolibooks.com
Website: www.rolibooks.com

Also at Bangalore, Chennai & Mumbai

Cover Design: Massand-Zimmermann Studio

ISBN: 978-81-7436-805-8

Typeset in Goudy Old Style by Roli Books Pvt. Ltd.
and printed at Repro India Ltd., Mumbai.

Dedicated to

Sundar, Mani, Murthy, Rafael Salan, Annie and Mathai Zachariah, Meera, Sandhya and Malli, Bharati, Joelle, J.J., Michael, Suryanandan and Mahalakshmi, Rajam Viswanathan, Ratna Raman and S.R. Iyer, and Mariam Paul, for their wisdom and love, many thanks.

I gratefully acknowledge *India Magazine* 1996, IIC Quarterly 2004 for publishing Chapter one from an early draft of this book, as 'From Death to Devotion' in 2003-04 Spring issue, and reprinted by Penguin in the IIC Collection entitled *Journeys*, Delhi; 2004;

French Information Resource Center and Rupa for publishing *Activism and Detachment* in 'Trajectories of French Thought' 2003-04;

Think India Quarterly for publishing *Pilgrims and Travellers* in Volume 9, Number 4, October-December 2006;

Indian Anthropologist for publishing *Dreams and Death* in Volume 38, Number 1, January-June 2008;

Samyukta for publishing an earlier version of chapter eight as 'Tsunami New Year' in their *Journal of Women's Studies*, Volume 7, 2008 and *Indian Journal of Human Development* for publishing a section of the conclusion in Volume 3, Number 1, January-June 2009.

CONTENTS

11
ACKNOWLEDGEMENTS

13
A VISIT TO RAMANA ASRAMAM

36
ACTIVISM AND DETACHMENT

71
DREAMS AND DEATH

85
RAMANA MAHARSHI

125
TSUNAMI NEW YEAR

148
RETURN TO THE SOURCE

161
ONE HOT SUMMER

192
MID-SUMMER

227
CONCLUSION

245
INDEX

250
REFERENCES

ACKNOWLEDGEMENTS

A book owes many things to many people. I wish to thank my many teachers and friends, and particularly my family who stood by me over the decades, in spite of the many crises brought about by time and temperament.

My friends at the asramam, to whom this book is dedicated, swept aside their anxiety about having a feminist writer, and allowed me access to the archives and to their minds. Their comfort and kindness is a zone to which I keep returning and my debt will never be repaid.

My family in Kerala, orthodox Mar Thoma Christians, were skeptical about my frequent returns but always happy to see me back in the South. Mathai Zachariah and Annie, Ivy and Raju, K. Kuruvilla and Asha, Geeta and Ari, Salome, Stanley and Jessy, Panthapathrayil Sam and Molly, Sally and Kunjootychayen, Hema and Manoj … thank you for your hospitality and kindness.

While the first visit to Tiruvannamalai, in 1996, was made possible only because Shiv Visvanathan held our three very young daughters while I disappeared into the far South, the remaining journeys were made to recover from the fact that fate decreed our lives were to be lived separately henceforth! I was diagnosed with multiple sclerosis, he lived a routine too turbulent for me to bear. Our friendship continues over our children's heads, though we rarely meet.

My sister Esther and my mother Mariam have always been there for me, as has Rajam Viswanathan; they understood me perfectly, that I was first a writer, and then whatever else. My children Meera, Sandhya and Mallika have been the reason for my great happiness and my extended life chances. Being with them, and on their wavelength which rapidly changed year by year as they grew up, has been a source of great joy to me.

To Ratna and Mani, and to Anil Nauriya, many thanks for their calm friendship.

My colleagues and staff at CSSS/SSS JNU have never doubted during these seven years that I was going on field work, and I'm glad that I could read papers based on this work at the Thursday seminar. I'm grateful to JNU for fieldwork grants, to Shri Bharat Kumar for much assistance and to the Centre for Communication and Information, specially Mr Chinmoy Basu, for help with scanning photographs for the book. Dr Mohammed Qasim, my homeopath has tided me through the many years of my illness and is the true representative of the dialogue of religions in his busy clinic in Nizamuddin. I am deeply grateful to Dr Prasada Rao and Dr Vinit Suri for their concern and medical help when I most needed it, and to my yoga teacher in JNU, Sri Ajay Shastri, who helped me with advice and ayurvedic treatments when I needed them.

Chitra Harsha, Jayati Ghosh and Abijit Sen, Praveen Jha and Smita Gupta, Neel Bhattacharya and Chitra Joshi, Ravindra Karnena and Geetika De pitched in for me substantially while I was away on trips to the South, and none of my work in JNU could have been done without their total support.

IIAS, Shimla provided me with wonderful library support, as did JNU, Nehru Memorial Museum and Library, and of course Shiv's books, both loans as well as gifts.

Bettina Baeumer, Fr Gispert, Fr T.K. John, Fr George Keeran, Sarla Kumar, Raphael Salan, friends at the MSH, Paris were wonderful in their encouragement of new writing. I must also thank Dayan Krishnan and Sriram Panchu, Nandini Sundar, Vidya Rao, Shail Mayaram, Shasheej Hegde and Edie and Satish Saberwal. I also thank Leela Dube, Sukh Pamra, Zarina and Idrak Bhatty, Huma Ghosh, Annie Paul, Neena Paul, Apeetha Arunagiri, Vijaya and Setu Ramaswamy, T.V.S. Subramanian, J.P.S. Uberoi, T.K. Oommen and absolutely everyone at Ramanasramam, Tiruvannamalai.

My grateful thanks to Pramod Kapoor, Nandita Bhardwaj, Neelam Narula, Namita Kala, and Supriya Saran for their concern in the production of this book.

1

A VISIT TO RAMANASRAMAM

I met Professor S.C. Dube, the sociologist and litterateur, the author of *Indian Village* (1955), just before he passed away. It was at his home.

He was sitting up in bed dressed in the most beautiful browns and fawns – the khadi kurta and Nehru jacket which that generation wore with such style. He had great difficulty with his breathing, but he smiled at me and in that small room, the world lit up the way it did when S.C. Dube and Leela Dube spoke of their days together: field-work, friends, conversations. S.C. then spoke of the hospital and the *Keralaputri* – 'the daughters of Kerala' – who had nursed him during his illness. He wanted to write a paper on them. He said, 'It will be about the symbols of integration.' He was to write on 'The Sociology of Narrative Forms' for a textbook for young people that I was co-ordinating, but he said that writing about the nurses who had become his friends, who had shared the stories of their lives, would be of greater sociological interest to him personally. Then he said suddenly, 'I dread not being able to sleep at night.'

'Have you tried to meditate?' I asked him. He stared at me blankly for a moment. He recovered his anthropologist's composure where nothing is 'peculiar' – neither polyandry nor cannibalism – not to speak of vision, trance or mysticism. Professor Dube replied, 'Meditation? No, I don't know how to meditate.'

'It might help,' I said cautiously.

And then I told him about Maharshi Ramana. I also told him that I had discovered Ramana quite by 'accident'. I was in grave trouble in 1984 – nine months of lying on my back, absolutely still – a time when I could not go out, work, meet friends, read or write. Towards the end of the ninth month of my pregnancy, I started feeling very frightened, and then one day an old gentleman appeared in my dream and smiled at me. It was a 'secular' dream, or so I thought at that time. It was a beautiful dream, the smile was the most amazing I'd ever seen, and I came through the last weeks of a first and dangerous pregnancy with tranquility. I didn't know who the old man was, but after he'd smiled at me there didn't seem to be anything called fear left.

Years later, I recognized a photograph of Ramana as being that of the gentle old man who had smiled at me.

It didn't change my life. After all I come from a long line of stable Christians, where visions and dreams are treated very matter of factly. We don't even discuss the fact ordinarily, that as a people, we may routinely 'hear' Christ's voice – miracles are a way of life amongst the St Thomas Christians of Kerala.

Professor Dube said, smiling, completely at ease with this story, 'What a great land is India. Christians see Ramana, Muslim musicians have visions of Kali, Hindus see Meenakshi in Mariam. Why should there ever be quarrels in our land if we can see each other's faiths?'

We drank the delicate tea Leela Dube always made and laughed over one thing or another. When I left, I said, 'I should like to come and see you again.' He shook hands with me and said in his formal gentle fashion, 'Please do,' but he didn't look at me at that moment, and though his hand felt strong and warm, I knew it was good-bye.

Following that encounter with Professor Dube, I realized I ought to go to Ramanasramam. I don't think my intention was anything other than anthropological. In 1990, I had affiliated with the Indian Institute of Advanced Study on a 'Religion and Culture' project. I spent the next six years writing a monograph on a French monk, Henri Le Saux, who had come to India and had met Ramana at Tiruvannamalai. Henri Le Saux ,known as Abhishiktananda, had became a wandering monk, a *sanyasi*. He had understood Ramana's life, and therefore attempted a doctrinal dialogue between Hinduism and Christianity. Thus Christianity and Advaita intertwined in Abhishiktananda's life in a strange and dazzling mix. I had to unravel the skein and did so using James Stuart's biography of Abhishiktananda and the latter's own writings. Stuart's work is like a travelogue – the *sanyasi* is constantly moving and in search, and Abhishiktananda's letters are both about the spirit and about the places which were important to him – Kulitallai in the South, and the Himalayas where he spent the last years of his life.

I had been an armchair anthropologist for so long that it was an effort, once I finished my book, to go to Ramanasramam. Would I be able to leave my daughters for two days, how would I go, how would I manage in an alien place? One gets used to a domestic routine, an equilibrium; and 'field-work,' even two days, is usually a life-changing event. I imagined struggling with bus journeys and strangers, and finally said to myself, 'It was structuralist analyses that I was engaged in' and 'Exegesis does not always require field-work experience' – glib phrases, which can keep journeys and adventures at bay.

Finally, my husband's sister's husband's brother's wife came to my rescue. She said she would take me to the asramam, and informed the office of our arrival the next day.

We caught one of those neat buses the Madras State Transport runs to Tiruvannamalai.

Anuradha and I had met just once before, in 1980. Now, this slender doe-eyed beautiful woman was widowed. She went to Ramanasramam every three or four months. She said the meditation there helped her, and she could cope with life without Raju.

We talked for four hours, and the long journey didn't seem so long. The countryside was beautiful – sparse, rugged, orange earth and brown hills, scrub and date palms, thatched roofs, swamps, morning glories growing wild. I had always made unfair comparisons when travelling by train between the topography of Tamil Nadu and my own extravagantly green 'native' land, Kerala. For the first time, journeying to Ramanasramam I understood this terrain and felt at home.

Suddenly, after five hours of travel, a hill appeared. It seemed larger than any hill I'd seen, because it appeared as if out of a frame, right against my eyes.

'That's Arunachala,' Anuradha said, as if she was introducing a friend.

The town was small, untidy and clustered at its base. There was nothing to distinguish it from any other bustling town. Tiruvannamalai, according to geological studies made by French academics, is built on charconite, which is a geological formation of rock associated with the Archaean age when the earth's molten mass condensed into rock, 3.8 billion years ago (*Ramana's Arunachala* 2004: 102). Thus the town is settled on rock which is older than the Himalayas.

> The Tiruvannamalai hill is an imposing landmark with an elevation of 2,634 feet and is the highest peak in the hill ranges, found conspicuously developed in the western and south-western part of Tiruvannamalai; the eastern and south-eastern part of Tiruvannamalai on the other hand is generally a gently undulating plain dotted with few knolls and mounds. (105)

There was the temple, in the heart of the town, one of the largest Shiva temples in India. Its history is recorded from about 750 AD.

> Tiruvannamalai was earlier known as Thiru Anna Nadu and the presiding deity was known as Thiru Anna Nattu Mahadevan. This region was called Thondai Mandalam and was ruled by the Pallavas. It then passed into the hands of the Rashtrakuas, a dynasty to which belonged to Krishna II who undertook important renovation work during the tenth century A.D. The region then came under the rule of chieftains like Kadavaraya, the Banas and Sambuva Raya. From the thirteenth to the fourteenth century, the Pandya kings ruled over it. Then came the Hoysalas who made Tiruvannamalai their capital while they waged war against other kings to establish their supremacy and sovereignty. The Vijayanagar kings who came after the Hoysalas spent enormous amounts of money for the worship and other requirements of the temple. Poets like Saiva Ellapa Navalar have sung in praise of the Naickers of Tanjore who came to power after the Vijayanagar kings for the great service they rendered to the temple. (109)

The authors of this collation comment on the jigsaw appearance of the temple where with every age and royal epoch, there were additions and permutations in the forms of architecture, that appeared as oblations to the gods.

We left our slippers at the gate of the temple and went in.

The editor of *Ramana's Arunachala* describes the structure of the temple thus:

> When we observe the general structure of the temple, we notice that there are five small gopurams on the inner boundary and four big gopurams on the outer boundary. The inner gopurams are known as Kitti gopurams. There are two gopurams in the East and one gopuram each for the other three directions. The first of the two Eastern gopurams is called Kili gopuram. There are indications that this was built in the eleventh century. The gopurams built during this period have no more than five storeys. The kili gopuram was built by Veera Rajendra Chola around 1063 A.D. (109)

The temple tanks, on that first visit, were green and clear and cool. The ground was so hot I could not bear it, but people walked upon the burning gravel as if it was part of the pilgrimage. The cave where Ramana had meditated, when he had emerged through the blinding light of realization, was warm and dark and womb-like.

Outside, the sun burst white. People crowded around the renouncers who heard their problems and gave advice, the ritual psychoanalysts of India.

Crushed jasmines, an elephant, outstretched hands, shaved heads, children sleeping, shards of coconut – all of these began to merge in one ritual moment.

We took an autorickshaw to the asramam. It was a hot bright morning, and everything seemed iridescent and sharply outlined. When I came through the gate I felt waves of excitement and happiness. Six years of writing, drawing from secondary sources and archives, delineating an imagined space, suddenly became real. A man was standing under a giant, centuries old tree, and there was a long line of mendicants to whom he gave food. Anyone who was hungry could come to Sri Ramanasramam and be fed. It was eleven o'clock. The man had a gentle face and an ascetic physical beauty which verged on the classical. Maybe he was a householder, but at that moment, standing under the tree, he belonged to all those people who needed him. He was certainly there because he had heard Ramana calling.

Inside the office we met V.S. Mani. Sri Ramanasramam is run by a Trust. Mani holds office by virtue of his involvement in family traditions and his calling to serve the pilgrims. He is a short delicate man, pale complexioned, with a long face, narrow eyes and a sharp beaky nose. He asked us our names, and said he was glad we had come. One felt immediately one was a valued guest, and that Ramana's home could be one's own for the brief while that was allocated to one by choice, destiny and asramam rules.

Dr Srinivasamurthy came in. He is a big-built man, very reserved and yet concerned, courteous. He spoke elegant English, a guttural nuanced Telugu and Tamil, also the Hindi so essential for communicating with pilgrims from North India. He gave us our keys and along with it we suddenly felt we were free, to follow the path we chose.

Outside peacocks called, and there were families of monkeys. The gardens of the asramam were wild and beautiful and birds rested in the shadows of walls and trees. I felt as if I had come home. It's a state of being, when you feel completely at peace, completely happy.

We went to the room allocated to us. It was newly whitewashed and there were two sturdy wooden beds with clean thick bed-covers, which didn't match. There was a picture of Ramana – the one I like best, because that was the way he had looked when he 'came to see me' when I was ill and exhausted and afraid, just before Meera, my eldest daughter, was born. Other than that, the room was bare, but for a printed notice warning one of thieves and monkeys.

We were late for lunch because the room was so peaceful and quiet that we just lay on the beds breathing in the peace of it all. I suppose the silence came like a shock to me. I lived, at that time, on the outskirts of Delhi 'across the river' and I hurtled to work everyday through miles of cacophonous city roads. Like most Delhi scholars, I entered into the summer with a complete sense of exhaustion and anxiety. Students' exams were just over and there was writing to catch up with, before University reopened. Everything in the summer felt as if it was in quick motion, and like a long distance runner I had got used to the loneliness and the missed heartbeats.

It was blazing hot outside and cool as an earthen pot inside the room. We felt no desire to move. Already it was, for me, a sense of what pilgrims describe as 'Lying in Shiva's arms' – contentment, ease, a quiet. There was no ritual about it, just an implicit understanding that it had actually happened, a state referred in theological texts as 'Being'.

We went for lunch to the main hall. My feet burnt on the sand again, and I had to cool them against the dark earth around the coconut trees, so it took quite a while to get to the main circle of asramam buildings. Everyone was seated on the ground in the spacious dining room, eating quietly. Anu and I felt ashamed at being the last to arrive. Mani, who was supervising with that quiet relaxed authority I grew to associate with him, immediately put us at ease. 'Come and sit here,' he said pointing to the single bench and trestle table against the wall. I wondered if that was where Ramana had once sat. Abhishiktananda, my French monk from Brittany, had described him as sitting facing his pilgrims. 'Oh, no, we'd rather wait,' I said, abashed.

'Please. It will be more convenient for our asramam servers,' Mani said.

It seemed to me then that in Ramana's asramam, all hierarchies disappeared – class, religion, gender, caste – everything was immaterial to Ramana's Advaita.

We sat down at the 'High Table' and when the clean glossy plates arrived – banana leaves – Anu sprinkled it with water and I did the same. It was a feast. The food was incredibly good, a tradition from the time when Ramana himself used to go into the huge adjacent hall to help prepare the meal, and sing odes to the 'frying of the pappad' and the coming into being of the soul! Everyone ate the various courses as if food was life. It wasn't greedy – it was as if people were hungry and being fed, and could eat till they were full.

I spent the rest of the day wandering about watching the monkeys and the peacocks. The peacocks had actually flared their fans and were screaming endlessly. I love that screech: the tax they paid for their beauty, defining 'Nature's sense of proportion'. Ramana was very close to the animals that lived on the mountain, and there were many stories about his love for the monkeys, squirrels, peacocks, cows, goats and deer that came to him.

At four o'clock, Mani saw me standing against a low wall looking at the mountain. I was trying to understand what it was about Arunachala that drew people either through love or curiosity. 'One is called' people said, 'Ramana still initiated through dream and vision.' Well. I was here.

'How long have you been here?' I called out, as Mani came out of some office.

'I don't conduct interviews at a distance,' he said.

'All right then, I'm sorry.' I went up the steps to where he stood. He was a retired professional who was related to Ramana and felt the intensity of obligation towards the places of Ramana's life. He took it all in his stride though – these trust duties were family obligations to carry out with courtesy and affection, his sense of hospitality on behalf of the asram was so fine and clear that I thought, with wonder, what effort must go into making every pilgrim feel welcome.

We went to the cowsheds where I was introduced to Ramana's cow's granddaughters. Mani stroked their heads gently. When one of them twisted her head and stared at me, rolling her big black eyes, I jumped.

'Cows are the gentlest things in the world,' Mani said.

I reached out and touched her head. Immediately she nuzzled and inclined her horns in order to be scratched. Mani talked to every cow and bull in that byre.

We went to the gardens where all kinds of bamboos grew with flowering trees.

'Where did you get these from?' I asked.

'Devotees like you,' he smiled.

I wanted to say 'I'm an Anthropologist' but wasn't really sure any more. So we discussed my earlier work *The Christians of Kerala* (1993) and the monograph on Henri Le Saux, which had brought me here. He knew about Abhishiktananda, but then there had been so many Western acolytes: Brunton, Chadwick, the Osbornes – and so many continued to come.

When we returned to the central maze of buildings I asked him how old he had been when Ramana lived.

'Eleven.'

'Did you understand the mystery of his being Bhagavan?'

'Boys will be boys, Susan. We were more interested in our games at that age. But I do remember we always felt at ease here, with him.'

We were standing under the great ancient tree, where the poor were fed every morning. Its boles are so curved and gnarled, its width like a huge round table. Srinivasamurthy was sitting on the verandah against a wooden column. Anu had been searching desperately for me for two hours after she came out of the meditation rooms, and was very relieved that I had not got lost. 'So you found her eventually,' he said and went back to his office.

Anu and I went for a walk to see if we could get closer to the hill. The ritual circumambulation – fourteen kilometres around the hill – can take three to four hours. In summer, the granite is too hot, one's feet can burn. I decided to return in the cooler seasons to climb Shiva's hill. For the moment it was enough that I had arrived here, that I knew this place existed.

It was dusk. I could hear singing in the hall. It was beautiful, a large spacious empty room, where the pilgrims came to sit on the shining mirror like floor. The songs were composed by Ramana. We sat against the walls, listening to the men and the women singing together and separately. I closed my eyes and almost immediately went into the state that I can only describe as darkness and fusion. One of the most beautiful things that Ramana taught was that one didn't have to lose the world, or leave the world to reach that state called Being. All dyads resolve in this moment, even the metaphors of dark and light are transcended. And of course, one needed to want to be in this state, otherwise one remained outside. For Ramana, being 'outside' was an equally valid state of being. In the end, 'there is no such thing as self-realization', only an understanding of what Being means.

I spent six years writing the text which inter-related the lives of my favourite mystics, Simone Weil, Henri Le Saux and Ramana Maharshi. I tried to understand what it meant to have 'interior' experiences, visions and trances. It had all been so abstract. I made this 'journey' using reams of paper, library space, ink, waking and dreaming hours – at the end of it, I wrote a small book. In 1996 I came to the asramam and realized in a moment that I needn't have taken six years over it. The knowledge that awareness, self-consciousness, the existence of a grain of sand or a grove of Buddha Bamboo at the foothills of Arunachala were all interlinked came to me as peacefully, as gently, as non-intrusively as rain falling or sea waves crashing.

I decided to leave early next morning. Bharati Mirchandani, a graphic designer who was there by chance at the same time, said, 'Susan, you can't go without eating the asramam breakfast. I can only describe it as blessed.' But I knew I had to leave – I would return, of that I was sure. I remembered what Henri Le Saux had said, 'When you are called to Advaita, you understand the experience of one-ness.' I felt in the contexts of the city in which I lived – disenchanted, rational, fleeting, individualistic – that the hill and the asramam were gentle spaces of retreat. Yet, I am a theoretician of dialogue: dualism is necessary for me. I understood Ramana, but I needed my structured world of distinctions and dialogicity, of identity and difference. I said 'Goodbye' to Mani who said, 'Come again, Susan' before he took off into the night and home, on his bicycle. The moon was exactly half a circle; it was 25 May 1996. Srinivasa Murthy only said 'Namaskaram', when I thanked him, and in a way I understood that pilgrims know they may or may not come across one another again.

That night as I lay securely, serenely, waiting for sleep I knew the mountain lay outside, large and softly awake – a mountain, but somehow even to my imagination, so full of power and tenderness: the embodiment of Shiva and Parvati in union.

II

After I returned to Delhi, I often remembered the heat and light in the asramam and longed to return. But it was not to be, for my obligations to my family were many and so also my duties at work. My three daughters were aged twelve, five and three years old, at the time of my first visit in 1996. There were years of growing up for them to do. My new work was somewhat different; I was writing a textbook on Theory and Society in India, which looked at peasant, tribal and industrial society (Visvanathan 2001). The work on mysticism was completed and appeared in 1998, three years after it was submitted, from the Indian Institute of Advanced Study in Shimla. It appeared also in a collected volume of essays, titled *Friendship, Interiority and Mysticism* (Visvanathan 2007). They were happy years, complicated only by academic temperament and the need to be continually balancing the duties of home and teaching. There was no reason for me to feel that I needed a quiet retreat – there was really no cause for me to return.

Then, unable to face the transition period of middle age, for Shiv and I separated in order to spend more time following our careers, in the year 2000, I had a cerebral stroke, and in 2001, I went to the asramam to recover. My life changed in its minutae.

This book records pilgrimage as therapy, a field of study encountered both in the Sociology of Mysticism as well as in that of Health and Well Being studies. To provide the reader with some space from which to understand historical and theological references in the reading of the biography as a social construct, I will first provide a biographical framework of Maharshi Ramana's life and work.

Following the introduction to a partial biography of Ramana, available in a large number of books, I shall discuss, in the three chapters which follow, some of the theoretical problems in the understanding of the life and work of Maharshi Ramana of Tiruvannamalai. These are questions of activism and detachment, of travellers and pilgrimage, and of reading the narratives of devotees, as an exercise in understanding the past.

In this book I am concerned with the way in which Ramana is perceived by those who feel close to him (devotees) as well as those who serve him, essentially 'workers' who communicate their total devotion, sometimes in silence, by their commitment to the ideas and work of Ramana, embodied in the organization, called Sri Ramanasramam. The three theoretical chapters are interspersed with data from the field. The remaining chapters are subjectively positioned in the methodologically entrenched frameworks of the sociology of knowledge. Some theoretical insights may be necessary to understand the narratives. As Lorraine Code argues, in her book *What Can She Know?*, interpretative knowledge has its dangers, but it builds bridges for autonomy and those feelings associated with privileging freedom and vision.

> Generalising an interpretive approach of this sort to other kinds of knowledge can afford a safeguard against dogmatism and rigidity. Knowledge of other people is possible only in a persistent interplay between opacity and transparency, between attitudes and postures that elude a knower's grasp, and traits that seem to be clear and relatively constant. Hence knowers are kept on their cognitive toes: the "more or lessness" of this knowledge constantly affirms the need to reserve and revise judgement Yet, ongoing personal and political commitments cannot be left undecided: they require affirmation that people know one another well enough to be able to go on. In the requirement that it accommodate change and growth, this knowledge

> contrasts further with traditional paradigms that deal on the whole with objects of knowledge that manifest a high degree of permanence. (Code 1991: 38)

Stability is one thing, permanence another. In the world that provides equilibrium to the seeker, permanence applies only to the conclusive nature of death, which is seen to be integration with all that is an Origin. For believers this is not myth, it is the everydayness of rituals and beliefs. 'We are believers!' is the cry from the heart which questions doubt or disbelief, or plain intellectual curiosity.

The sage Maharshi Ramana is associated with the sacred mountain of Arunachala, which is the epitome of the joyous consummation of Shiva and Parvati, and of the *tejolingam*, which is the appearance of Shiva as a column of fire. The town is midpoint on the map of South India, being four hours journey by bus from Chennai, and six hours from Bangalore. An important pilgrim town, it has now reached the zenith of its commercial development, but has since mythic times been associated with the need for transcendence, creatively assumed in the form of annihilation of the Self and in the implicit recognition of the Self. This is a well-known refrain in the theology associated with non-dualism. Psychologically, this means that all desires are fulfilled.

In the second chapter, 'Activism and Detachment', I will discuss some aspects of Ramanine theology in the work of Henri Le Saux, a Christian mystic who struggled past the conventionalities of the Benedictine order to live the life of a labouring monk, where he disseminated through his writings the nature of the mystical path. In Europe, Le Saux is one of Ramana's most famous devotees. I will introduce the problem by looking at the problems of action and renunciation which often are related in an oppositional sense, like two sides of a coin. The figure of Dom Le Saux is still problematic in many Christian circles, Orthodox, Catholic or Protestant, but his is a celebrated presence in many radical circles, whether in the Church or outside it.

III

Sri Ramana Maharshi was born on the night of 29 December 1879, in Thiruchuruli, a sacred temple town thirty kilometres from Madurai. The event of his birth was seen as auspicious. It coincided with a temple festival, when the image of Lord Shiva was garlanded and taken in procession with ritual drumming, conch blowing and music. The moment Shiva entered the temple was the moment the child, who became one of India's greatest and most revered sages, was born to Sundaram Ayyar and Alagamma.

Sundaram Ayyar was what Arthur Osborne in his book, *Ramana Maharshi and the Path of Self Knowledge* (2004), calls a rural lawyer. He was a man who loved people and was hospitable and generous. His house was always open to guests, not just friends and clients, but also passing strangers. It was perhaps in response to a family legend, that when a sadhu had knocked at the door of an ancestor's home, he was sent away without food, and had prophesied that one member of the family would in every generation from then on become a renouncer.

> Curse or blessing, the pronouncement was fulfilled. One of Sundaram Ayyar's paternal uncles had donned the ochre robe and left home with staff and water-pot; his elder brother had gone ostensibly to visit a neighbouring place and from there slipped away as a sanyasin renouncing the world. (Osborne 2004: 3)

Life was peaceful and happy till Sundaram Ayyar suddenly died, and now bereft, the children – Nagaswami, Venkatraman, Nagasundaram and Alamellu – struggled with the sudden change in their circumstance. They went to live in Madurai with their father's brother Subbier.

Venkatraman, who was later known as Ramana Maharshi, went to Scott's Middle School and then to American Mission High School. He was bored with his studies, but had the gift of great imagination and a good memory, which allowed him to cope with the demands of school. He was athletic and had many friends. He had one quirk, which was deep sleep. He slept so deeply, that enemies could wreak vengeance for one act or another, and he would never know. About one such incident that happened in Dindigul, he told Devaraja Mudaliar:

> I was left alone in the house. I was sitting reading in the front room, but after a while I locked the front door and fastened the windows and went to sleep. When they returned from the temple no amount of shouting or banging at the door or window would wake me. At last they managed to open the door with a key from the house opposite, and then they tried to wake me up by beating me. All the boys beat me to their hearts content, and your uncle did too, but without effect. I knew nothing about it till they told me in the morning ... the same sort of thing happened to me in Madura also. The boys didn't dare touch me when I was awake but if they had any grudge against me they would come when I was asleep and carry me wherever they liked and beat me as much as they liked and then put me back to bed and I would know nothing about it till they told me next morning. (cited in Osborne 2004: 4, 5)

Ramana Maharshi had had a death experience in mid-July in the year 1896. Sri Sadhu Om writes *In the Path of Sri Ramana* (1997),

> Venkataram was sitting alone in a small room upstairs. Though there was no sickness in the body, a great fear arose in Him that he was going to die. It happened not merely as an imaginary or superficial fear, but as an actual experience of death. He was not perturbed by this. He did not even inform anyone of it. He boldly welcomed the forthcoming death and ventured to scrutinize it and find the result of this scrutiny for Himself. "Yes, death has come; let it come. What is death? To whom does it come? To me. Who am I? What is it that is dying? Yes, it is this body that is dying; let it die." Deciding thus He lay down stretching His arms and legs. Closing His lip tightly and remaining without speech or breath, He turned his attention very keenly towards Himself. Death was experienced! What did He come to know at that time? (4)

This experience was a reflexive one, where the boy thought to himself that it is not I who dies, 'I am not this perishable body. I and it are different. I am the indestructible "I" (Self.) Of all things, I, unbound by the body alone, am real. The body and world are meant only for destruction, but I, who transcend the body, am the eternal Supreme Thing!'

Venkatraman was having difficulty in school, getting regularly in trouble with his teachers. He was bored and was given useless punishments. Sadhu Om writes,

> One day his teacher gave Him an imposition to write three times an English grammar lesson which he had failed to learn.
>
> Next day, it was a Saturday, the 29th of August 1896. Sri Ramana had written the imposition twice when He felt a dejection towards this useless work. Throwing away the pencil and notebook, He sat up and closed his eyes in Self-Absorption (nishta). Nagaswami, who was sitting nearby was saddened at seeing this. (7)

Hearing his brother rebuke him (which implied that Venkatraman was enjoying the comforts of home and world while enacting a renunciant's obligations) the boy decided to leave home.

While the imposition from Bain's English Grammar and his brother's criticism might have been the overt catalyst, in Ramana's own reading, it was perhaps the working out of destiny. Destiny and the realization of the

Self were the two basic strands which devotees saw as the clearest indeces of Ramanine teaching.

> Venkataraman recognised the truth of the remark and, with that ruthless acceptance of truth (or justice, which is applied truth) that characterised him, he rose to his feet to leave the house there and then and go forth, renouncing everything. For him that meant Tiruvannamalai and the holy hill, Arunachala.
>
> However, he knew that it was necessary to use guile, because authority is very strong in a Hindu household and his uncle and brother would not let him go if they knew. So he said he had to go back to school to attend a special class on electricity.
>
> Unconsciously providing him with funds for the journey, his brother said, "Then take five rupees from the box downstairs and pay my college fees on the way." (Osborne 2004: 19)

His aunt gave him his food which he ate hurriedly, and five rupees, which he took for his journey, leaving behind two rupees and a note, saying that he was on a virtuous path, no one need look for him: 'I have set out in quest of my Father in accordance with his command.' The note, which is exhibited in the asramam archives, also says that the college fees have not been paid. A seventeen-year-old boy ostensibly going for a class on electricity in 1879 would encourage much sociological analyses. Emile Durkheim in his *Elementary Forms of the Religious Life* (1917) argues that the origin of scientific thoughts lie in religious ones! 'Current' and 'power' are terms sharply defined in both fields of discourse. For the young Ramana Maharshi, yet to be acknowledged by the world and his family in terms of the worth of his dreams, Arunachala represented the culmination of his desire. His father had died, his mother whom he always saw as beautiful and holy, represented the space of indivisible conjugal joy, which death had not divided. In Arunachala, where Shiva and Parvati are conjoined in conjugal bliss, or *kalyana*, he would find bliss again. Osborne argues that the Ramana whom devotees loved had become one with the father, He was the Father. For the anthropologist, the tactile quality of popular faith and the intensity of believing is a given. Analyzing this, we may have our own models, which may or may not harmonise with 'conscious models', but we cannot doubt the significance of faith.

The story of his journey to Tiruvannamalai has been told over and over again. It has the quality that characterizes all pilgrimages – mistakes, new encounters, courage and an unceasing desire to reach the goal. He left home at noon for a train that was due to arrive at that hour. Luckily, it was late. He raced down the list of stations, having looked at an outdated itinerary at home. He bought a ticket for Tindivanam, though if his eye had just travelled a little further, he would have seen that Tiruvannamalai was already on the Railway map!

Osborne says,

> The events of the journey are symbolical of the arduous journey an aspirant (sadhaka) makes to his goal: first there was the favour of Providence in granting the money and allowing the train to be caught, although he started out late; then the provision made was exactly what was needed to reach the destination (ticket to Tiruvannamalai was exactly three rupees) but the heedlessness of the travel lengthened the journey and caused hardships and adventures on the way. (22)

While in the train, a kind maulvi told him the shortest route to Tiruvannamalai, which was to get off the train at Villipuram. He remained at the station till dawn and then decided to walk to the temple town. At the rest house where he ate his breakfast, the innkeeper told him to keep his money, and informed him that Mambalapattu was on the route to Tiruvannamalai; the young Venkatraman went back to the station, caught a train to this town which he reached in the afternoon. He started walking and reached the temple of Arayaninallur. Here he sat in a pillared hall, and saw a bright light.

> Thinking it must be an emanation from the image of the God in the inner sanctuary, he went to look but found that it was not. Nor was it any physical light. It disappeared and he sat down again in meditation. (23)

The boy hoped for food, but there was none. He went to Kilur, with a group of devotees, and by the time the puja was over, he thought he might be fed.

> It was nine o'clock by the time the puja was finished and they sat down to supper. Again Venkatraman asked to be fed. It seemed at first that there would be nothing for him, but the temple drummer had been impressed by his appearance and devout manner and gave him his share. He wanted water to drink with it and, holding his leaf-plate with rice, was shown the

> way to the house of a sastri [pandit] nearby who would give him water. While standing in front of the house, waiting for it, he stumbled on a few paces and then collapsed in sleep or faint. A few minutes later he came round to find a small crowd looking on curiously. He drank the water, gathered it up and ate some of the rice he had spilled, and then lay down on the ground and slept. (25)

He was still twenty miles away from Tiruvannamalai on 31 August. It was Gokulashtami, the birth anniversary of Lord Krishna. He arrived at the house of one Muthukrishna Bhagavatar, hoping for food and the chance to exchange his gold earrings set with rubies for money. The lady of the house made sure he ate every morsel of the food she served him, and Bhagavatar accepted his story that he was a pilgrim who had lost his luggage, and took the earrings for pawn. Venkatraman was given four rupees and the address of the house to which he had come unannounced, so that he could claim them.

> As soon as he left the house he tore up the address, having no intention of ever redeeming the earring. Finding that there was no train to Tiruvannamalai till next morning, he slept at the station. No man can end his journey till the allotted time. It was the morning of September 1st 1896, three days after leaving home, when he arrived at Tiruvannamalai station. (25)

He entered the temple, all the gates were open, there was no one about, and in that moment of unity with the mountain, the quest ended.

However, the ordinary things of life would always accompany Ramana Maharshi. People would always call out to him.

A barber invited him to shave his hair. After paying him, he threw the remaining money he had from pawning his earrings into the temple tank. The wife of Bhagavatar had given him sweets which also he threw into the tank. Then he went into the thousand pillar hall where he meditated ceaselessly.

Venkataraman was known in this period as the Brahmana Swami. Seshadhri Swami, who was one of the most renowned swamis that Tiruvannamalai gave shelter to and had arrived some years earlier, began to protect the young boy. He himself was a magnetic personality with a reputation for granting miracles and being eccentric in nature. Seshadhri asram is adjacent to Ramanasramam and is well known for providing rooms and board to those who arrive in Tiruvannamalai without prior plan. However, being protected by Seshadri Swami, who was a mendicant who gave people what they wanted, and who could become divinely possessed in a moment, was not entirely an advantage!

> Seshadri Swami made the impression of being slightly deranged and thereby drew on himself the persecution of schoolboys. They now extended their attentions to his protege whom they called "Little Seshadri". They began throwing stones at him, partly out of boyish cruelty, partly because they were intrigued to see one not much older than themselves sitting like a statue and, as one of them put it later, wanted to find out whether he was real or not. (29)

Sethu Ramaswamy in her work *They Spoke with God: Saints of Tamilaham* writes of Seshadhri Swami, considered to be one of the greatest saints of Tiruvannamalai. Narrating how Seshadhri Swamy came to Tiruvannamalai, she writes:

> … in the middle of 1889 (Seshadhri Swamy) reached Arunachala or Tiruvannamalai. He was then only nineteen years old. He spent forty years in Tiruvannamalai performing innumerable miracles, and by merely looking at a person bestowed his grace on him and transformed him. By a mere touch he could heal. He behaved like a mad man, but the people of Tiruvannamalai knew that he was an extraordinary saint.
>
> His behaviour, which is described as utterly eccentric if not insane was seen to be a view of the world that was divinely inspired.
>
> Swamigal sometimes spoke in conundrums. No one could understand what he meant, but to those who were close to him, the meaning would be clear – they may be prophetical or philosophical, but to hear it one would think it was nonsense. (Ramaswamy 2009: 108, 111)

It was this 'mad' saint who protected the boy Ramana from intruders and violators, keeping them at bay with sticks.

In the Patala lingam in the Arunachala temple, Ramana began a period of samadhi, which was so fulfilling that he did not notice anything, neither the darkness nor the heat nor the tormenters who continued to oppress him. He lived his life as if it was a moment in the sight of god, but the people who came protectively to guard him were horrified by the condition they found him in. They carried him out from the underground vault to the Subramania shrine.

> For about two months the Brahmana Swami stayed at the Lord Subramania shrine. He would sit motionless in Samadhi (absorption) and sometimes nourishment had to be put into his mouth as he paid no heed when it was offered to him. For some weeks he did not even trouble to tie on a loincloth. He was looked after by a Mouni Swami (one who observes silence) who also lived at the shrine. (Osborne 2004: 30)

The Mouni Swami would bring for him a glass of milk everyday, which was mixed with water, turmeric, sugar, bananas and whatever went into the washing of the shrine of the Goddess Uma. The priest noticed and started to send pure milk for the Brahmana Swami, as Venkataraman was known then. Yet, all his life Ramana was not averse to accepting whatever devotees offered him as food. Sometimes the frugal offerings of shepherds and old women were mashed into gruel and drunk. He really did not mind. All his life he would communicate that food was *Ana*, holy, and it should be received with pleasure and redistributed. Even while in the precincts of the temple, hardly aware of his surroundings, he always shared what he received. It was a Malayali sadhu Palaniswami, known for his austerity and his devotion to Lord Vinayaka, who became the first of a loyal band of devotees who would circle Ramana and recognize he was Bhagavan, 'One who has attained Union with the Divine is sometimes worshipped in the same manner as a temple idol, with burning camphor, sandal-paste, flowers, libation and chanting' (35).

When Tambiran (one of the devotees) was at Gurumurtam (where Ramana had shifted because of the difficulty with sightseers and stone-throwers), he worshipped Ramana in this manner, but the next day Ramana had written in charcoal the words in Tamil, 'This is service enough for this', meaning that the bringing of food was sufficient.

Discovering that the boy could write, the circle around him began to pressurize him for an answer regarding who he was. He wrote in English 'Venkatraman, Tiruchuzhi'.

> His knowing English came as a further surprise, but Venkatrama Iyer was puzzled by the name Thiruchuzhi in English transliteration, especially by the "zh".
>
> The Swami therefore took the book on which the paper had rested to see whether it was in Tamil so that he could point out the letter that is commonly translated as "zh", a letter midway between "r" and "l" in sound. Finding it to be the Periapuranam, the book which had had so profound an effect on him

> before the spiritual awakening, he looked up the passage where Tiruchuzhi is mentioned as a town honoured in song by Sundramurti Swami and showed it to Venkatarama Iyer. (36)

Over a period of time, friends and family came looking for him. Venkatraman tried to send them away in the time-honoured religious tradition of those treading the mystic path. Rangan, who was a fervent devotee, whom Maharshi could never dislodge, although he often reminded him of his obligations to his family, records his mother's visit. They had been neighbours of the Maharshi when he was a boy. David Godman, the British spiritualist, gives us devotees' accounts in his valuable collection of memoirs of devotees (2002), of which Rangan's witness is one of the most important:

> My mother had visited Bhagavan when he was residing in Pavalakundru in the 1890s…
>
> My mother had already told me about her first visit. It seems that on that occasion she had asked Palaniswami whether Bhagavan would eat some fruit if she offered him some. It did not occur to her to address Bhagavan directly because at the time she did not think he was conscious of her presence. However, Bhagavan heard her remark and responded to her query by stretching out his hand. My mother peeled a banana and gave it to him. Bhagavan ate it.
>
> "Does he walk?" she asked Palaniswami.
>
> Bhagavan got up and walked a few steps to demonstrate that he could move about.
>
> "Does he speak?" asked mother, still dealing with Palaniswami.
>
> Bhagavan did occasionally speak, but on this occasion he kept quiet. Many years later Bhagavan told me about this incident.
>
> "In those days," he told me, "I was speaking only one or two words with Palaniswami. It was difficult to speak even those few words, so I spoke rarely. I would have spoken to your mother, but I was afraid that if I spoke and my family heard about it, they would drag me back to Madurai. So I kept quiet.
>
> "When your mother came for the first time to see me, she was frightened by my ascetic appearance and attire.
>
> "She asked me, 'Have your father's philanthropy and charity fructified into this?'
>
> "My hair was all matted, my body was completely covered with dust and I was sitting on the rocks on the mountain. She went away because she could

> not bear to see me in this state. Also, she felt that she could do nothing to help me." (Godman 2000: 2)

Ramana stayed at Gurumutham for a year and then moved to a mango orchard in the vicinity owned by one Venkatarama Naicker, who provided shelter to both the sage and his attendant, Palaniswami. The latter was interested in ideas and struggled with books, and Ramana with his photographic memory and his lucid understanding helped him with his reading.

> His prior spiritual experience enabled him to understand at a glance what was expounded and his wonderful memory retained it when read, so that he became erudite almost without effort. In the same way, he later picked up Sanskrit, Telugu and Malayalam by reading books brought to him in these languages and answering questions in them. (Osborne 2004: 36)

I have seen notebooks in the Ramana archives, where Ramana had copied out sentences over and over again, in Malayalam, in order to learn the language. Entranced by his attention to script and neatness, and the monotony of learning, I asked one of the archivists how this occurred, and he replied that 'Bhagavan slept very little.' This desire to understand the need of devotees is a very important part of future translation studies.

Meanwhile, his mother was desperately looking for him. In August 1898, at the funeral of Subbier, the uncle with whom Ramana had been staying in Madurai, the family heard from a mourner that he had heard one Annamalai Tambiran speaking with great reverence of a boy who had achieved great heights of spiritual grace, and was probably Venkatraman. Nellapier, one of the brothers of Ramana's father, went looking for him and was denied admission into the mango orchard by the owner, who said that the boy was a mouni, so why disturb him?

> Nellapier wrote on a piece of paper that he had with him, "Nellappier, pleader of Manamadura, wishes to see you."
>
> The Swami showed already that keen perception of mundane affairs coupled with complete detachment from them, which was to characterise him later and which surprised so many devotees. He observed that the paper on which the note was written came from the Registration Department and had some office matter on the back of it in the handwriting of his elder brother Nagaswami, from which he deduced that Nagaswami had become a clerk in

> the Registration Department. Just the same in later years, he would turn a letter over and examine its address and postmark before opening it. (39)

From the mango orchard, he shifted to the Arunagirinathar temple. He had refused to explain himself to Nellapier who took the sad tidings to Alagamma that her son had been found, and was not communicative and had no intention of returning to the family fold. In fact Ramana tried to shed Palaniswami off as well, saying that he should go begging in one direction, and Palani in the other, and they should not stay together any more. But Palaniswamy was distraught and could not bear the idea of a separation, and thus was found to have returned in the evening to the Arunagirinathar temple, and was allowed to stay (ibid 40).

It was during this time that Bhagavan became a familiar sight in Tiruvannamalai, and not one street was left unvisited by him in his search for food! Sethu Ramaswamy, (whose nephew, Captain Narayanan, serves at the asramam) recounts the time that Ramana used to visit her relatives. 'He would clap and my aunt would come out and feed him' (personal communication, April 2005).

When Alagamma found from Nellapier that her son was at Tiruvannamalai, she waited for the Christmas holidays when Nagaswami, her younger son, would be free to accompany her, and then went to Tiruvannamalai. She tried desperately to have him return with her, but he ignored her. She wept. The devotees then persuaded Ramana to communicate with her.

> He took the pencil and paper and, in utterly impersonal language, wrote: "The Ordainer controls the fate of souls in accordance with their prarabdhakarma (destiny to be worked out in this life, resulting from the balance sheet of actions in past lives). Whatever is destined to happen will happen, do what you may to prevent it. This is certain. The best course, therefore, is, to remain silent." (41)

Osborne immediately comments that this is similar to the relationship between Mary and her son, Jesus. He also asserts that Ramana had begun showing signs of 'normalcy' and had started once again to be concerned with temporal things such as food and shelter.

> The mother returned home and the Swami remained as before. And yet not quite. During the two and a quarter years that he spent in temples and shrines

> at Tiruvannamalai the first signs of a return to an outwardly normal life were already appearing. He had already begun to take food daily at a regular hour and then, so as not be dependent on anyone, to go out in search of it. He had spoken a few times. He had begun to respond to devotees, to read books and to expound the essence of their teaching. (44)

The Virupaksha cave still emanates a sense of radiant peace, while the internal cloister where Bhagavan meditated has an intense and heavy-laden vibration. It has a density which is apparent to the viewer, and there is a juxtaposition of light and ephemerality, where the sky is the only roof, and inside, it carries the vividness of being closed inside a cave or a womb.

It was in the Virupaksha cave in 1903 that the great scholar Ganapati Muni came to visit him. And a lifelong friendship, with differences, arose. Virupaksha cave, while being a masculine and renunciatory space, was open to seekers who came looking for Ramana's advice or blessing. Even today, it carries euphoria of sunshine and peacefulness.

Virupaksha cave was where the woman who used to cook for Bhagavan would turn up with her offerings. Echammal was pursued by misfortune, but still believed in the goodness of existence, and the love of the sage for her. He wept with her over the many deaths which were to afflict her.

His own mother, Alagamma, who had been tested in a similar fire of loss, returned to Tiruvannamalai in 1916, fell ill with typhoid, recovered by the beseeching prayers of Ramana Maharshi. She went back to Manamadura, where sadly, her younger son Nagasundaram's wife died. Then, renouncing everything, she went to live with Ramana (Osborne 2004: 77). This is a complex series of events, and to decode Alagamma's suffering we must also remember that she had now no home, for her brother-in-law Nelliapier had also died, leaving the family in some difficulty, and the house in Thiruchuzhi had been sold to pay debts (ibid 77).

Thiruchuzhi, Ramana's birthplace was well known for its temple, dedicated to Bhuminathar and Sahayavalli. Madurai, too, has its famous temple and in this town Ramana Maharshi had his death experience in Chockappa Naicken street. By returning to Tiruvannamalai, again, Alagamma hoped to live with her son. She must have been reflective, in the nature of her destiny. This heroic woman later became the centre of a cult, the deified mother, the manifestation of divinity as a representation of Ambika, Sahayavalli, Bhuminatha, so representing the resolution of non-dualism in everyday practice as the substance of tantric pujas at Sri Ramanasramam.

Devotees were afraid that Maharshi would leave the place when his mother returned. Osborne writes, 'However, there was a great difference, for now it was she who had renounced home, not he who was detained there' (Osborne 2000: 78).

She stayed in the beginning with Echammal. Soon, the Skandasramam was established for it was more conducive to Alagamma's needs. It was on an overhanging rock crop and directly above the Virupaksha cave.

Devaraja Mudaliar chronicles in his book *Day by Day with Bhagavan* (2002) how this happened.

> Bhagavan said that the old disciple Kandaswami was anxious to build a separate Asramam for Bhagavan. He inspected various places on the hill and in the forests to select a site, and finally suggested the present Skandasramam site and then Bhagavan also approved of it. Thereupon Kandaswami began converting what was a thick forest of prickly pear on the mountain slope. The result of his labours, unaided by any at the time, is the Asramam we see now. He added, "You cannot imagine the state the site was in originally. Kandaswami worked with almost superhuman effort, achieved by his own hands what even four people together could not have done. He removed all the prickly pear, reduced stone and boulder to level ground, created a garden and raised the Asramam." (66)

Skandasramam continues to be one of the loveliest sites on the hill. It is maintained by Ramanasramam in much the same way as during the time of habitation by Bhagavan and his mother. Her room is narrow and overlooks the great Shiva temple. The sounds from the temple and horns from the traffic and music from the megaphones come across echoing up the hill. A breeze always blows, the plants are always well watered, and the drinking water is sweet. Bhagavan's chamber and meditation rooms communicate the aura of a still and beatific spirit. The pilgrims come and go, hoping to return, and the garden and the rooms where Ramana lived till the time of his mother's death are sanctified by memory and ritual.

After the mother's death, Ramana moved to where her body had been interred, as she was, according to him, a Realised soul and therefore was buried not cremated. It is there that the present asramam is situated.

2

ACTIVISM AND DETACHMENT

Henri Le Saux came to India in search of the transcendent mystery – the Grail. As an anthropologist, I am concerned with the journey he undertook with a belief that Maharshi Ramana was catalyst in the discovery of his life's goal. Following the work of Marcel Mauss, and his mentor Emile Durkheim, I would argue that 'Ideas are real'. However *imaginary* the 'Grail', the consequences of the search are facts which can be analysed. The debates on the dialectic of subjectivity and objectivity are too complex to analyse here; let us admit that as specialists, we know that the work we do affects us, influences us, changes us (Meister 2000). I will not, therefore, introduce yet the question of how the work on mysticism affected me, for that is another kind of writing, specialized in itself; a campfire of anthropologists' dreams, longings and discussions of failure and success. The real truth is that there are no failures, all data goes into the beehive format of our collectives lives, and is classified as experience. Whether there is consensus of how this experience can be shared, reflected or disseminated is another experience (Geertz 1973).

Henri Le Saux perceived his encounter with Ramana in January 1949 as a life-changing moment, tranquil in its apparent manifestation (the sage was like a 'kindly grandfather').

Yet, this one meeting resulted in transformative visions, affecting 'zones of paraconsciousness' and he described this as a 'call which pierced through everything, rent it in pieces and opened a mighty abyss' (Stuart 1989: 62). The dreams continued and in these Ramana continually appeared to him. After the Maharshi's death, Le Saux visited the asramam several times. 'If Ramana was indeed great, how much more so must be this Arunachala which drew Ramana to himself?' (23).

Out of these several pilgrimages (and in fact, Le Saux's life itself became one of total pilgrimage), many works of theological interest appeared. Today, these writings have tremendous sociological significance. In times of great stress, religions cannot remain exclusivist (Baeumer and Dupuche 2005). Indeed, the comparative analyses of religions lead to greater understanding of the many composite cultures we are now part of, when post-modernism has given way to globalism.

Why should we be interested in a monastic's search? The answer is because the path which he elaborated is a contextual one and pertains to our times. Secularism is a political construct, drawing its meanings from the specificity of culture and history. In reality, people proceed towards religious experience in one way or another. Whether the state disciplines people *for believing* or for *not believing* (the latter being the case for religious fundamentalism), the people's life and world will have a velocity of its own, in the Rabelaisian or the Bakhtinian sense (Bakhtin 1968).

The question that is most often asked of anthropologists is, why do people turn more and more to religion? Daniel Bell would have said 'fear and trembling' which is the affectual core of Durkheim's definition of normlessness or anomie (Bell 2001). So within the statistical analyses of religious motivation, conversion to various religions is of substantial interest. The state can neither promote nor suppress religious experimentation – it is, as Durkheim would say a social fact *sui generis* (Durkheim 1966). As social scientists we can merely study it – including those new forms of mysticism that appear without an umbrella. Previously mysticism always had an adjective – it was Hindu, Christian, Muslim and Shamanistic. Now in the popular parlance of modern media, mystical experiences can be had through music, appreciation of nature, hatha yoga, drugs – well being, adventurism and mysticism have thus become confounded. Diana Eck, while writing on the need for religious dialogue, says that Heinrich Zimmer had written of the spiritual crossroads that the West had reached, and India was an important anchorage for spiritual striving.

> Our cultures are thirsty for whatever it is that is named with the word spirituality. Our lives are busy. Our days hurtle by with a roar. Our rooms are piled with books to read, filled with the sound of televised new reports, with minute-by-minute coverage of baseball games and national and international disasters, filled with music as we like. There is so much to keep up with, that

> stopping for periods of real stillness is increasingly difficult. We have practiced the routes of having, doing, going, making, getting, and keeping so frequently that we know the terrain by heart. The ways of watchfulness and attention will take both learning and unlearning. (Eck 1993: 151)

Learning from the quest of others is an extremely important part of the routines of Ramanasramam. Visitors are emphatically reminded that the peacefulness and rhythm and the order may not be disrupted. The residents who have invested all their emotions in the upkeep of the Sri Ramanasramam's traditions, in memory of the Master, have a code of silence which they are happy to break when visitors are being dealt with, and initiated into asramam practises.

The anxieties of living in bondage to the sacred is conceptually well handled by an excerpt from one of the entries in a collation by W.H. Auden, *A Certain World*. This is a monk's entry, and Auden has taken it from Helen Waddel's *The Desert Fathers:*

> Our sixth contending is with that which we may describe as tedium or perturbation of heart. It is akin to dejection and especially felt by wandering monks and solitaries, a persistent and obnoxious enemy such as dwell in the desert, disturbing the monk especially about midday, like a fever mounting at a regular time, and bringing its highest tide of inflammation at definite accustomed hours to the sick soul. And so some of the Fathers declare it to be the demon of noon tide which is spoken of in the Ninety-first Psalm...
>
> It will not suffer us to stay in our cell, or to attend to our reading: we lament that in all this while, living in the same spot, we have made no progress, we sigh and complain that bereft of sympathetic fellowship we have no spiritual fruit and bewail ourselves as empty of all spiritual profit, abiding vacant and useless in this place; and we that could guide others and be of value to multitudes have edified no man, enriched no man with our precept and example... Towards eleven o'clock or mid-day it induces such lassitude of body and craving for food as one might feel after the exhaustion of a long journey and hard toil, or the postponing of a meal throughout a two or three day's fast. Finally one gazes anxiously here and there, and sighs that no brother of any description is to be seen approaching ... one's mind is an irrational confusion, like the earth befogged in a mist, one is slothful and vacant in every spiritual activity, and no remedy it seems, can be found for this state of siege than a visit from some brother, or the solace of sleep. (Auden 1971: 3)

In Auden's choice of a soliloquy of penitence and boredom, the enchanted garden is rendered a prison. My own entry point for analysis has been substantially different, as this book will proceed to show. I use the category of 'experience' as a sociological variable, following my previous work (*Friendship, Interiority and Mysticism*) where I argue that as scholars of the comparative method in sociology, we may understand 'believing' through the time honoured methods of language, symbols and rites. Yet, the analysis of all narratives on religion is about performance and art. Richard Schusterman writes that 'we must remember that every description of a work of art involves an interpretation of it, since it involves a selection of what to describe, what aspects of the work are important enough to be worth describing. No description describes everything egalitarianly reflecting all that can be said truly about a work. But what more acutely undermines the idea of any firm and definite distinction between descriptive truth (presenting the work's core of incontrovertible properties) and interpretative elaboration is that what is taken as descriptively true (the so called hard facts on which interpretation is based) will often shamelessly depend on which interpretation of the work we come to adopt' (Schusterman, in Iseminger 1992: 71). The problem of subjectivity, of selection, of bias will always be part of sociologist's repertoire. 'The simalucrum of a brilliant conversation cannot be willfully substituted for a brilliant conversation and be a genuinely rewarding experience' (Noel Carrol, in Gary Iseminger 1992).

When it comes to work and worship, and the analysis of these categories, are we sure we have understood one another? Carrol suggests that we do not have the possibility of a real conversation unless we are sure we have understood one another. All conversations must presume the presence of community, and communication rests on this.

> A fulfilling conversation requires that we have the conviction of having grasped what our interlocutor meant or intended to say. This is evinced by the extent to which we struggle to clarify their meanings. A conversation that left us only with our own clever construals or educated guesses, no matter how aesthetically rich, would leave us with the sense that something was missing. That we had neither communed or communicated. (118)

Carrol argues that this is not just true of personal interaction, but the writing of texts. The problem here may be posed as a common one for writers: who is the audience? The most interesting example is perhaps provided by Jersy Kosinsky in his novel, *Being There*, when what the protagonist says, and the meanings received in his utterances, are completely at variance with one another (121). But these are the unutterable difficulties of every day life and of dualist practice and are the real preoccupations of those who are on the path of a mystical search for fulfilment. Carrol tells us, 'We would not think that we had a genuine conversation with someone whom we were not satisfied we understood. Conversations, rewarding ones at least, involve a sense of community or communication that itself rests on communication'(118). The intention of conversation, serious conversation according to Carrol, is to create a sense of shared community whatever its differences.

Yet, sociologically, the thought process of monastics when inscribed through writing, and published, affect the everyday ramifications of religious policy. Jean Leclerq (1961) wrote that grammar and spirituality are the two frames of monastic thought. For Dom Henri Le Saux (known to us as Abhishiktananda) this translated in an experientiality which he believed was communicable. He had seen something, felt something, and he wished to tell the world about it. It is this which marked his activism – the 'telling of' his experiences. Curiously, it does not fit neatly into the conventional texts of evangelization and conversion. It is the analysis of personal metanoia, or transformation of the heart that my work has been largely concerned with.

Sociologically, I see no difficulty with the analysis of the charisma of Dom Henri Le Saux, or the study of religious pilgrimage, or of the asramam as a haven of rest for pilgrims. Similarly, that the symbols of womb and cave, of logos, and the search for the father predominate, are not conceptual problems in themselves. So also, the 'mountain' as the unity of principles, the symbol of co-habitation, fusing the dualism of the one and the many, the opposition of male and female, the transcendence of here and now was stabilized by Le Saux's experience of Advaita. The holy mountain Arunachala became the symbol which transcended the biological differentiation of persons, to attain the androgynous state of fulfilled desire. As Richard Davis has so brilliantly argued, sacred things have meanings for devotees, and they are alive ... they are not merely objects for aesthetic appreciation or anthropological conceptualization (Davis in ed. Meister 2000: 93). All of Abhishiktananda's published work thus became an invitation to prayer, to detachment, to the endless fulfillment, which comes from what

Leclerq, with other theoreticians, has called 'desire and possession' (Weil 1987 a, Leclerq 1961).

It is here that I wish to remember the work of Simone Weil. France produced many brilliant writers, and Weil's thought is paramount in its ability to draw the threads of a Durkheimian obsession ... modes of thought and types of work. If society is the source of all that is sacred, then how may we assert the magnetism of our own biography in relation to the cosmic? To be everything, is indeed to be Nothing. Both Weil and Le Saux understood the essence of desire and possession, or its other side which is waiting and patience (Visvanathan 1998, 2007).

For Abhishiktananda, the activism of waiting lay not in clearly defined trajectories of criticism, but in providing a map for living in the world. He was a writer, he travelled constantly, met people, wrote drafts, rewrote them, chased publishers, got angry with himself and them when his work was not understood. He certainly believed that he had to share what he had felt and seen. Every mystic understood the uniqueness and singularity of his/her own experience, understood that the body mediates. For the mystic, the freedom is not from the rules of the gravity of the earth, but in understanding these, living with them, interpreting them, and very occasionally being allowed to transcend them. The intensity of this experience can only be had through solitude, and it is to be sought for purposefully, and it is dangerous. But there is no way that the state, the family, the neighbourhood, the structured religious organization can stop those who seek the grail. Because it is a shift away from objectivity which is comprehensible and shared, to a subjectivity that is total, but can indeed, be described and shared, and is feared. William Hocking argues that this intense subjectivity is dangerous, because of the existence of the razor's edge, but it often results in complex forms of social service and in forms of art (*Hocking in Woods* 1980: 233).

Karen Jacobs in *The Eye's Mind* (2001) says very sharply that the very existence of writing is a looking back, which, following the work of Marc Blanchot, she calls Orpheus' Gaze. It is the 'backward glance which condemns Orpheus's bride Eurydice to the underworld for the second and final time'. Thus it may seem that interiority is intrusion, and encompasses both surgical penetration as well as the ethnographic gaze (Jacobs 2001: 28):

> ... the intent of the participant-observer method was to produce a wealth of empirical ethnographic data made possible by the field-worker's divestment

> from his own cultural biases and assumptions in order to see from a monolithically conceived "native point of view". (29)

The functions of writing, according to her is nostalgia, and archival interests. She brings to our attention the traps of the participant observation method, and while James Clifford is perhaps the best known of the interlocutors of field work and participant observation, feminist writers have brought the problems of sharpened affectuality to the forefront of their work (115). Like photographs (each according to legend capturing more than a thousand words) that are always available for scrutiny should they be preserved, the ethnographic record in the manner of its inscription strives to fulfil the tasks of memory.

One of the other interesting forms of writing is polemic, and the tract. While it differs from ethnography, it still manages to convey the sense of a time, and the currents of opinion and events characteristic of a period. What photography and writing have in common are not just fixity and aesthetic and mimetic qualities, but also the power to develop connotations of authority through 'a transparent subject-lens which itself represses the evidence of that production' (Jacobs 2001: 29). Joseph Brodsky, in his brilliant essay on Marcus Aurelius which combines travelogue with historical analyses and reminiscences, argues that black and white photography as well as sculptures with their pupil-less gaze into eternity are similar because of the role the imagination plays in perceiving the play of light and colour, darkness and memory, past and future. We can never inhabit the past but through an act of the imagination, yet the past is always present unless mnemonics are destroyed or displayed differently (Brodsky 1994). In this book my anthropologist's notes will be a dominant thread of intervention in the narrative analyses of mystics', devotees' and observers' writings.

It is not a method sociologists are unfamiliar with. Andrew Abbott, in his work *Time Matters: On Theory and Method* (2001) writes in an essay titled 'From Causes to Events':

> In the last decade a number of writers have proposed narratives as the foundation for sociological methodology. By this they do not mean narrative in its common sense of words as opposed to numbers and complexity as opposed to formalization. Rather, they mean narrative in the more generic sense of process or story. They want to make process the fundamental building blocks of sociological analyses. For them social reality happens in

> sequences of actions located within constraining or enabling structures. It is a matter of particular social actors, in particular social places, at particular social times. (183)

Methodologically, this is my intention in this book. Abbott goes on to say that while in the mid '90s narrative positivism was isolated,

> Today it has become clear that these efforts make up a fairly coherent assault on a central set of methodological issues, and more broadly, an attempt to refound methodology on a clear articulation with sociological theories of action. (205)

It is in this context that I remind readers of the work of Simone Weil, for Le Saux was aware of her writings. Simone Weil was Jewish, a trade unionist, a philosopher, a teacher and a mystic. She was born in Paris in 1909, entered the Ecole Normale Superieure in 1928, taught at a secondary school for girls in 1931. The war years were fraught with danger, and in 1942, she was in Casablanca, trying to see her parents to safety in America. In August 1943, she was dead at a sanatorium in England and the last sentence she is believed to have written was 'The most important part of education – to teach the meaning of – "to know".'

Ricoeur in *History and Truth*, first published in 1955, argued that human beings ('Man' specifically) embody work and word, praxis and theoria. And this we call biography (Ricoeur 1977: 4). We also, within this frame, transcend *logos* and *eros*, objectivity and subjectivity, love and coercion, manual labour and mental labour. An 'objective' reading, Ricoeur would point out, has subjective reasons – the so-called acknowledged 'bias' in Weber's *verstehen*. The 'historian's craft', he argues, is to decide between good and bad subjectivities. What goes into this dialectic that informs the reading of the chosen biographies? It is the judgement of importance, the selection of events and factors, what Raymond Aron called 'the theory that precedes History'. He presumes there is a cultural context in reading data, defined by him as 'the popular conception of causality'. Clearly, the framework is the debates on secularism and or fundamentalism. Within this, we presume there is the 'phenomena of historical distance' or to notate what has changed, what has become 'other' or has continually been 'othered' (26-28).

Exegesis attempts only at collage, but within the collage there is a motif. It is the social scientist's imperative need to understand, to explain, but not to judge. James Clifford (1988), providing an exegesis of Marcel Mauss and his followers in an essay called 'On Ethnographic Surrealism' argues that juxtaposition produces what Roland Barthes called the effect of the real (Clifford 1988: 133).

The problem for us, then, in the analysis of mysticism is to engage with a theory of work and life. It may be argued that the organizational principles Le Saux worked with centred in the writing, translating, decoding, and from these the parallel structures which were set up in terms of discussion groups and the contributions of friends to a way of life that was monastic, but deeply rooted in the world. It can be called the quest for freedom. The dangers of mystic experimentation, however, are only too well known. Mysticism has often been the social response to war, the degradation of industrialism and to the existential tragedies of modern existence. Tiruvannamalai, the site of mystical revelation as the embodiment of the holy mountain Arunachala, to millions of people through the centuries, has also been the site of misplaced religious fervour, madness and death. Armies of mendicants and beggars appear here, also travellers, pilgrims, tourists and the homeless. Arunachala has been known to be the refuge of those seeking benediction and the solace of divine love, also those, in secular terms, who are running away from home. Malevolence, drugs, prostitution, murder, rape, suicide, theft, all of these may manifest in any pilgrim or tourist town, but the analysis of social pathology is not the subject of this work.

In 2005, I heard of a young Frenchman who died in a cave in Tiruvannamalai. For many years he had walked in the streets of the town wearing a calfskin loincloth, tawny, muscular, broken ... yet striving to find that space of consummation. Do we have the terms by which we can understand such experimentation, or are we to close our hearts and minds to the occurrence of deaths in pilgrim towns? It is imperative to anthropologically record this death, and for both our countries, India and France, to examine the ways in which industrialism might call upon some to make the mystical search. Also, are madness and death the only resolution to this search?

My notes for the winter of 2003, at the Ramanasramam are presented here. Should the social anthropologist intervene, when he or she sees something untoward? This is one of the most significant problems for the professional scribe, who plays a shadow role, in order to observe.

There is a wild boy who is dressed like Mowgli, a handsome, long limbed tawny fellow who is completely naked, except for a garment made from what looks like the spathe of coconut. He is long haired and manic, and he appears in the long hall but the guards whip him gently and throw him out. He staves off their batons with which they prod him, by yelling that he is a mahayogi and he needs a place to meditate. He is furious at the asram but the devotees are relieved that he has been chased off. One afternoon I come back and hear the door of the cave monument near my room open. I look out and see that the hillock has some carvings like window apertures, and inside I know having checked it out myself – there is a steep staircase. If one can get in through the tiny door, one can enter the cave. It is disused and dirty, so no one usually goes in there. I wonder if I should tell the management, but somehow I don't. I'm scared that the wild boy will come back, and I'm embarrassed that I saw him leave. Anyway I don't have the words right then to describe the expression on his face, when I saw him leave the hole … smeared in what looks like mud abundantly happy, though. I keep the doors of the room I'm lodged in locked, feel scared, but do nothing.

I think it's because the French hermit, of whom I know nothing, had got his wish, and because he looked happy, as if all that he had most longed for had occurred. There is a section of le Saux's work which describes mysticism as more dangerous than drugs or psychoanalysis.

My notes for December 2004 and January 2005, continues recording of this tragic story.

The surge of the tsunami follows us everywhere. We are never ever free of its shadow. Yet the asram protects one from every possible upheaval … from sorrow and tomorrow, and that is why one longs to return. What was Thomas Mann's Magic Mountain *about? It was about a sanatorium where the heated up and the despised go for a while … and the young man tormented by his desires, finds good company with a Jesuit. Here, too, one knows that everyone who is here is here because they have been in crises. I am told by my friend, Prerna (name changed), one evening, that a young Frenchman was found dead in the rock cave where he was hiding. He had been dead for some days when he was found, and his body had turned blue. I felt horror and regret … I should have told the asramam's trustees that I had seen him disappear into this convoluted turret … but I myself had been so afraid when I saw him emerge covered in slime, looking around like some branded wolf afraid of humans, that I had not said a word. He was such a beautiful golden long limbed youth, so desperate to meditate, till the light he longed for would bombard, brighter than a thousand suns, who can survive that moment of encounter? Yet, how was I to know that he would die? I only knew that he longed to meditate in Ramana's sacred garden and whenever he was found, the guards would chase him away, and he would turn violent, yelling, 'I Sadguru! I Ramana!'*

Now, I feel that if we accept the concept of destiny, all battle and all reason are taken away from us, and we float in that space of freedom, so ungovernable and without boundaries or trajectories. This is why the asramam is so careful about vetting everyone's desires to be there, and you have to constantly prove that you belong. Prerna told me that the young Frenchman had a University background, and that he was sent money by his family. But he would keep a couple of hundreds, and the rest he would hand out in fistfuls to the beggars. He had apparently given thirty thousand rupees to one beggar woman ... 'But then,' Prerna says, 'he died in a cave in Tiruvannamalai, in Ramanasramam, that in itself assures him a good rebirth.'

Prerna, a French citizen, has been living in Tiruvannamalai for many years, visiting the asram for prayers in the evenings. She is always happy, though oddly the stories of physical distress are frequent (landlord, broken pipes, dreadful falls and broken limbs) and it all culminates in the distress of her son and his family to her exile in some strange and unknown place in south India. They do not understand, nor does the State, so sometimes there are problems with her pension. And as for banking, she goes all the way to Pondicherry to handle that ... Devotees accept the call of the enchanted mountain as the culmination of their lives, a self-fulfilling prophecy as Marx would say. Experienced forms of religious effervescence are hard to circumscribe!

This time I turn to the writing of a devotee named Nagamma to orient my work. Here was a woman who wrote letters ... the same length every time, probably written on inlands ... she wrote almost every day to her brother, because he demanded news of Bhagavan and the asramam (I come to know later that it was a diary). She is really interesting ... companion to Bhagavan in some odd and intellectualist way, recorder of the circumstances of the latter years of his life, a friendship and love that blazons the pages ... what shame is there in loving? That's the interesting thing about this work ... we have no veils to hide the quality of our feelings when we are on the mountain, yet we are asked to don these veils, so that the light on our faces will not dim our recognition of routine tasks. Those routine tasks must continue, and we become known by the work we do. Mine is, I fear, only to appear and look around and be startled by the Annamalais, and particularly Arunachala ... clouds, plants, creatures which inhabit this ancient hill range. I feel no threat, and the oscillation between subjective experience and objective record are the anthropologist's trademark.

Andrew Abbott in *Time Matters* (2001) writes there are methodological turning points in writing theory. He says turning points are processes and thus have a time duration. They are often located in narrative structures and are marked as catalysts. Reading narratives thus embarks the subject upon a journey. Abbot then goes on to speak of boundaries. He believes we should focus on the links between boundaries. Fixed entities exist, but process is to be understood through linkages and the question of time or duration. Thus, '… social entities come into existence when social actors tie social boundaries together in certain ways. Boundaries come first, then entities.' As spatial maps go, this is not hard to follow. He goes on to say continuity between boundaries is of significance, rather than synchrony and logical relationships. We thus analyse, in a fixed world of institutions, where the web is galvanized by actors (Abbott 2001: 263). Neighbourhood would then be seen as sites of proximity but also some difference. For the mystic and the activist, the earth condenses into a neighbourhood, where all people converge as familiar and intimate. There, however, *is* a theory of distance built into a cosmos where all are seen as brothers or sisters. Abbott would answer this problem by bringing in the category of an 'adjacency structure':

> That is, we imagine some kind of metric or propinquity that places institutions or boundaries. Examples of these metrics might be professional mobility between areas, or career, structure linkage between areas, or relations of division of labor, or client exchange or whatever. It seems to me that we should for the present leave the nature of propinquity open. I simply underline that I have assumed some kind of propinquity measure, which may or may not be independent of the dimensions of difference. (269)

He returns us to the sociologically valid category of actor. Abbott says that the yoking between boundaries takes place through events, which are unique and historical but when repeated form a pattern. He uses the term 'scripting' to explain how narratives are formed. Scripting does not produce an entity, but is one of 'several ways of conducting the action that pulls together a set of boundaries into a social entity' (276).

Narratives, thus, not only describe a world, they sometimes bring a world into existence. Comparative sociology has always seen this to be the central motif of its task. I shall now discuss why Simone Weil believed the recognition of the needs of others is the first step to shared humanity. The boundary between social work, political action, and mysticism is sometimes blurred.

II

Simone Weil argues that the first quality of being human is to recognize hunger in another. Human rights – food, shelter, clothing, education, medical facility, community, these appease hunger. But there is the hunger that arises from the moral condition of humans as well.

This is where the question of obligation becomes most evident. Privileges accrue towards oneself – obligation is towards the other. There is a dialogicity that is set up as soon as we recognize the needs of others – this would then be conversations rather then a monologue. 'A man left alone in the world would have no rights, he would have only duties' (Weil 1987b: 3).

There is, for Weil, a dialectic between the subjectivity of rights and the objectivity of obligations. The needs of the spirit are real, for Simone, for she says they are difficult to recognize or to count, but everyone knows they exist. There are the palpable and different forms of cruelty 'a conqueror can exercise over a subject population; such as massacre, mutilation, organized famine, enslavement or large-scale deportation', and there are forms of cruelty which 'can injure a man's life without injuring his body', such as the loss of freedom, or the fear of the loss of freedom' (7).

For Weil, the collectivity is sacred in the Durkheimian sense, as are rules, and institutions even more so. These institutions must be protected, they are 'unique and irreplaceable', for they are our link with past generations, and are the conveyor of ideas (8). But she beckons us to beware of those collectivities which demand unspeakable sacrifices, and those 'dead collectivities' which without devouring souls don't nourish them either (9). She recognizes the difference between needs and desires, whims, fantasies and vices. 'Man requires not rice or potatoes but food'. The maintenance and representation of order is paramount. Like Durkheim's work, there is fragility to this position, a possibility of compromise or mitigation. Order, like symmetry, can become an end in itself.

That search for order she defines as a journey. This journey is often in the dark, without a light, and sometimes without a guide, demanding the ultimate sacrifice, but it is characterized by hope – this is what makes us human and pacifist.

In order, contradictions are reconciled and there is a fine balance between antithetical poles. Hunger and appeasement. Desire and waiting. For Weil it is the ability to choose that is the greatest attribute of freedom. Yet we are encircled by rules. These rules must be comprehensible to the people who are thus bound by them. People must understand their usefulness, their applicability and their necessity. They must be simple enough, so that people who adhere to these rules are not confounded, every time they wish to apply them or think about them. This right to information, it would seem, is an inherent human right for Simone Weil (13).

The plank on which mysticism can be read in the modern world is thus around anti-war, anti-bureaucratization, anti-capitalism and anti-consumption. If anyone was concerned with re-enchanting the world, it was Simone Weil. She was sensitive to the degradation brought about by the machineries of war. So also was Abhishiktananda, who had escaped by bicycle in disguise, and had 'interred himself' in the monastery in Brittany through the war years. Simone Weil wrote that 'God has created a world which is not the best possible but which contains the whole range of good and evil. We are at the point where it is as bad as possible because beyond is the stage where evil becomes innocence' (Weil 1987a xviii). But it is also the stage where love is just possible, where it is a great privilege .... For the mystic on the other hand, the closeness to god was translated in the need for solitude and the desire to love and care for others.

In mysticism, our reading of boundaries begins to transform. Sometimes the engagement with what is community care, or social work, highlights itself in the co-operative work of the residents at a religious organization or a company of mendicants. Here, the question as Andrew Abbott argues, the quest of transformation sharply posits itself. Boundaries are what are formed at specific historical moments, and professionalization is the result. 'And it is my contention that the separations themselves emerged as interdependent unconnected boundaries long before it made any sense to speak of social work as a social entity' (Abbott 2001: 268). Abbott encourages us to think of 'sites of proximity having some difference'. If we think of functions, rather than specialized roles, similarities might overarch differences. Philanthropy, redistribution, reciprocity, care, organization, nurturing – all might be marked by 'propinquity'. This feature of closeness across difference, involving categories of the 'local' and 'adjacent', helps us to understand relationships of difference, as well as division of labour, clientship, dependence and autonomy. He suggests the metaphor of 'yoking' or linking between the mosaics of difference. It is a hard core sociology that suggests that scripting action leads to action. There is a relationship of great dynamism between given texts and what historians call 'events'. In my work, Paul Ricoeur's imperative that we look at language as if it were action, and C. Wright Mill's preoccupation with culture, biography and history will prevail as emblems of the sociological imagination.

In the third and fourth chapters I deal with the social anthropology of tourists and pilgrims and the narratives they leave for us as witnesses. I specifically discuss the event of Maharshi Ramana's life and death in the context of women's narratives as a particular type of record keeping. Here, death is experienced, understood and transformed by the Maharshi into a cerebral space of detachment and transcendence. This indeed is the spine of his theology. After this moment, there is no death, there is only absorption. Thus the actual historical moment of mortality becomes a further re-articulation of the advaitic understanding of death, which is merging into the great light. I shall use the record of Suri Nagamma, who is one of Bhagavan's devotees. The key problem, as with much of narrative analysis, revolves around the question of memory. Raphael Samuel in *Theatres of Memory* (1994) writes that 'Memory, according to the ancient Greeks, was the precondition of human thought' (vii). Yet, the narratives of the marginalized are always open to doubt, even if published by the home press. Nathaniel Mackey, interestingly, calls this kind of writing 'discrepant engagement'. Much feminist writing and first person testimonials may fit into this category. Those who want their stories told see themselves as marginals and hope to be included in conventional formats of articulation. 'Discrepant engagement, rather than suppressing resonance, dissonance, noise, seeks to remain open to them. Its admission of resonances contends with resolution' (Mackey 1993: 20). Such a verb function, of which writing is such a dominant expression, takes on fixed nouns, monolithic structures, contests categorizations which are given and is always against monolithic forms of knowledge (21).

3
TRAVELLERS AND PILGRIMS

Claude Levi-Strauss begins his *Tristes Tropiques* (1976) with the damning statement that he hates travelling and explorers. This is probably based on the assumption the records of missionaries, administrators and travellers are dangerous for anthropological writings. In 1955, when *Tristes Tropiques* was first published, the author had a terror for nostalgia, or for describing the routine dangers an anthropologist must face, 'periods of hunger, exhaustion, sickness perhaps' (15). As he continues with the task of documenting the manner in which he collected data on Brazil, in the mid '30s, he becomes bolder, and chronicles the truly terrorizing incidents of fieldwork. I will not go into them except to list them for the curious ... bees which did not sting, but sucked at the eyes and lips and nostrils (353), a 'putrid opthalmia' which affected the victims, tribals and ethnographers (including his wife who was a team member) with the dread of blindness and paralysis (395), jokes and distancing mechanism which included mumbling and pronunciation distortions (366), the extinction of the group studied (382), worm infested food, dreadful hunger, or survival by eating lizards and armadillos (420). There was also the question of transport over rivers and through jungles. 'Moreover, out of the thirty-one oxen I had started off with, I had only seventeen left, and they were in such poor condition that it was impossible for them to carry on even over easy territory' (422). Part of the team, with Claude Levi-Strauss as member, shifts to boats to complete the journey.

> All we had to do was to follow the Rio Machado downstream. Months of drought had made us careless, and the first evening we did not bother to put our hammocks under shelter, but merely slung them between trees on the

> river bank. The storm broke in the middle of the night with a noise like a horse galloping; before we were even fully awake, our hammocks had been transformed into bath-tubs; we fumbled about in the dark trying to unroll a waterproof canvas sheet to serve as a roof, but it was impossible to fix up in the torrential rain. Sleep was out of the question: crouching in the water and supporting the canvas with our heads, we had constantly to keep an eye on the folds which kept filling up with rain, and empty them before it came through. To pass the time, the men told stories.

It is these stories, which were transcribed for us in the volumes on kinship and aesthetic representation, particularly narratives, which form the backbone of anthropology courses. We might have tired of binary oppositions, preferring Marcel Mauss' early preoccupation with tripartite structures, or Victor Turner's focus on mediation as a central heuristic device, yet the claims Levi-Strauss has on our imagination is renewed by reading *Tristes Tropiques*, which is truly the celebration of the spectacular. It deals with questions as diverse as body painting, and its aesthetic dimensions, to questions of love and family, the relationship between the colonizing impulse and the decimation of the natives. Interspersed among these very carefully crafted chapters is a digression which takes us to a recently partitioned subcontinent. On India, soon after partition, Levi-Strauss' memories are devastating, and at the same time full of the subcontinent's optimism and resilience. The years of the visit are not certain (1948-50?). It is a newly partitioned country, and the traveller captures it in the thirty closely printed pages titled the *Magic Carpet*, *Crowds* and *Markets*. Like most popular writing on the Indian subcontinent, the themes are garbage, beggars, sycophancy, corruption and exploitation. Karachi, Dacca, Calcutta merge in this one exhalation. Like Katharine Mayo, before him, his report describes the alienation of the city as

> ... filth, chaos, promiscuity, congestion; ruins, huts, mud, dirt; dung, urine, pus, humours, secretions and running sores: all the things against which we expect urban life to give us organized protection, all the things we hate and guard against at such great cost, all these by-products of cohabitation do not set any limitation on it in India. They are more like a natural environment which the Indian town needs in order to prosper. To every individual, any street, foot path or alley affords a home, where he can sit, sleep and even pick up his food straight from the glutinous filth. Far from repelling him, this filth

> acquires a kind of domestic status through having been exuded, excreted, trampled on and handled by so many men. (169)

The anthropologist as traveller encounters a world quite unlike any he has attempted to capture in his painstaking records on Amazonia. He sees this as 'clinical symptoms of a life and death struggle'.

In case the reader feels that a flying visit is an obstacle to recording social life, Levi-Strauss assures us that:

> I have visited all kinds of markets; in Calcutta, the new and the old ones; the Bombay Bazaar at Karachi; the markets of Delhi and the Sadar and Kunari in Agra; Dacca, which is a series of soukhs, with families living huddled in the nooks and crannies between the stalls and craftsmen's workshops; Riazuddin Bazaar and Khatunganj at Chittagong, all those at the gates of Lahore: Anarkali Bazaar, Delhi, Shah, Almi and Akbari; and Sadr, Dabgiri, Sirki, Bajori, Ganj and Kalan at Peshawar. At country fairs in the Khyber Pass along the Afghan frontier, and at Rangamati near the Burmese frontier. I have visited fruit and vegetable markets, with their piles of egg-plants, pink onions and burst pomegranates releasing a heady guava-like smell; flower markets where florists intertwined roses and jasmine with tinsel and angel hair; the displays of dried-fruit merchants, brown, tawny heaps on a background of silver paper; I have seen and smelt spices dry and curried, pyramids of red, orange and yellow powder; mountains of peppers, emitting a pungent odour of dried apricots and lavender which was enough to make the senses reel. I have seen meat-roasters, the boilers of milk-curds, the pancake-makers – nan or chapatti; tea and lemonade sellers, whole-sale date merchants with their produce piled up in sticky mounds of pulp and stones suggesting the excreta of some dinosaur; pastry-cooks, who might have been mistaken for vendors of flies, presenting their wares on a base of cake; tinkers who could be heard a hundred yards away because of the loud rumble of their hammers; basket makers and rope-makers with their yellow and green straw; hat-makers who had arranged the gilded cones of kallas, resembling the mitres of the Sassanid kings, in rows interspersed with turban cloths; textile shops, hung with lengths of freshly dyed blue or yellow material, as well as with saffron and pink artificial silk scarves in the Bokhara style; cabinet-makers, wood-carvers and laquerers of bedsteads; knife grinders pulling on the cords of their grinding-wheels; scrap-iron fairs, separate from the rest, and cheerless; tobacco vendors with their heaps of golden leaves, alternating with russet masses of tomabak, alongside bundles of chilam tubes, vendors of

> sandals, stacked in hundreds like bottles in a wine store; sellers of bracelets or bangles like pink and blue glass intestines lying higgledy-piggledy as if they were the product of a recent disembowelling; potters shops, with oblong, varnished, chilam water – vases arranged in rows; jars fashioned out of micaceous clay, and others painted brown, white and red on a background of tawny earthenware, with vermicular ornamental markings; and chilam bowls strung together like rosaries; flour vendors sieving flour all day long; gold and silver-smiths weighing tiny fragments of precious braid in shop fronts which were less brilliant than those of the nearby tin smiths; calico-printers striking the white cotton fabric with a deft, monotonous movement which left a delicate coloured pattern and blacksmiths working in the open air. All this formed a swarming and ordered world above which rose a forest of multicoloured children's windmills, mounted on sticks and fluttering like leaves stirring in the breeze.

If one accepts the virtue of these thousand words, which today we can still capture in a photograph, without much change of its visual content, Levi-Strauss' intentions to record must be accepted.

In my published essays on the pilgrim town of Tiruvannamalai in South India over the last ten years, I too have noted the garbage accompanying the great symmetry of the mountain Arunachala and the temple dedicated to Shiva and Parvati in their consummation as Ardhanareeswara. In subsequent visits, I noticed that the temple is now very clean, resembling in fact photographs from the 1930s, when the crowds were fewer.

Court cases putting the onus on the Tiruvannamalai municipality to clean up the area, a public interest litigation and suggestions from the Archaelogical Survey of India have had some part to play in the general cleansing of the town and temple complex. An essay by a devotee in the *Mountain Path*, the official journal of the Ramanasramam, describes the garbage and noise as the chief detriments to meditation, but that skimming over it, or delving beyond it, the devotee recognizes the meditational joy of being with the Lord. To me, it seems, that anthropology is still dependent on traveller's accounts, and that we merely need to bring to it the objectivity of our gaze. A resident of Ramanasramam, Captain Narayanan, brilliantly describes the activities pertaining to the lighting of the Beacon, and then prosaically says, 'The old order gives way to the new, yet the devotion of the people has remained the same. In fact it has increased manifold, for amidst such noise and bustle, the devotee is able to inwardly experience peace and tranquility…' (*Sri Bhagavan's Devotees* 2004: 78).

As an anthropologist and traveller who participates in the nature of pilgrimage, my notes for 2003 are:

Winter's Light in the Year 2003

Sunlight too, on a winter's day in Delhi. The days have been volatile – rainy, windy, cold and suddenly the sun bursts again. I've just returned from three days in Tiruvannamalai.

I was driven down to this temple town from Bangalore, at hundred miles an hour by a young knave who didn't know the way, and had us trapped for one hour and more at a toll-booth. He did not know that transport officials in India take lunch-breaks with no substitutes functioning in their place. When we reached the gate, at Hosur, there were about thirty trucks and as many cars and vans. I was at a pitch of exhaustion, after having finished correcting examinations scripts before setting out on my journey, and therefore, succumbed gracefully to fatalism. In any case I was carrying with me Thor Heyrdahl's Kon Tiki. *This is that fabulous anthropological work on how contemporary Nordic sailors retracing the route of ancient Peruvian sailors to the Easter islands found serenity and wonder in isolation and danger. One of them had taken around seventy-three books on sociology on the raft, which he proceeded to read with the waves sloshing around him.*

Finally, we reached the asram at night, instead of dusk. The roads were jammed with people, hundreds of them, jubilant that after three years of drought, the rains had come at last and the wells were full, almost to the brim. It was almost impossible to cross the road.

'It's an agricultural fair,' Dr Srinivasamurthy informs me. 'The local farmers sell their produce, including cattle.' Indeed, there is a fourteen kilometre rural market that encircles the hill.

A fire is lit on the Arunachala mountain. It is a fire so intense, so immense, it can be seen for miles. Peasants and urbanites throng to this sacred pilgrimage town, from all parts of the South and the rest of India and the world to see the flame which is thought to have been present from the earliest times.

The librarian at the asramam, J. Jayaraman, explains the significance of the fire. It commemorates the conjoining of Shiva and Parvati, it also symbolizes the unitary principle that sets aside hierarchy, when Brahma and Vishnu quarrel over supremacy with one another, and Shiva appears to them in a column of fire. 'It's an eternal fire, which requires some human help to keep it stoked' he says. 'The pilgrims bring their share of ghee to pour in the cauldron at the top.'

On this trip, I feel full of an intense sense of purpose. I have my camera, notebooks, and several pens. I arrive early in the morning, looking purposeful, at the asramam office. V.S. Mani is busy, but he laughs when I tell him that I want to engage with the rituals at the temple. 'I'll have to make a very important phone-call' he says reassuringly, but then he realizes that the crowds are such that it will be impossible for me to reach the sanctum in the temple without standing for several hours in the queue. I see the truth of this myself, later in the morning, when I venture out and the crowds are so multitudinous, that there is no negotiable space. I will have to leave it for another time.

I decide to visit the office of the Mountain Path *on the first floor of the office buildings. One of the staff agrees to speak with me.*

'The Mountain Path *has a completely new format. Many of the old subscribers have died, and their children write, saying that they don't want to continue with the* Mountain Path. *The new devotees have different needs, they are from different parts of the world, they have more sophisticated and cerebral needs, and the* Mountain Path *was beginning to cut and paste from earlier issues, so the asramam felt that the new editor was the best person to steer the magazine into a new space. Besides he knows many people and has many friends everywhere.' Just then, the editor walks into the air-conditioned, book-lined, computer-endowed office. He agrees to give me an interview at 4 p.m., probably thinking how obdurate the anthropologist is. It is difficult to get access to anything unless people trust you. I'm not yet sure if that trust in me as a person or as an anthropologist has yet been established.*

A man and a woman come into the main office, which is open to visitors from 8 a.m. to 12 noon and then again from 2 p.m. to 8 p.m. The man is very disturbed, and the woman is weeping. Their pockets have been slashed and they have lost 1800 rupees. The man wants fifty rupees to go home by bus. The woman is dressed in fine silks, and the only thing the man has in his pocket is his identity card, which he keeps pointing to, saying 'I will money-order the amount on my arrival in my home-town.' The chief accountant, who was a resident during Ramana's time, listens to the story, then while I wonder nervously whether the couple would be refused, he takes out three hundred rupees and gives it to the husband and wife, and says, 'Return it after you reach home'. The evening before, Dr Srinivasamurthy, who deals with five thousand guests to the asramam lodge every year, told me, 'Go out if you must, but be careful of your bag and your keys. Be careful of knives.' Alas, the morning proved quite conclusively that the doctor was being as practical as always.

Chastened by my experience of the real world, where robbers strike where they will, I set out to go on the pradikhshanam (circumambulation of the hill).

I am caught in a web of laughing, talking, eager people. It is a pilgrimage of joy, successful harvest perhaps to look forward to, for the rains have been miraculous. After the hard summer, when the water in the wells have touched rock bottom, the damp earth and the filled wells are a miracle. Pongal is around the corner.

I move in step with the people. The women who have brought grass fodder for sale, smile and clutch the green stalks as a tribute to the art of perseverance. They look like they are from the third century poems that A.K. Ramanujan translated for eager English speaking readers. There is a laughter and voluptuousness to them, a sense of love and the memory of war. I often think that the people of India, the peasants and the poor, are never put out by the vagaries of the State. They live out their lives in a particular space, and in ways which are adaptative to time, but nevertheless, communicate a resilience to homogenization. The pilgrims seem concerned only with the essential tasks of pilgrimage, oblivious to any other subtext.

The fourteen kilometres route of the Giri pradikshanam is lined with shops on either side. This is the real heart of the town's commerce. At festival times, the peasants of the hinterland and the merchants of Tiruvannamalai rake in enough profits to allow them to subsist for the remaining part of the year, which is also focused around the pilgrimage to the great Shiva temple – the Arunachaleswara temple. There is rentier capital as well, besides shops, and agricultural land which is either owned or laboured upon.

I walk and walk, first with the intensity of the anthropologist's gaze... a seeing which records details, which is observation and classification, compounded by the delight in people's differing ways of life. The hill seems very distant to me, composed as it is of the multitudes who are calling out to one another, to the vendors who shout louder than them and the general sense of food, flowers, ribbons, books, audio-cassettes blaring. I see however that without this effervescence of people's belief, happy memories which they take back home, the re-vitalising aspects of people's pilgrimage cannot be understood. So much of Mikhail Bakhtin's work recorded just this aspect of the second life of the people.

The crowds are immense. Mothers carry overgrown children who do not wish to walk anymore, young husbands hold the hands of their even younger wives, there is a surge of people, but none of it is mildly threatening. Clearly pilgrimages are states of holiday making, and the ardour of faith is matched by the delight in the locale itself. I am convinced that this is due to the myth itself – the unification of two volatile lovers, Shiva and Parvathi, and also perhaps the unifying of three principles, Vishnu, Brahma and Shiva. Why is annihilation more powerful than creation or preservation – I will never quite understand, but practically I suppose it is something which is daily affirmed to us.

At six o'clock that day, the lamp is going to be lit in the narrow space directly outside the large hall in the asramam. It is Deepam, the annual Karthikeyi festival. People have gathered while a space has been cordoned off for the objects of ritual. These are placed on a table, a lamp which is a wick placed in a bowl dripping with ghee, a large portrait of Ramana Maharshi, and a pair of binoculars along with the begging bowl which had belonged to him. Kanakamma, one of Ramana's devotees, told me Bhagavan would sit on his chair without moving, and watch the flame, through the binoculars. The people gathered there would watch without speaking, and his concentration was so total there was not a whisper, not a floating leaf to disturb him in his meditative gaze.

On 7 December 2003, people have gathered together in anticipation of seeing the flame. There are devotees in the crowd who have never met before, but are immediately engaged in conversation about the primacy of devotion. One says, 'Modallae Bhagavan' (Bhagavan comes first!) and the other says 'Modallae Arunachala' (Arunachala comes first!). The mysteries of non-dualism have escaped them for the moment. But when the fire is visible, that first moment when it comes into view on the mountain, the sense of beauty and calm is as visible as the love between two people who will never be separated. It is the suddenness of the fire that takes everyone by surprise though many of them would have seen it a lot of times before. From where we are, it is not a large flame, it is a deepam – the light of a candle, but so consistent with Jesus' saying, 'A light on the hill that cannot be hid....' I understand people like to believe in the idea of eternity and their part in it.

II

A pilgrim is often the best of travellers. He or she carries with him or her the idea that the place of pilgrimage is one goal among other greater transcendant ones. One of the best writers, in the genre called *pennu eyarthu* or women's writing, is a devotee of Ramana Maharshi called Nagamma. She was born in August 1902, in a village in Guntur. She was married at eleven years of age, and widowed at twelve. She spent many years in religious devotion, and slowly educated herself in the vernacular religious literature. She had a vision of Dakshinamurthy, who is associated with Arunachala, as early as 1913. She began to practice visible religious austerities from 1918, while staying with her brother who was a lawyer in Vijayawada. Her brothers were progressive, and did not stand in her way, though others were censorious, since she did not shave her head. While her family was supportive, yet her *desire* to be an ascetic was so strong that she became fatally ill. She went to her father's ancestral home in Kolanukonda, which had been lying vacant for a long time.

> Hence, snakes, scorpions and other poisonous reptiles had made it their home and were freely roaming about. We had to live together, but we did not interfere with one another. They used to come out in the night time and left me in peace during the day. Our life together was very amusing and it gave me ample opportunities to lead a life of friendliness towards all living beings.

During this time of recuperation which included natural foods (*jowar* flour, vegetables, no spices) performing *pujas*, reading and explaining the Bhagavatam to those who assembled at her house, she prayed for a guru. Her brother D.S. Shastri had met Sri Ramana Maharshi on one of his travels, and encouraged his sister to meet him. In July 1941, she boarded the train to get to Tiruvannamalai. It was 8.30 p.m. when she reached the town. She slept on the verandah of the house of a lady she had just met, whose husband served at the asramam and who advised her to meet a Telugu woman called Subbulakshmi who would take care of her, while she visited the asramam.

The record of her days as described in *My Life at Ramanasramam* (Nagamma 1993) conveys a sense of a deep happiness and a life well spent. What we have here is the pilgrimage of interiority.

> After I got the grace of Bhagavan, like Ahalya getting rid of her past ignorance with the touch of the dust of the holy feet of Sri Rama, my mind became clear with the dispelling of its darkness. It turned inwards and began a sort of Self-Enquiry. I now realized that whatever spiritual practices I had followed till then were only the paths leading to this Self-enquiry. (21)

Whenever she had a problem, she would consult Ramana Maharshi, who had very early admired her intellectual and spiritual verve. He had once introduced her, saying, 'Look. Her name is Nagamma, it seems. These are verses on saranagati. Paste them in the book' (15). Four days afterwards, she wrote three verses on Ramana and the asram. To her delight, these were also accepted and pasted in the book. Her prowess as a writer became confirmed when she started writing a record of asram

life in the form of letters to her elder brother. He had gifted her with a diary to record everyday events, since he enjoyed hearing about it, but it was not an oeuvre she felt comfortable with.
Her brother responded,

> "Never mind about writing a diary. You are anyway writing to me now and then about various happenings in Bhagavan's presence. In the same way write letters addressed to me but keep them with you. We will decide what to do with them in due course. We shall change them suitably if necessary." Accordingly, he brought a pen and a bundle of writing paper and left them with me. (31)

Other visitors to the asramam also begged her saying that,

> "We all come and go. Please take up the writing work as your duty, assimilate and pass on to us the voice of Bhagavan." I agreed and accordingly commenced writing the letters in November 1945 after praying to Bhagavan for success inwardly, as I had not the courage to tell him openly about it. (31)

Devaraja Mudaliar, another devotee, was writing a diary at the same time. One day, he came across Nagamma polishing her letters of which she had written five or six, read them, was delighted with their quality and told Maharshi about them. He asked Nagamma to read them to him, so she made fair copies and carried them to the asramam.

> In the first letter, I had written about Bhagavan as follows: "What is there for him? Should he bundle up his belongings? A walking stick, a kamamandalam and koupeenam; that is all he has." When he heard this, Bhagavan said jokingly, "Ayyayo. What about this towel? She has forgotten all about this." Everybody laughed. (32)

By July 1947, a dozen advance copies of *Letters from Sri Ramanasramam* published in Madras were ready. Two weeks later a thousand copies were received in the asramam along with favourable reviews in the newspapers, and orders for copies began to come (47). But along with it came jealous responses which grew so vivid that Chinnaswami (the brother of Ramana Maharshi) requested her to 'Stop with this now.' Since the practical matters of the asramam were run by him, she stopped reading aloud on the next afternoon itself. When Bhagavan asked her why she did not read, she said,

> Chinnaswami asked me not to, I replied. "Is that so?" he said and looking at Rajagopal Iyer, who was nearby, remarked, "Our asking someone to read and their asking them not to do so is curious. It means we should not ask anybody to read." (48)

Chinnaswami explained that he only wanted the writing of letters to be stopped. To maintain peace in the asramam, under pressure from jealous witnesses, he took away the library keys from Nagamma, and copies of unpublished letters. She was unconsolable and told Maharshi who comforted her saying, *'Never mind. Let that work go'* (49).

> I gave up the library work without much regret but I was very sad indeed that I had to give away all the letters I had with me. I had heard that some years before, the asram authorities had confiscated the diary of Sri Venkarramayya and so, as matter of caution, the original letters which formed Part II of the series had been taken away to Madras by my brother a week earlier. Hence I had with me only carbon copies.
>
> Anyway, I felt I should obey orders... We found Bhagavan sitting leisurely with outstretched legs. There was absolute quiet in the hall. I entered trembling all over, placed the bundle at the feet of Bhagavan, folded my hands and with shaky voice said, "Here are the letters. I have been asked to hand them over to the asram. I have bundled them and brought them here. It is not merely a bundle of letters. It is my heart's treasure. Bhagavan may do whatever he likes with them. I never did the work for fame or wealth." As I said that, tears rolled down my cheeks in abundance. Bhagavan looked at me with sympathy and received the bundle with both his hands. He turned it over and giving it to Rajagopala Iyer remarked, "Here it is. She has brought all the letters duly bundled. Take them and give them to the office." Meanwhile, I wiped my tears and sat in the front row reserved for the ladies. (49)

The tears did not stop, however, and Nagamma stayed away from the asramam for ten days, since all the work she was used to doing had been taken away from her. She describes this as a period of tears and madness, which broke only when she started writing verses in honour of Maharshi, which she offered in person to Maharshi.

On the third of these occasions he broke his silence, and gave her a *stotram*, which someone had dedicated to him, to read.

> After I finished reading he began telling me all that had happened in the last ten days as if he had tied the news up in a bundle which he was opening for my sake. He went on like that for over an hour. All were surprised at the sudden change. I felt happy and contented.
>
> From then onwards, he himself used to call me and talk to me. I showed him the song I had composed, namely "Palukave okasarei Ramana" (Wont you speak for once, O Ramana!) thinking he did not know anything about it. Laughing at me for my foolishness, he said, "Yes, I know. Keep it." I felt ashamed of my stupidity. (51)

These letters describe the details of life at the asramam with such lucidity and tenderness that the identity of the writer and her subject seem to merge. One of the most powerful of such writers was Paul Brunton who brought many pilgrims to Arunachala by the verve of his writing. It's not unusual in the Ramana archives to come across a writer who says, 'I had read Brunton's book *A Search In Secret India*.'

Brunton's work is of significance even today because we get a marvellous and literal line drawing of the topography of Ramana's asramam and the vicinity of the Arunachala temple.

See for example, Brunton's description of Maharshi's darshan:

> The divan is but a few paces away from a broad high window in the end wall. The light falls clearly upon the Maharishee and I can take in every detail of his profile, for he is seated gazing rigidly through the window in the precise direction whence we have come this morning. His head does not move, so thinking to catch his eye and greet him as I offer the fruits, I move quietly over to the window, place the gift before him, and retreat a pace or two.
>
> A small brass brazier stands before his couch. It is filled with burning charcoal, and a pleasant odour tells me that some aromatic powder has been thrown on the glowing embers. Close by is an incense burner filled with joss sticks. Threads of bluish grey smoke arise and float in the air, but the pungent perfume is quite different.... There is something in this man which holds my attention as steel filings are held by a magnet. I cannot turn my gaze away from him. My initial bewilderment, my perplexity at being totally ignored,

> slowly fades away as this strange fascination begins to grip me more firmly. But it is not till the second hour of the uncommon scene that I become aware of a silent resistless change which is taking place within my mind. One by one, the questions which I have prepared in the train with such meticulous accuracy drop away. For it does not now seem to matter whether they are asked or not, and it does not seem to matter whether I solve the problems which have hitherto troubled me. I know only that a steady river of quietness seems to be flowing near me, that a great peace is penetrating the inner reaches of my being, and that my thought-tortured brain is beginning to arrive at some rest. (Brunton 2003: 141)

Another passage records their further meeting. On one hot afternoon, when most people are resting,

> I enter the large hall and sit down near him. He half reclines upon some white cushions placed on the divan. An attendant pulls steadily at the cord which operates the punkah-fan. The soft burr of the rope and the gentle swish of the fan, as they move through the sultry air sound pleasantly in my ears.
>
> The Maharishee holds a folded manuscript book in his hands; he is writing something with extreme carefulness. A few minutes after my entry, he puts the book aside and calls a disciple. A few words pass between them in Tamil and the man tells me that his master wishes to reiterate his regrets at my inability to partake of their food. He explains that they live a simple life, and never having catered for Europeans before, do not know what the latter eat. I thank the Maharishee, and say that I shall be glad to share their unspiced dishes with them; for the rest, I shall procure some food from the township. (143)

In this essay I am concerned with the resources provided to social scientists by those who record pilgrimages. I do not enquire into the nature of indoctrination as Barbara Goodwin (1978) would have us do, or the critical light-hearted interpretation of *Pilgrims and Other Travellers* by Makarand Paranjape (1999). My concern in juxtaposing different fragments of pilgrimage accounts is to argue that while we do have methodologies for taking care of biases, the data provided by such writers goes a long way to establish the primacy of certain kinds of data. As anthropologists in the field we are subject to sense experiences that we call 'subjectivities' and sometimes these pervade our accounts (Meister

2000). To be ashamed of them is unnecessary in the new genres of writing that are increasingly made available to us.

Gary Snyder in his *Passage Through India* (1983) gives us a description of his stay in Tiruvannamalai in the early '60s. The Osbornes are his hosts,

> Here we were met by an Englishman, Arthur Osborne, and his Czech wife. Osborne and his wife have a house hard by the asram ... The Osbornes put us up in a little room on top of their house, from which we could look about the landscape and through a mass of bougainvillea up toward Arunachala. We had our lunches at the asram dining hall, sitting crosslegged on the stone floor, putting a platter of a few leaves stitched together with fiber before us on the floor. A server came along and put rice on the platter, then another fellow came and poured some curry sauce and some ghee on the rice, and put a brass cup of water down. This we ate with our right hands. Afterwards the leaf platter is thrown away, and one washes his hand at a faucet outside. After the meal, coffee is served in a brass cup. South Indians always drink coffee, mixed with milk and lots of sugar, and poured back and forth between two brass pots until it gets frothy. The south Indian curries are very hot, but never actually inedible, and in a way rather fun. The dining hall had about thirty people eating, loincloth dressed sadhus with long hair, layman-type asramites with white dhoti or sari, and a Swiss lady in white sari. Many old pictures of Ramana Maharshi on the walls, including one giant portrait of him standing by his cow Lakshmi. Since Maharshi is no longer there, it is the aura of his previous presence which brings people here, or as the asram pamphlet described it – "Saturated with the Benign Presence of Shri Ramana Maharshi the asram confers the unequalled blessing of peace, bliss, and happiness to the devotee whatsoever the religion he may profess." Many devotees gather morning and evening in the old hall and in front of the Samadhi (tomb) for silent meditation and prayer ... Mrs Osborne wore white sari, and was constantly being greeted by peasant women along the way. She speaks very good Tamil, it seems, (which is rare – everyone says Tamil is terribly difficult, and few foreigners know it, whereas everyone in northern India who's been there a year or so can speak Hindi.) She was great friends with peasants because she is a homeopathic medicine expert and gives treatments free. (24-27)

In 1996, when I first visited the asramam, it was not very different from Snyder's account for 1962! The changes brought about by the twenty-first century have been dramatic, and I record them for the readers.

3 December 2006.
I am back in Tiruvannamalai for Deepam, and this time the change is enormous. A million people turn up in this small temple town, and it bursts at the seams. The sounds of traffic screech endlessly through the night, particularly since it is Deepam, also a Sunday, and Purnima (full moon). Right through the night and day, people walk around the hill. The nature of the crowd has changed, very different now from the crowd I walked with in 2003... it is a carnivalesque crowd, and hurrying and jostling, it spells both euphoria and danger. I step momentarily into the crowd, twenty lakh people swirl around the hill on the first three days, and immediately I know that as a city born person used to discretion and silence, my instincts of self preservation are higher than my desire to understand the crowd. There is revelry and carnival here, disobedience and gaudyness, it is about danger and lust and the swirling quality of life itself. I step back in to the quiet of my room, and the order and regulation of asram life. It is an artificial world that we take recourse to ('us' and 'them') but nevertheless, my sense of survival depends on it. So much of sociological work has hinged around Durkheim's definition of effervescense and collectivity, has depended on being somewhat silent about the nature of crowd life. Is the crowd a sociological category? In this shifting floating mass of people can one perceive institutional structures? The market dominates, and the vendors have found a new way of pulverizing the silence and the calm. For old timers, like Captain Narayanan, whose devotion to Bhagavan and the holy mountain is well known, the noise only serves to highlight the peace within the heart. 'Even the heretic and unemotional spectators are awed and moved by the sublime sight' (Sri Bhagavan's Devotees 2004: 85).

But the underbelly of a carnival town is more than evident now. Beggars have been astounding in their ability to represent mortality and fecundity as the index of corporeality. This time, one of my informants tells me that twenty thousand prostitutes are brought into the town during Deepam. She says that the trucks lined up are the rendezvous for illicit sex. Commerce has become the most visible element of Deepam, the rustic aura is quite gone, it's like a Marquez township, immediately dismantled after the festive days are over.

Asramites don't even consider swimming with the crowd. Hands reach out to touch women, unknown hands, young, eager, quick, and terrifying. Again, one of the women who has lived here for fifteen years, a French citizen, says she can't bear to cross the road and come to the asram on such days, for fear of the crowd. Her body, (she is in her sixties), is pinched and touched and felt and mauled, and she feels degraded and desperate, longing for the tranquility that she left her home and family in Paris for. The asram staff takes the crowd as part of the reality of the message, the success of the sales of books and calendars, of pujas and flowers and momentos. Exclusion is not the principle of Ramana Maharshi's faith. Yet the workers look exhausted, working far beyond their physical stamina. The visitors leave such a trail of garbage which has to be swept up that the cleaning women look quite aghast every morning. 'We are the crowd' is what I have been saying to myself, for these past events of festival. This time, I feel cowed by the numbers. M.N. *Panini, my colleague at the Jawaharlal Nehru University, says that the only way of dealing with shifting densities which are anonymous is to use the idea of 'confluence' as the unit by which such ebbs and flows can be understood. The crowds are not exactly anonymous. Each person like me has a home, a history, an identity, a family. Those crammed in these buses are coming from somewhere, their aim is known to them, and they are excited and fearful even if they have been visiting the temple town of Tiruvannamalai for years.* (see *Bauman* 2006)

On this trip, I have caught a bus from Pallakad, a lovely town on the border of Tamil Nadu and Kerala. I go to Coimbatore in comfort, in an express bus. I presume that it will be connected to Tiruvannamalai, but I am disappointed. I must travel to Salem.

In Salem the bus was rolling along well enough through the congested city, where suddenly the bus stopped. Tyre puncture. Fortuitously, or was it intentional, the bus stopped directly near a tyre puncture repair shop. The driver and conductor had been setting off on a five-hour journey, without a stepney or a spare tyre apparently.

So we all got off. And there we stood helplessly in the sun. Finally it was fixed and we took off again. We passed the most marvellous forests, mainly bamboo, which were dark and sullen and in some odd way, pristine and prickly. I'd never seen forests like that before, and the Annamalais rolled into view with the lovely agricultural land around it. Tamil villages are verdant in winter with rice and fruit and flowers and vegetables riotous in the fields, amassed in the markets. Half the population goes to build roads in metropolitan towns, and the other half grows food. At Harur, some three hours from Tiruvannamalai, and fifty kilometres from Salem, the road was disrupted with granite rubble, pits and holes, and the tyre which had been patched up with water and glue and spit and hope, gave up again. Once more we were close to a tyre repair shop. Clearly, punctured tyres are great business in small hamlets. Immediately a mechanic came, efficiently unplugged the huge tyre and rolled it off. We sat in front of a locked up temple dedicated to Durga and ate our lunches. The bus-driver put us in a country bus and with difficulty we all got into an already packed bus. I put my bag on top of a sack of rice blocking the alleyway.

Two hours down the road, the rice merchant picked up his sacks, roaring at every one in the way, and in the melee threw out my bag as well. I clambered off the bus and got it back. Frightened to death, I sat quietly after that, next to a sweet faced swami, ancient and creased in his new white clothes, going to Arunachala temple for the first time. The bus went on for hours, since country buses have no fixed route. And at last, at 6 p.m. when it was night, and all the lights of the temple town were lit, we got off at Arunachala temple.

All the people struggling in these over packed buses, what do they hope to achieve? The theorists of pilgrimage have always argued that the journeying is the most important ritual.

To me it seemed that losing my bag, with money and documents, was a moment of sheer fear, (loss of identity, my Parisian friend Karuna said!) I had got off tired and was pleased to go to my room and sleep ... but then, the megaphones outside disrupted every neuron in my head till I was ready to scream. Later in the week, I met the old swami who had sat next to me in the country bus. When I said 'Namaskaram' to him, he held my hands and said, 'Why did you go away without saying goodbye? ('Cholladu poyachu') You must never do that.' I had only been in a desperate hurry to get my things off and get an autorickshaw to the asram. His face remains in my memory ... fragile, so wise, so gentle, so old! These are the so called 'anonymous faces in the crowd'. He had told me that he had had an attack of chikungunya, the new disease which brings excruciating pain and fever, and yet, he had kept half the weight of my bag on his shriveled knees, so that I could sit comfortably.

Journeys are punctuation marks in the routines of our busy lives. For the researcher, like the pilgrim, they are not merely experiential zones but are much more acts of inscription. Combining both aspects has made this book what it is, ... a palimpsest of past and present, my own and other peoples. In the reading of cultural products and diffusion, we know that things, including ideas, move about because people do. In the following section, I use Roland Barthes' preoccupation with the structure of narratives as prescribed in *Image Music Text*. While a manuscript is collaged together with a specific theme in mind, the interpolation of criss-crossing materials, of journeys and dramatis personae which interlink catalytically various parts of a larger project may indeed be relevant for presentation. This continues with the preoccupation that I had in *The Christians of Kerala*, namely who is the ethnographic subject, who is the actor, and why a series of events may be interlinked in the fabrication of a narrative. Do we forget actors when we do not write about them?

WHORLS WITHIN WHORLS: FOLLOWING SWAMI ABHISHIKTANANDA'S TRACKS IN OCTOBER 2006

Bettina Baeumer, who with Raimundo Pannikar and Mary Rogers composed a translation of the Vedas, *Mantramanjari*, which brought to English speaking readers the 'experience' of the Vedas, invited me to visit her inter-religious asram near Phulchatti, in Uttarakhand. We met at the Indian Institute of Advanced Studies Shimla, where she was a Fellow. The library has an interesting collection of books on mysticism and religion, also on language and experience. The sunsets were splendid, and made me understand the value of Psalm 121, 'I will look unto the Hills' and the later verses which say, 'The Sun shall not smite me by day, nor the Moon by night'. Time becomes muted in eternity when we understand that the essence of being human lies in the desire for calm, and our seeking of it, as well as our quest in understanding it.

From Shimla, Bettina (who had for long been the president of the Abhishiktananda Society and editor of its newsletter, *Setu*) and I went to Dehradun, where we visited the Agnes Kunze Home, which is called Kurukshetra Kendra. Here we met the weavers who produce the most brilliant weaves of colour. Reds, blacks, tropical blues, forest browns, sunshine yellow and vivid oranges – the colours spill out in bales of cloth for all purposes, including mats and carpets. There is a consignment all ready to go to Italy. The hall is large and cool, outside there are lovely gardens of canna flowers, a variant which make them appear like forked orchids. Butterflies and grass and wild flowers thrive. The workers are former lepers, maimed and occasionally disfigured, but once healed, they are completely rehabilitated as weavers. Agnes Kunze was paralysed for fourteen years in the last phase of her life, but she continued the work she had done for decades in Kurukshetra Kendra, where the trust in god and one's abilities was profoundly passed on to victims of leprosy, who once cured became brilliant weavers. The struggle in the cause of rehabilitating lepers continues. Afflicted as they are with their past illness, medically certified as cured and non-contagious, they have to struggle for their subsistence. Weaving gives them dignity, but they still live in poverty, hoping that by educating their healthy children, their old age will be provided for. Lalli, whose fingers are bent and decapitated, makes us tea and boiled eggs. She served Ms Kunze in those fourteen years of her paralyses and still misses her and longs for her presence. She guards her grave, having planted evergreen trees (conifer) around her grave, and in her fat adorable granddaughter's hand she shoves a clutch of fragrance sticks, which are burning. The child is frightened of the flame, but out of love for her grandmother, she waveringly holds the joss-sticks. We have driven eight hours through the mountains from Shimla (it is October) through roads which are so unknown that only the locals are there, loyally mending the roads in their tattered garments with small buckets of tar. Adjacent villages, so obscure, are named by its inhabitants, 'Yahan' (Here) and 'Wahan' (there). They are in stark contrast to a rubble road which has a village called 'Kahan' (Where). Close by flows the river called Renuka and nearby a picturesque stop for tea. The love of the country in which one lives unites us regardless of our status or our origin. When we leave Dehradun, Bettina Bauemer is nostalgic for Agnes' abiding friendship. The Kurukshetra Colony had asked her to head them but she told them she was a writer and not equipped for social work. She had lived amongst them for days when Agnes was alive and they now greeted her whenever she arrived with hugs and cries of joy. A Frenchman who came to India after the Student Uprising of 1968 in Paris has lived among the lepers for decades, co-ordinating between the Western countries which import the co-operative's handlooms, but he needs help with the everyday dealing which requires bilingual or trilingual skills.

Henri Le Saux, a devotee of Ramana Maharshi and an exponent of Hindu-Christian dialogue, was a friend of Agnes Kunze and Bettina. Le Saux visited Kurukshetra Kendra often.

From Dehradun, we drove to higher reaches, of which I had read about and written about (through archival work on Swami Abhishiktananda, published in 1998 and 2007) but never seen, and never quite imagined. Past Laxman Jhoola it got very dark and then the full moon was out and we drove on and on for another eight kilometres, where buses are rare, and service jeeps occasionally take the pilgrim up. Past Phool Chatti, we came to the Trikha Inter-Religious Asram, which Bettina runs with friends. Dr Sarla Kumar was there to greet us. She had arrived hours earlier and was wondering where we were! The moonlight was bright and the hill above us gleamed and the river roared over white rocks which we could see through the trees. Fireflies roamed, and there was no sound other than the continuous rush of water over rocks. I slept perfectly through the moonlight and the silence, and woke up to a bright clean sunshine and the blessings of tea brewed by Sarla in a teapot with leaves. She had written a thesis on Doris Lessing in the '60s on the contribution Lessing made to feminism. 'It's all behind me, now that I write on mysticism.' Sarla and Bettina were putting together a book on their teacher Swami Laxman Jhoo for publication to commemorate his birth anniversary. To me it seems amazing to meet a scholar who wrote on Doris Lessing in the '60s, and I keep pursuing her with questions. But the calm of the mountains entrances us and Bettina joins us for tea since she has completed her meditations for the morning. When I return to Delhi later in the day, I think how lovely the Ganga looks in her light turquoise density. I have washed in the rivulet behind the cottage, and the water is warm and clear, and the man who drives me to Laxman Jhoola says it is melted ice.

Claude Levi-Strauss in his *Tristes Tropiques* galvanized a whole generation of writers, trained in the last decades of the twentieth century, to look at fieldwork as a consummate type of travel writing which surpassed the genre of travellers' accounts. The implicit suggestion was that fieldwork was the symbol of the anthropology of travel between countries or between regions. The art of cognition was mobilized to include language, aesthetics, rituals and beliefs as well as structures.

4
DREAMS AND DEATH

When Maharshi was diagnosed with cancer, he was already old and frail and there was an unnerving sense of his own death which his devotees were shocked by. Yet, the texts of detachment were such that he was able to withstand the most enormous degree of pain. It has been testified by many writers that Ramana was always able to send them away comforted. Here I am only concerned with providing the record of the progression of Maharshi's cancer. The real story can perhaps never be told, because of the precept of silence, which was part of the sage's life and work.

Susan Sontag, who suffered from cancer herself and described it as a metaphor of the 'encroachment' of modernism, writes that the task of the writer or artist is to make the recipient believe that the unanswered questions are not significant, and in this 'highly manipulated quest for knowledge' what they don't know, 'they can't know or shouldn't care about knowing.' In a narrative of this sort, opacity and multiplicity are legitimate, and sense is not lost by the narrative being porous or intermittent, clumsy or concealing. 'The use of displacements are valid' and it is the intention that must be honoured. Problematic though such a reading is, it has its worth because it means taking the artist's intention at face value (Sontag 1976: 133).

I have argued in an earlier work that Ramana Maharshi communicated that dying was only dreaming without the body (Visvanathan, 1998, 2007). He took away the mortal fear of dying by showing how the body was separate from the Self, and that we are the Self and therefore we never die. Dreaming is thus essential to Ramanine theology. Because we are trapped in the plane of dualism, we see the opposition between the 'gross' body and the subtle body. Shri Sadhu Om, in an interesting representation of Bhagavan's teaching, says, following Ramana,

> What happens to the body of an ordinary person when it is left behind as a corpse? It loses its form by being decomposed into the five elements of which it was originally composed. That is, the body is left in one of the elements, whether in fire, in the earth, in water, or in the open air, and that one element gradually separates the other elements in the body, thereby merging them into the surrounding elements. ... Since the body anyway has to lose its form and disappear, what does it matter how it loses it? (Sadhu Om 1997: 29, 30)

If death is a dream, how can we imagine it? Salomon Resnik in *The Theatre of the Dream* (1987) describes the nature of interiority as poetry. Love and mysticism are both aspects of such poetry. The darkness of night is illuminated by the dream. 'All experiences that are out of the ordinary, whatever is extraordinary, amazes or frightens us. Hence the need to name, to represent, to symbolise' (Resnik 1987: 171). What we will see in the writings of witnesses and devotees is just this. Resnik further informs us very perceptively that:

> The loss of the loved object is always the representation of the drama that has already been presented. Analytical work tries to bring to light a sense of absence, helps us to become familiar with darkness, absence, mourning, with everything that comes to us from our secret, hidden dimension, the unconscious. The experience of discovery is a way of unmasking the unknown, of illuminating darkness: an experience that is expressed through the sense of amazement. (171)

It is in this context that the diary of Suri Nagamma is to be read, for it is both an official document as well as a contested site of authority and dissent, as it is spelt out in a woman's record. We will see here both marginalization as well as legitimacy, and structurally therefore, the connotations of life and sustenance in the domain of death and intimations of immortality.

Suri Nagamma is one of the most interesting of writers. She was encouraged to keep a diary by her brother to record the days she spent at the Ramanasramam. She found it a medium that she was not comfortable with, so she resorted to writing letters instead. These were so communicative that they were read out to Bhagavan and other devotees present. They were also published and found an immediate audience. Suri Nagamma described Ramana's struggle with cancer in a manner we may benefit from, since it describes not only the nature of physical agony but also the miraculous axes of detachment and coping, which still remain in the twentieth century, the only way, by which we may understand this marauding disease and its violent appearance.

Nagamma writes that at the beginning of 1949 a small tumour appeared above Bhagavan's left elbow and soon grew as big as a marble. Shankar Rao, the asramam doctor and Srinivasa Rao told Bhagavan that it should be operated on. He was unwilling, and said, 'It does not give me any pain. Let it be as it is. Why meddle with it?' (Nagamma 1993: 73).

After that first operation, Bhagavan appeared looking tired, covering his bandaged arm with a towel, and sat on the stone sofa, which was a throne that had been built for him. Blood began to ooze and drop on the ground, which Nagamma saw as a sign of great disaster. By mid-March, the tumour had resurfaced. After speaking with the asramam doctors and the office, Nagamma hoped that ayurveda could be started as a line of treatment, some plasters were used and discontinued, and ayurvedic medicines were received but not used. By the end of March surgery was again confirmed and Ramana said, 'Yes. Whatever is to happen does happen. It will not stop even if we want it to. All right. Let things take their own course.' (81)

Nagamma records here that, 'Having learnt that the operation would be performed without anaesthesia we all sat down in the Jubilee Hall anxiously looking towards the hospital. Ramana came back from the hospital looking fatigued. He was spending day and night on the sofa, and was available for darshan. 'The daily routine was going on as usual, and there was no limit to the questions' (81). In a conversation with Mahalakshmi Suryanandan, (5 May 2006) the daughter of K. Swaminathan (editor of Mahatma Gandhi's collected works in 100 volumes and who was a devotee of Maharshi) I came to know that Mahalakshmi's sister, at that time a medical student, was present as a witness during one of the bandage changes. She came back saying, 'Only god could have borne the pain of those bandages being ripped off.'

One of Ramana's relatives came to visit him, and when he noticed that she had a growth like his on her arm, he gifted her medicine that had been earlier brought for him. She took it with veneration and applied the plasters with some green leaves and cotton dipped in milk and the tumour disappeared. In Maharshi's case, the tumour grew and bled continuously. He described it as a cobra hissing, a cobra which had been disturbed from its habitat. On one occasion Murgunar the poet and Nagamma began to weep begging him to save himself, and the Master looked at them with compassion, but remained silent (85).

Like Christ, Ramana is lost in the wonder of god, remains in the temple, devotees gather to hear his stories, his mother constantly follows him, the suffering at the end may not be (like the bitter cup which it is) taken away from him.

By now Radium treatment had begun and Ramana told Dr Anantanarayana Rao that the Jnani always looks forward to the time when his bodily *karma* comes to an end (86). He compared it also to the leaf which is thrown away. He had said he had no desire for a miraculous cure. 'There must be something called mind to create a desire but there is no such thing,' he had said. 'How then can a desire be got? That which is non-existent, how can it be secured, developed and retained?' (87).

Bhagavan refused the suggestion of amputation, accepted the ministrations of an Ayurved called Valliavan *thatha* who had treated him for a broken arm in 1943 (and had cured that fracture in three days!) but this time, the old man said the cancer was too far gone and Bhagavan should cure himself.

Fever set in, and Raṃana called it Nataraja's dance, tandava darshan.

In spite of pain and fever, Maharshi continued to be present for darshan and ate at the dining hall. Following the withdrawal of Valiyavan *thatha's* leaves because of the fever they had caused, Dr Guruswami Mudaliar prescribed homeopathy and suryanamaskaram. Devotees starting circumambulating the hill and to perform suryanamaskaram, but since there was no cure for cancer, Bhagavan's condition worsened and his arm had to be bandaged twice a day (95). On 31 July 1947, ten doctors arrived to examine Bhagavan. They confirmed the diagnoses as cancerous. Nagamma records,

> On 5 August the Morvi guesthouse was cleaned up for the doctors who were coming the next day. With the government's permission, X-Ray and other electrical equipments for the operation were transported from the Royapettah Hospital, Madras, in a lorry. Everything else necessary was brought in the cars of the doctors. With a desire to make use of this opportunity to serve Bhagavan, a total of thirty medical men came with Dr Raghavachari. It seems there was never an occasion when the equipment of a government hospital had thus been permitted to be taken out of the

> hospital premises. Moreover no charges were levied for the use of the equipment. Actual expenses for transport were met by a devotee. (96)

Nagamma further records that Bhagavan was kept on a liquid diet to prevent vomiting after the operation, X-rays were taken which confirmed that the cancer had not spread. Present was an electrical engineer Narayana Rao who made sure that there was uninterrupted supply of electricity by telephoning to Mettur and arranging this for the operation (97). Even after the operation Bhagavan insisted on being accessible to his devotees. On 7 August, after being operated upon, Bhagavan sat in the verandah, and the next day as soon as the doctors left, Bhagavan came walking to the new hall saying, 'if he stayed in the hospital, devotees would be inconvenienced as also the patients coming for treatment' (99). All his devotees, including Nagamma, were always desperate for darshan and continuously communicated their longing to see Bhagavan. Meanwhile, the tumour rebounded back and another operation was scheduled for 19 November. In spite of it, by 9 February, the tumour was visible again. Prayers to Goddess Lalitha were offered, and on 15 February Dr Raghavachari the chief surgeon said that nothing else could be done, 'and that the patient should not henceforth be troubled by being given all sorts of medicines and strict dieting' (109). Doctors now came and went, so did astrologers. In the face of continual panic, Bhagavan remained calm saying, 'What if it has sprouted again? It comes and goes' (109).

By March 1950, an ayurved from Kerala who had been called in felt disheartened and composed a hymn in praise of Ramana and gave it to him. He arranged for the Vishnu Sahasranama (repeating of the thousand names of Lord Vishnu) and some devotees began reciting the Mritunjaya japam. According to Nagamma, the Maharshi was detached, since he was a jnani, and rituals were unnecessary to him. A woman who was present told Ramana that there was a man in her village who had the power of mantras and she said, 'He will first offer you a 108 coconuts and later break them throughout the asram' (113).

Suri Nagamma records that Bhagavan smiled and said, 'He breaks only coconuts? Does he not also slay hens and spill the blood all over the asram? Will he not also tie an amulet and smear vibhuti?'

By this time the asramam was bustling with what Nagamma calls *japam*, *homam*, *stotras*, and on 16 March an astrologer said that Bhagavan would pass away in a couple of days. 'If that was really the case, I felt would not Bhagavan tell me about it in some manner or other although it was a foolish sentiment, it somehow persisted in my mind' (113).

On 18 March, the eve of the Telugu Lunar New Year, called Ugadi, she presented Bhagavan with the new towel and loin cloth for his personal use, as she always did. He said, 'Oho! Ugadi is come?' in such an ominous way that her heart felt ripped apart (114). She asked him, 'I was wondering whether I should stop this practice of offering clothes and so on to Bhagavan, but felt it would be a grave error on my part to do so. I did not know what to do. I have merely brought these clothes.'

As with other times, she kept asking him how he felt, and pleaded with him to cure himself of the cancer, and then exclaimed, 'How can you be that indifferent?'(115). To this Bhagavan remarked, clearly and unambiguously and with compassion, 'How can there be a cure at this stage?' She wanted him to ask a crucial question, ('How would the devotees manage?'), but before she could find her voice or wipe away the tears which were blinding her,

> ... people from the office rushed in to have some differences of opinion amongst themselves settled by the Sage. That was my misfortune. Like a deer frightened by the sudden appearance of tigers, I was horrified by the way they all entered. I could not ask what I wanted to and left to go home with profound grief. (115)

It is interesting that in spite of Suri Nagamma's profound irritation with the management of Ramanasramam, her diaries have been reprinted and are available to us! The account is continually poignant, respectful, intimate and it gives us a rare glimpse of Maharshi's life from the pen of an erudite woman who was fearless.

> On the morning of the Telugu New Year Day, I went to the asram early with the chutney of neem flower and a copy of the new panchangam. I served the chutney to the devotees and to Bhagavan with their breakfast and waited on the verandah of the new hall with an idea of giving the new panchangam (calendar) to Bhagavan personally. Bhagavan had put on the new koupeenam and towel but while he was about to enter the bathroom stumbled over the doorsteps and fell down. Shouting that Bhagavan had fallen down, I rushed to the place where he was. The attendant who was close behind him was trying to lift him up but Bhagavan was shouting at him not to do so. I was too afraid what Bhagavan would say if I touched

> him and so stood by the side, stricken with fear. His koupeenam and towel were blood stained. Hearing my shouts, a close devotee rushed along and tried to lift Bhagavan up. However he did not allow the devotee to touch him and keeping one hand as support got up by himself. It seems there was some small fracture of the backbone but the attendants were strictly instructed not to tell anyone about it. Furthermore, pus had formed at the bruise and gave immense pain to Bhagavan but this was not allowed to be disclosed till the very end. Though he had fallen down and hurt himself, Bhagavan went to the water closet as usual, came out and sat on the verandah by 9 a.m. I then offered the panchangam. That is all! My going to Bhagavan and hearing his nectar-like voice was over forever on that day. His asking me in surprise whether the Ugadi had come was perhaps to indicate the abrupt end of the wonderful time I had been in the past few years listening to his sweet voice. It was as if he had said gently: "With this new year my conversations with you will come to an end." (116, 117)
> *(From then to his death on 14 April, the Tamil New Year, Bhagavan could not meet devotees as he had previously, they filed past him for darshan in queues.)*

A respondent to my queries during the anniversary of Samadhi on 14 April 2006 said that someone she knew would keep going back to stand in the queue because no one was allowed to stand in front of Bhagavan for more than a moment!

> We had to content ourselves with having darshan from a distance. Anyway, I did ask my brother and others to go to Bhagavan and obtain from him a last message but they did not succeed. Somehow they found themselves unable to open their mouths in the august presence of the sick Sage. I was standing at the gate and was watching them. When I asked them what happened, they said nothing. (117)

In an extremely perceptive essay titled 'The Maha Nirvana', Quilkey, editor of the *Mountain Path* describes the last days of Bhagavan Sri Ramana. 'One of the many treatments which Bhagavan patiently submitted to was the herbal remedy that was started on 18 July. The green paste actually aggravated the disease and sepsis set in. At some point during these months the failure to contain the spread of the tumour led to the spread of the cancer cells through the blood stream and lymphomatic system .... During all this time Bhagavan gave no indication of pain or discomfort.' T.N. Krishnaswami, who was an eyewitness, describes it as a kind of detachment, 'There is severe intolerable headache,' he said as he was going into a slow uraemia and his kidneys were failing. 'The Maharshi never described the symptoms in a subjective manner' (cited in Quilkey 2004: 11).

II

In an imaginative reading of Freud, the great theologian philosopher Paul Ricoeur in the Terry Lectures (published as *Freud and Philosophy: An essay on Interpretation* 1978) discusses the relationship between Eros, Thanatos and Ananke (Love, Death and Work). These are the Titans, the great struggling heroes of existence. Ramana Maharshi put all of them to good use in his life and provided his devotees a stability of vision from where they could view their lives and actions. These three principles, Death, Love and Work also contribute, as we can see from the Tiruvannamalai and Arunachala sacred tales, signifying the unification of the trinity, (Shiva, Visnu and Brahma) and the transcendence of dualism (the conjunction of Shiva and Parvati) simultaneously. (See *Sri Bhagavan's Arunachala* for a legendary and devotional history of Tiruvannamalai, 2004).

The syndrome of anxiety runs through mortals when they cannot accept that Thanatos has the final word, but love and wisdom work as restraining and creative principles in order to regulate anxiety. Ricoeur asks, 'What is the death instinct and how is it connected with negativity? What is pleasure and how is it connected with satisfaction? What is reality and how is it connected with necessity?' (Ricoeur 1978: 311). I have chosen a feminist text for the representation of the tussle between mortality and immortality, although many such narratives are available such as that of devotees like Kanakkammal, Cohen and Mudaliar. The risks involved in reading the intense and personal voice of an afflicted woman's record is deep subjectivity, but that is where narrative becomes as analyzable as a dream. It is a method which Ricoeur endorses, when he argues that fiction or biography can reflect the subconscious as sharply as a dream narrative. Ricoeur writes. 'No reader can be insensible to the uncertain, winding, and even 'limping' character of the speculation and its set of heuristic hypothesis' (311). We apply the method to myth when we accept the play of biology.

Describing Freud's stand, Ricoeur says, 'Further, do we not feel that we are listening to one of the pre-Socratics when Eros is called that "which holds all living things together, the preserver of things"' (312).

Ramana Maharshi, while being the greatest devotee of Siva, in the form of Arunachala, is seen to be like Vishnu, a preserver and lover of the peacock, and unutterably desirable to both men and women. The principle of non-dualism, however, also demands that the Trinity and its manifestations be assimilated in the historically profound presence of Bhagavan.

For Ricoeur, the negation associated with the death instinct is derived from the character of substitution. For him substitution is about play, about aesthetic-creation, which is the stuff of myth, and what he calls reality testing itself. Theoretically he puts it thus, 'The death instinct is not closed in upon destructiveness which is, we said, it's clamour; perhaps it opens out onto other aspects of the 'work of the negative', which remains 'silent' like itself (318).

The death instinct for Freud is the principle of constancy, the pleasure principle arouses the categories of restraint and satisfaction, which Freud calls the 'nirvana principle'. The nirvana principle, a term borrowed by the pioneer from Barbara Low, is the tendency to remain calm in the face of danger, and is described as the *effort to reduce, to keep constant or to remove internal tension due to stimuli* (319). Freud also understands the death of the self in order to integrate with the collective body as an erotic sacrifice. Ricoeur reads this to mean that:

> If Eros is the "preserver of all things", it is because it "unites all things". But this enterprise runs counter to the death instinct: "Union with the living substance of a different individual increases those tensions, introducing what may be described as fresh 'vital differences' which must then be lived off."

Paul Ricoeur's reading is useful because it unites the triptych of Shiva, Brahma and Vishnu, and it also explains why the death of the ego submerges the self into the calm of the universe. This is the essence of Ramana's worldview.

Freud himself suffered from fatal cancers of the mouth, which terrible journey was recorded by his physician Dr Schur. In his chronicle, Schur presents a letter that Freud wrote to his intellectual partner Fleiss, about fear of death in one of their patients,

> From your description poor S reminds me of one of the most vexing aspects of our modern medicine. The art of deceiving a patient is certainly not highly desirable. But what has the individual come to, how negligible

> must be the influence of the relation of science, which presumably has replaced the old religion, if one no longer dares disclose that this or that man now must die... The Christian at least has the last sacraments administered to him a few hours beforehand. Shakespeare says: "thou owest Nature a death." I hope that when my time comes I shall find someone who will treat me with more respect and tell me when to be ready. My father knew it clearly, said nothing about it, and retained his beautiful composure to the end. (Schur 1972: 192)

The manner of dying, the composure and the gracious comfort offered to the mourners is the clearest indication of Ramana's belief that there is no death, only the active and unified cosmic spirit remains in harmony with the universe. This equilibrium is probably the greatest lesson for mourners. For Freud, hunger and love were the two most motivating elements of human action (195). In his own journey, he was accompanied by a loving crowd of family and friends. But the physical torment was vivid. Schur writes,

> Freud's physical state, which varied only from severe discomfort to real torment, persisted more or less constantly over the next 16 years. Pain and discomfort were of course more intense during the first year after the radical surgery until the wound was finally covered by a combination of newly formed mucous membrane and scar tissue, the prosthesis was gradually adjusted to the remaining anatomical structures, and Freud adjusted to the prostheses. It took a long time for him to learn how to take it out and put it in again. I vividly remember what a complex manoeuvre this occasionally required even after years of use.
>
> Freud also had to learn gradually how to eat, smoke and talk. (365)

Schur quotes Freud to show how his suffering helped him to elucidate the nirvana principle as a pleasure principle. The libido was the representation of the pleasure principle, but when it unites a life instinct with death instinct it appears as the nirvana principle ... the nirvana principle (and the pleasure principle which is supposedly identical with it) would be entirely in the service of the death instincts, whose aim is to conduct the restlessness of life into the stability of the organic state, and it would have the function of giving warnings against the demands of the life instincts – the libido – which try to disturb the intended course of life (cited in Schur 1972: 371).

Freud argues that we do not have a physiological understanding of how the death instinct is tamed by the life instinct, but that there is 'a very extensive fusion and amalgamation, in varying proportions, of the two classes of instincts which takes place, so that we never have to deal with pure life instincts but only with mixtures of them in different amounts.' (372)

Schur's argument that the work that reveals these insights could only have been written while Freud was suffering with cancer, 'the wish to die and not suffer any longer could be in a precarious balance with the wish to live and carry on the struggle. It is generally known that the wish to live plays an important role in the course of any serious illness' (373). Wish, however, is different from instinct, and Thanatos and Eros are part of Freud's delight in dualism, mediated by Ananke as destiny or Moira.

On his sixty-eighth birthday, according to Dr Schur, Freud writes to his confidant Lou Andreas-Salome,

> I have admired your art more than ever this time. Here is a person who instead of working hard into old age ... and then dying without preliminaries, contracts a horrible disease in middle age, has to be treated and operated on, squanders his hard-earned bit of money, generates and enjoys discontent, and then crawls about for an indefinite time as an invalid.... And you can still praise me for bearing my suffering so well. Actually, it isn't quite like this, although I have weathered the awful realities fairly well, it is the possibilities that I find hard to bear; I cannot get accustomed to life under sentence. It is now six months since my operation and the attitude of my surgeon, who allows me to travel far afield in summer, ought to lull me into something like security – so far as such a feeling is admissible, considering the doman non c' e certezza (of tomorrow there is no certainty) which affects us all.
>
> Six hours of psychoanalysis, this is all I have retained of my capacity for work. Everything else, especially social contact, I keep at bay (Of course Romain Rolland, who has announced himself for tomorrow, I cannot refuse... (380)

To another friend, Marie Bonaparte, Freud wrote in 1926, just before his seventieth birthday,

> I must continue my morning drives in the Viennese spring, and find it truly beautiful. What a pity that one has to become old and sick to make this

discovery. How fortunate that you did not have to wait for so long in your garden ...

He then quotes a poem by Uhland to her,

The world grows lovelier each day,
We do not know what still may come,
The flowering will not end,
The farthest, deepest valley is abloom.
Now, dear heart, forget your torment,
Now everything, everything must change. (392)

III

When Ramana Maharshi comforts his followers by saying at his deathbed, 'Where can I go? I am always with you', he is actually conveying what he had always believed that he and the Godhead are one, and that there would indeed be no change in that. The calmness of his garden is an assertion of that belief; it is a palpable and tactile aura of contentment and joy. One of the Ramanasramam residents said to me that, 'For those of us who are believers it is another domain, which we do not question, for our faith is such. We are believers.'

IV

While Samadhi Day was celebrated on 14 April 2006 very quietly, in the evening, with the recitation of the work known as Marital Garland, Aradhana or New Beginnings was much more flamboyant. It is the announcement that Bhagavan is always with his followers. The hall was decked with flowers and all the workers wore new clothes. The asramam was abuzz with activity. At 7 a.m., the hall was bright with streamers, and devotees packed the grounds. Flowers were used to decorate the main hall, long trailers of jasmine (white) and kanakambram (orange) and mint (green) were linked together and the effect was delicate and pretty. Musicians, nageswaram and tabla players were announcing the start of a new day. A thousand people sat for breakfast which was elaborate and filling. Twenty additional cooks called for the occasion ran about busily serving the guests *vennu pongal* (rice cooked in butter), *uppumav* (a savory made of fine cereal), and strong coffee.

The priests recited prayers all morning. The lingam was washed over and over again with water, milk, curd, ashes. It was decked with fine cloth and flowers. Ornate silver utensils, with mango leaves, celebrating the New Year, commemorating Maharshi having left his body but promising the devotees he would always be here, were the dominant aspect of the ritual. He had said, 'Where else can I go?' and the silver seshadhri (cobra) is placed on the lingam. A large and elaborate circle of flowers like an arch is placed behind the lingam. Above, the streamers made of jasmine (white) *kanakammbram* (orange) and mint (green) merge in a lovely nationalist hue. Everything looks tasteful and pretty and quite grand. People swirl around the samadhi like a colourful stream. Little children laugh and play. The asramam looks scrubbed and clean and shiny.

Lunch is served on the cow dung-plastered floor outside the dining room. I had watched the floor being prepared. Six women had covered the red gravel with diluted cow dung water. One woman mixed the water with the cow dung, another threw bucket upon bucket of this thin brown water on the gravel, covering it slowly. As it dried, the remaining women swept it and fashioned it with their broom. Back-breaking labour, but so carefully done. Layer after layer is fashioned like this, and it quickly dries and forms a hard beaten floor.

One of the trustees passes by. When I say, 'These women are such perfectionists!' he nods and laughs and says. 'Yes, it's interesting, isn't it!' Then next moment, he goes and shouts at them in a loud patriarchal tone for not raising the floor saying, 'If the edge is not higher, the rain can wash it away.' The tone is authoritative. They take it in their stride and continue their work.

Two upper-caste women sit on the steps, composing and singing a song for Ramanamaharshi. They practice over and over again, compulsively and loudly, prettily and perfectly. The workers with cow dung stop to stare. Then they return to their work. The class differences among the two sets are evident. The workers, however, are happy and comfortable in their hitched-to-the-knees sarees, and their bright but mis-matched blouses. The upper-caste women are gorgeously dressed. They are quite impervious of the women labourers, only their music matters to them. They are going to be singing the hymn to Bhagavan at his shrine in the main hall.

On Aradhana day, 200 of us sit on the earthen floor, the rest have been accommodated in the dining hall. The cooks have energy we cannot imagine, running with heavy buckets here and there in a manner that makes it certain that they believe everyone's appetite must be fully satisfied.

The whole day goes by in great and fulfilling joy. Those who have arrived to spend the day are expressive in their ardour of emotion. In the night a woman sings. She is in her thirties and is very beautiful. She is accompanied by a violinist and a mridangam player. She is a recipient of a state title, and when she suddenly smiles, she is transformed. She comes from a family of Ramana devotees.

The following day the makeshift shelters are taken down as are the flowers and streamers from the previous day. It took days to get everything ready for the thronging pilgrims. The dismantling is fairly quick. The boys who take down the temporary shed work very fast. The day is hot, but they work unprotected from the heat, seemingly comfortable astride the poles like acrobats. They have to unravel each knot which keeps the poles together. They are young boys working almost absent-mindedly and tranquil in the glare of the afternoon sun. Each pole is unraveled and then slid out.

May Day, culminating a fortnight of ritual, is celebrated enthusiastically in the Ramanasramam with the conch ceremonies. One hundred and eight conches with water are passed down by a series of priests to the main priest who uses the sacred water to wash the lingam. The mango leaves and hibiscus flowers which accompany the ritual provide colour and beauty to the delicacy and pale transluscence of the shells. No one asks any questions about wages and rights, a benevolent paternalism envelops everyone. Workers receive new clothes and food on festival days, but the work of looking after larger and larger number of pilgrims is beginning to show on exhausted faces.

On 3 May 2006, Bhagavan's monthly Nakshatram birthday or Punarvasu is celebrated, and thus the creativity of a new ritual year is inaugurated. Mahalakshmi Suryanandan, whose father K. Swaminathan was a pillar of Ramanasramam, comes to sing for two hours, though now she is in her eighties herself, and is frail. By sustaining these rituals, the idea that we share in immortality and that Bhagavan shows the believers the transcendence of here and now, life and death is clearly annunciated ... the moment of *sahaja* or happiness is compounded by understanding the ritual.

Mallika and her mother Sugandha who are from Bombay explain the importance of rituals to me, as we walk the fourteen kilometre stretch in moonlight around the sacred mountain, Arunachala. 'It is a grammar. Without the grammar we would be quite lost!' Between styles of devotion and practice is a line as thin as that between language and speech, complicated in Ramanine theology by a call to silence.

5
RAMANA MAHARSHI

One of the methods of analyses is to use memory, mine as well as that of other writers and devotees in general, to come to an understanding of a way of life which survives institutionally. Is there a way in which one can understand the charisma of the mystic, when the forms of routinization are not embodied in one successor, but is found in the witnessing of hundreds of individuals?

In his seminal collection of essays, *Towards an Anthropology of the Body* (1976) John Blacking summarizes the work of Silvan Tomkins to assert that affectuality can be analysed, that it is not 'obscure' or 'internal' but a primary human response that can be understood, through gestures, signs and facial responses. He argues that these can be read and analysed, primarily because the signaling between human beings is more understood than misunderstood. Affectuality is reflected in action and cognition, and vice-versa. Feelings are the mediator between body and mind, because they impact individual behaviour and the selection of what shall be shared and conceptualized from what remains 'private'. Blacking draws substantially from Max Weber's sociology, from questions of empathy, identification with the other, rational analyses of shared subjectivities. He provides us insights into the analyses of religious experience. In all societies there is a great emphasis on 'transcendental somatic states and experiences of bodily communication, the oneness of true fellow feeling. It is that loss of self which becomes most eagerly sought – the flowing along, the sharing, and the communitas.'

In contrast we have the work of Hannah Arendt whose commitment was towards participation and theory as two sides of the same coin; that of living in the world. It was this preoccupation with the understanding of authority and of violence that made her a critic of intellectualism, and demanded that we return to common sense. Kate Soper, in *What is Nature: Culture, Politics and the Non-Human*, sets up a similar problem while stating that a concern with the supernatural alone may make us fatalistic towards ecological politics.

In Ramana's life (which we may describe as a living theology) the preoccupation with non-thought on the intellectualist plane and with everyday matters in a practical sense is pre-eminent. For the devotee there is the call to submit, to destiny (*prarabdha*) and to the love of God, but in Advaita, God is present in the Self, and we find God by seeking within ourselves. The devotee is thus asked to surrender to that 'I' who is more significant than personal egoism.

Judith Stills, in *Feminine Economies* (1997) writes that 'Utopias, economies of abundance, beneficence' have a problematic relation to Eros, and sexual regulation is its primary index (Stills 1997: 120). Thus, in an order of companionship, where householders may also have a rightful place, members enjoy the bonds of love and membership, free of eros. The subjugation of passion may never be spoken about. Family bonds are sustained, by those who are in conjugal relationships, the bearing of children permitted, but lust is controlled by the ritual calendar and the presence of monastics.

In the following section, I will delineate the curious circumstance of my return to Ramanasramam after six years of absence. My first visit in 1996 was an act of anthropological curiosity, since I had encountered Ramana's ideas through the work of devotees (Visvanathan 1998, 2007). I returned in 2001, as someone seeking the dream time of recovery.

One of the interesting dilemmas in this book arises from the fact that by using the accounts of devotees, who use the written and/or the oral medium of communication, one cannot tap the larger resources of those who have ideologically accepted the path of silence. Consent to be interviewed is a major difficulty in a milieu where the text of silence is the most comforting of palimpsests. Both the questioner, as well as the respondent, know in their hearts that once it is understood, the significance of explaining it to one another diminishes. But it is the recurring vocation of the anthropologist to record, and that responsibility is larger than the privilege of understanding. Max Weber's methodological dictum holds true, that there is much in social action that may at some time be incomprehensible but that does not preclude our ignoring it.

The trials of meaning and construction are well interpreted by Renato Rosaldo when he says, quoting the work of Charles Frake, 'an ethnography should be a theory of cultural behaviour in a particular society, the adequacy of which is to be evaluated by the ability of a stranger to the culture (who may be the ethnographer) to use the ethnographer's statements as instruction for approximately anticipating the scenes of the society. I say "approximately anticipate" rather than "predict" because a failure of an ethnographic statement to predict correctly does not necessarily imply descriptive inadequacy as long as the members of their described society are as surprised by the failure as is the ethnographer. The test of descriptive adequacy must always refer to informants' interpretations of events, not simply to the occurrence of events' (Frake cited in Rosaldo). This generally means that there must be some fit between our record and the opinion of its veracity, by those whom we study, and a further possible concurrence with the objective views of other inscribers.

Rosaldo also discusses the problem of affectuality and thought in the recording of ethnographic materials. He draws here from the work of Raymond Williams in *Marxism and Literature*.

Raymond Williams is describing those things we call 'impulse, restraint, and tone, specifically affective elements of consciousness and relationship; not feeling against thought, but thought as felt and feeling as thought: practical consciousness of a present kind, in a living and inter-relating community' (Raymond Williams cited in Rosaldo, 1990: 106).

Rosaldo asserts that thought does not create this binary opposition between affect and cognition, we do. 'Ideas are felt, and feelings are conceived. Related parts held in tension, these forms are in transition between being experienced as private and becoming recognized as social' (107). It is conceived of in Durkheimian sociology as 'currents' which affect the mind and behaviour, 'religious effervescence' being our best example (Durkhiem 1979).

Here, we also confront the contestations of class formation, consciousness or antagonism. The routinization of charisma in organizational forms of mystical cultures results in strict notations of who is welcome and who is not. Class formation is according to Rosaldo a continuous process, and there is interplay of structure and agency. If there is a presumption that spiritual life is about equality, the social aspects of such equality have never been evident. Ramana Maharshi was very clear that human beings, by the circumstance of their birth, are born in particular situations and that they continue to operate within the vocabulary of these. Thus, he suggested that it would be impractical to have a casteless reference point when it came to seating arrangements. If devotees practised caste distinctions at their home, why come to the asramam, to reform? (See *Sadhu Arunachala* 1994: 34). Today, caste distinctions are not apparent, and the only visible difference is between workers and guests. In truth however, segregation continues in terms of gender, age, marital status, caste and class for people tend to converge in terms of their familiarity with social labels, which custom and conventions dictate. These are not rigid in any sense, only underlined by what in South India are known to be rules of propriety, where age, gender, religion and occupation are still heavily laden with traditional meanings.

Reading through old issues of the *Mountain Path*, one draws insights from the poetry found within the pages which describe the ecological and social impetus of the lives of devotees spent in maintaining Bhagavan's garden, as if it were the body of the Lord.

Robert Duncan in *Roots and Branches* writes,

I think of my element, it is not of fire,
Of ember and ash, but of earth,
Nor of man's travail and burden
To work in the dirt, but of the abundance,
The verdant rhetorical. Servant of the green,
The Garden of the Hesperides returns sometimes
No more than pompos of the poem,
A claim I made on some mortal prince
I thought I had seen so real he was mine
Received in the music-magic of Sitwell or of Stevens,
Robed round in sound rich as a tree
In full foliage of metaphor and fruit.
(Duncan in Mackey 1993: 71)

The reminiscences around Ramana Maharshi have the same mythopeoic quality, where nature and humans interlace in some way decipherable only if one wishes to read the signs. In a more technical work, Louis Marin draws our attention to narratives around the Sun King. Racine writes a poem to his King, there is a fire, the manuscript is lost! Yet fragments remain. Marin, who is France's most astute narrative analyst, writes of chance and rhetoric, the keeping of records and the pivotal place of the narrator. The narrator seeks to trap the reader in the text, by setting up the vital place of interaction and meaning (Marin in Blonsky 1986).

Shiv Visvanathan in a seminal argument, *Unravelling Rights* (1995) discusses the appearancc of the commons, which become in Ivan Ilyich's terms the notation of shared and respected spaces. Visvanathan writes that a great deal of human sharing is about the understanding of suffering.

> Modern man without locality, nature, dwelling, motivated by the utility, mastery, uncertainty has created in the notion of rights his only poem. Modern rights theory pretends to be a science instead of a cry of grief uttered in loneliness. It is a science of estrangement, a contract for strangers. Vaclav Havel caught its basic problem when he stated recently "the idea of human rights and freedoms must be an integral part of any meaningful world order yet. I think it must be anchored in a different place and in a different way, than has been the case so far."
>
> For this, a rights discourse must locate itself in a world beyond strangers and the contract. Humans who perceive each other only as strangers no longer dwell upon the earth. It is only when we are embedded in dwelling that we see the outsider, the wayfarer not as a threat but as a pilgrim. Pilgrims need hospitality. The world itself then becomes a dharamshala, a refuge, an invitation, a theory of hospitality. The world of Cain and Abel becomes not a genocidal opposition, but a theory of two ways of being human, two metaphors of living, of the wayfarer and the dweller.
>
> It is only by understanding dwelling, that the current notion of property can be altered. Possessing property is a one-way relationship; it is a matter of mastery. (Visvanathan, in ed. Kumar 1995: 39)

The difficulties of faith and of belief in a milieux where no standardization is sought is probably the greatest imperative to keep returning. How can one prove that one belongs to an association of believers when the very act of commitment is an act of self abnegation? To be a member one must repudiate the arrogant self and assert the identity of the godhead within oneself. Miracles abound, and Ramana's way has always been to assert that once one has given of oneself, one cannot deny the Master. Non-dualism or Advaita, as it is more familiarly known, denies the possibility of questioning, once the goal has been reached. Luckily for us, as devotees, we are only human, and we all fall off the path and have to learn to struggle to get on again, something which the philosopher

Indu Gandhi once described to me as 'oscillation'. Every sociologist knows that the pilgrimage is as important as the grail, getting there is as fruitful as revelation. I will now use the feminist mode of subjectivity as a primary tool of sociological analyses, whereby autobiography splices the text to make meaning more personal and public at the same time. It is not polemic necessarily, but the dream time of existential work, which sees images and collage as necessary tools in the crafting of a story.

Tests by fire are mythic, and I do not see myself in that category, but it is a Ramana Maharshi narrative, so I must tell it. As a child, struggles with death were frequent, but with the wisdom of someone who suffered nightmares often, I never spoke about it. It was the struggle to wake up from sleep that frequently characterized my childhood. Quite like being caught in the talons of a giant bird and struggling to be free – relief when I awoke and saw that I could breathe, recognize the room around me. The most frightening of these was of course the wild flapping of angel's wings which I fictionalized in one of the stories in the collection titled, *Something Barely Remembered* (Visvanathan 2000). But there were other dramatic episodes too. One long set of sequences affecting my life-chances began on November 1984 and ended in March 1985, coincident with the killings of Sikhs in Delhi and the miasma of destruction which followed. I can still recall the smoke rising in Delhi, from those large-scale deaths that occurred with the torching of members of the Sikh community, as acts of revenge for Indira Gandhi's assassination, by crowds of looters and murderers.

I was reading in the library, a researcher and lecturer, with a very new baby, when I heard the words in my head which said, 'Be Still and Know that I am God'. My brain felt heavy, like a dead mussel in its clam – there were many waking dreams, all of them caught in the warp and weft of many divine spaces. During that phase I was asked to leave the world, renounce my family, and go into the mountains. I fought the voices with a fury equaling the strength of their demands. The divinity of the first realm of experience had been replaced by the most horrific and the most bizarre, as I continued with the steadfastness that my responsibilities to my family were my primary promise and I would stay constant with that. I was blinded by the white light that emptied my head, suffused my body. The images continued in kaleidoscope fashion, but I kept my job at Hindu College, Delhi University, where I taught Sociology, and managed to remain tranquil. Between March and May of 1985, I healed myself, by doggedly reading the texts of Carl Jung, and then the space of mythic consciousness, and laughter at fear, became healing spaces. Meanwhile blood-curdling migraines followed me, and dreams were my second nature. Nothing frightened me; though there were times I could not bear the physical distress. I did not seek medical help for the simple reason that I did not believe I would survive a battery of tests. My reading and writing on mysticism were therapeutic spaces and Ramana's theology the safest space to glide out from.

After a serious cerebral stroke, which I had in October 2000, there were evidences of these earlier episodes in the scar tissue which appeared in my brain for my neurologist, Dr Vinit Suri, to read. It was my second day in the ICU when he said, 'There is evidence that you have suffered episodes like this before,' and I said glibly, 'yes, but my brains grew back.' There is a child-like quality to those who suffer intense physical or mental pain, and who survive because others will them back into health, or they struggle to clamber back, and the grace of god, and what Ramana calls destiny is the cloak in which all our pitiful meanderings are located. On this occasion, in the October of 2000, I was paralysed, my speech was lost, (some burring sounds, barely decipherable took its place,) and so the clot on my speech centre had to be rapidly dissolved. I was treated with L-dopa, the lost brain mapping was resolved with cortisone. There were ten days of dreaming, and the experience of travelling on, forever on, seemed permanent – when my physician Dr Prasada Rao, told me very gently, that the 'experience of dying was not the fact of dying'.

There was one day in the hospital, when I *knew* I was dying. At that moment, the weight of the mountain Arunachala lay on me – a weight I cannot describe. I said to Shiv who was in the room with me, that 'I have three minutes more, and then I will not move for seven thousand years and this is mythic time.' That desperate hallucinatory rambling was perfectly clear to him. When I looked sideways he had shrouded his head with a blanket, and curiously it was not him that I saw, in what I thought was my last terrible moment, but Ramana Maharshi. Arunachala moved away, I presume, and I lived to write this story. I did write about what had occurred to V.S. Mani and Dr Srinivasamurthy, who immediately invited me to come to the Ramanasramam. Mani wrote a letter saying, 'You must now look after your body,' which intuitive concern was Ramanine theology at its most empathetic.

I had separated from Shiv in November 1999 for ideological reasons, since I could not adjust to corporate academic life and the pace of his work style. We still remained completely respectful of each other's individual identities and work interests, and each of us understood the importance of one another's work. We had become emotionally destructive to each other and being intelligent rational modern human beings, separation seemed better than the lethal rage which underlay our laughing and malicious conversations with each other.

In the long months which preceded my return to the asramam, for the last time had been in 1996, I struggled with journeys to the moon – accompanied by voices which told me that the disease I had was so terrible it could not be described, but that those looking after me would be as angels. I had been diagnosed in October 2000 with multiple sclerosis, (the same time as my first book of fiction *Something Barely Remembered* had been released) but by December, the MS had become asymptomatic. The dream landscapes of death were so frightening and deafening that I preferred not to sleep at night, but right till the end of January 2001, I was walking in the frozen silver street outside my house on campus, willing myself to stay alive, because my children were so young. My mother and sister, my three children and my friends stayed by, while I fought to come out of the speech paralysis which finally disappeared without a trace. By March 2001, I was back in the classroom. I had begun a long term treatment with the eminent homeopath Prof. Mohammad Quasim, and Ayurvedic treatment with our JNU yoga guru, Shri Ajay Shastri, as soon as I was discharged by my doctors, Prasada Rao and Vinit Suri from Apollo Hospital, in November 2000. I recovered enough in May 2001 to make the long journey to Tiruvannamalai.

On reaching Ramanasramam, days of peace and contentment followed, as they always do in the asramam and I returned home completely happy. I returned to Tiruvannamalai again a few months later, and the desire to write a book on Ramana Maharshi, which had followed me since 1995, now became a very conscious desire. In this book, which is the culmination of twelve visits to Tiruvannamalai in six years, I record several journeys to the asramam, and the things that I saw and the people I met. It is both a travelogue as well as a sociological exercise. Sometimes the narrative is presented as journal entries, sometimes as sociological essays, replete with jargon, for which the lay reader may forgive me, and sometimes as reminiscences and meditation. The following section records a visit in October 2002.

4 October 2002

I am now at the Ramanasramam. This is my fourth visit. I came first in the summer of '96 for one day, then in May 2001 for ten days, then again for nine days in November 2001. Now I am here for seven days. I got here after a five-hour bus ride from Bangalore. One has to go on the Hosur road, and get on to the highway to Pondicherry. The route is very beautiful, the rice is about to be planted, and one is far away from the blitzkrieg of soft-drink ads. The fields and markets are full of yellow flowers and jasmines, sugar cane and that mussel-like fruit of the palm called nong. The bus is for backpack travellers, labourers and those like me who are witnesses – others take a taxi from Bangalore or Chennai. The agricultural workers and domestic servants going home carry their valuables back home in gunny bags. The women wear white stones set in gold in their ears and both nostrils. They talk loudly all the time to one another, both their longing to return home as well as the list of traumas they have experienced in the city. For five hours at a stretch, each can go on about the same kind of occupational problems – food cooked by them in grand households which is never appreciated, coffee which is watered down for the domestic, saris for whose loss she as maid-servant has been accused. The litany of woes sound like a dreadful drum beat, at times it becomes sharp and rattling like gun-shots, at other times it sounds like a whimper and tears fill their eyes. It is a story of a civilized sort of slavery, a story of continuous bereavement, where the soul is left adrift and the body hinges together around meal times, hand-me-down nylon saris and a monthly salary. At certain points in the journey, young women dressed in flamboyant colours, with jasmines in their hair, their faces golden with turmeric tinted oil get on the bus – young, gay, newly-married, sometimes accompanied by thin rapier sharp men with white dhotis (sarongs), gold watches and moustaches. Then the eyes of the older abandoned women, forced to work as domestics, fill with tears again because that was a world they once knew or did not know at all. Sometimes, there are newborn babies with feet like the Krishna, in the bus, travelling with their grandmothers, while their very new mothers look out of the window at the stunning scenery as bare low hills, green fields and the saffron coloured earth pass by. Black goats stare ominously at black cows, tethered in the green fields. Crows cross the road leisurely, flying a little when the bus approaches.

The road is like a narrow ribbon of tar, so constricted and threadlike that the bus has to limp on to the red earth, to the side, every time a truck or a car or bus comes from the other direction. But these are few, and in fact inter-state buses such as the one I am in do not stop for local passengers. Most villagers seem to walk wherever they have to go, or have local buses which serve them occasionally. A little girl dressed for a wedding gets on in one of the market towns – she's wearing pearls and a new silk skirt and her eldest brother holds her in his lap. Life seems normal and good, and poverty does not seem terrible when it is as simple and honest and trusting, as these people seem to be. Human nature seems suddenly recognizable; emotions are shared, mutually recognizable. There are no beggars, though occasionally a woman mad and dishevelled appears searching the garbage. At the bus stop a mystic with a blank face places a peacock feather on each of our heads and places an urn of sulphurous incense. I turn my head away and he places his peacock feather fan for a second time on my head. Blessing or curse? I have no idea, and those who are frightened of his grim-faced catatonia immediately give him money. The rest of us cough and wish he disappeared. Fat children like a babble of monkeys appear selling over-ripe speckled bananas and are shouted at by the conductor, who takes his job very seriously and counts heads every time we set off from a rural town with new passengers.

I have brought hibiscus as a gift for the asramam. When I get off, the conductor very kindly disentangles himself from the foliage and passes my luggage to me. The passengers are looking forward to idlis and coffee at the terminus before taking another bus to their 'ur' or village. Tiruvannamalai is a pilgrim town – teeming with people and goods.

I leave my belongings at the steps of the office, for it is 'lunch time'. Dr Murthy, who handles accommodation for devotees and visitors, is washing out the main Samadhi hall with the help of four workers. They have thrown buckets of water and are sloshing the mosaic. I watch for a moment, but am told to 'kindly wait at the office'. When the floor is cleaned, it is like a mirror. Dr Murthy is a physician by training, but he clearly believes in the ultimate space of the 'whole man' or what is called 'well-being' as an index of general health of the community. Manual and mental labour is combined, handling brooms, Vedic texts, large amounts of cash – nothing disturbs him.

Later in the afternoon, I meet one of the trustees, V.S. Mani, who thanks me for the potted hibiscus and is discussing some detail about the buying of barbed wire with a worker, but stops to ask about my work, my health, and my children. I had a paralytic stroke two years ago, and it was Mr Mani, a grand-nephew of Ramana Maharshi, who wrote to me asking me to spend some time at the asramam. 'We cannot escape prarabda, (consequences of past actions) but now you must look after your physical body, forget the spiritual journey for the moment.' Diagnosed with multiple sclerosis (though it is asymptomatic now), I walk a tight rope and my nerves threaten to burn like unsheathed electrical wire when I'm under pressure. He asks me about my writing, after I explain to him that my teaching is going well.

'I'm writing a book on Ramana Maharshi,' I say.

He looks skeptical, but he smiles as I continue, 'I know there is an industry around Ramana Maharshi,' – it sounds rude, so I go on breathlessly – 'it's very difficult to cut a new space. I'm going to take very small steps.'

'Take the big step,' he suddenly says.

Bharati Mirchandani, the designer, who is also a Ramana devotee, told me that the Cartier Bresson photographs might be interesting to study. I first saw copies of Ramana's funeral photographs, when my youngest daughter Mallika gave me a folio from the Hindu, *which had these classic pictures of death and mourning. Though she is only ten (in 2002,) she is concerned with my work, and my two other daughters Meera and Sandhya have also pitched as substantially into my reading of Ramanine theology as any research community supportive of shared interests.*

So here I am at Tiruvannamalai. At first, I'm startled by the smallness of the hill, at the courtyard quality of the asramam. Have I left home and children for Arunachala? I think not. I'm definitely a devotee, but a detached one. Detachment to devotion, detachment to the site of power – only an intellectual can play with terms and their meanings. I beg Arunachala, the Holy Mountain, embodiment of Shiva as agnisthal, to forgive my absurd and playful state of being. 'Oh hill of concupscience where Shiva and Parvati are rolled into one, won't you let me remain an anthropologist?'

We all have dinner – fabulous as always, after the stunning evening rituals. The colours, the flames, the bells, the songs, the flowers – the senses are filled and one comes out to a night sky so packed with stars one cannot imagine them moving. I come to my room and suddenly the electricity goes off. It is pitch dark, suffocating, sclerosis makes me sweat in panic. I stumble down, going by the back gate, on the main road, through to the front, to the temple complex where a generator runs. I lie down in the open verandah at the main hall, there is a woman fanning herself there. All the visitors have left. Dr Murthy is locking up and there are eight boys waiting for him to finish. They help him in the gardens, village boys with broken English and a terrific sense of fun. They assist the staff in the dealings with guests. I ask Dr Murthy if he can allot me Room 27, the room I stayed in earlier, because it has larger windows. He is non-commital because the juggling of days and rooms and visitors is a complex job. He says, 'Tomorrow', but from his tone I think it's unlikely since as devotees we must be detached from the trivialities of personal comfort. I walk back through the black night clinking my large metal key and ring, hoping that the sound will ward off snakes. I take the path through the asramam gardens past the lemon trees, jasmine shrubs and clumps of grass, not the main road.

I come to the large lemon tree, with its outsized leaves, and think, 'Now I must turn left.' I misjudge my step and fall into the cement trough just adjoining the temple pond. It's a bad fall but I don't break any bones. I'm just terrified, and keep saying, 'Jesus, Jesus, imagine falling into the pit. I can't believe this.' I'm blaspheming and frightened. Luckily, my room key has not fallen into the water and I find it almost immediately. I hoist myself out with some effort, the way we climb a wall, heaving up with one's back to the wall. I'm out. I'm scared. I knock at the nearest cottage and a lady comes out horrified to hear what has happened. She comes upstairs with me to my room. It is pitch black in the room as well, but shivering with fear I bathe and put turmeric based antiseptic cream on my bruises which sting all night. I'm lucky to have got off so easily. All night I keep waking up to check if I'm paralysed – I feel I might be. But at last, its 5.30 a.m. – my usual waking hour. A new day has begun, the cuts on my ankle and knees have formed neat scabs and I'm ready to face the day.

6 October 2002

I wake up to find it is raining. Heavy rain which mixes with the red earth and falls on trees and the temple pond with a distinctive smashing sound. I lie in bed and feel I'm in a bower of green – the tree outside my room seems to have crept in. I make myself some tea (no anthropologist sets out without tea making apparatus) and eat some crackers without looking at the time. I think it's about five o'clock but then I look out from the corridor and see two old ladies dressed in rich magenta and leaf green hurrying out barefoot in the squelchy mud and find my watch to see it's 7 a.m. – breakfast time. I'm a little panic struck because there are few expectations at the asramam from devotees but punctuality at meal times is one of them. In any case I get warm water from the solar heater tap which is located on the mezzanine. Yesterday the water was boiling hot, today after the rain, the water is merely comfortably warm. Outside the sadhus and the children are bathing in the temple tank. The tree, which overhangs the tank, is crowded with gnarled knobs of suspended roots and saffron clothes. The mothers and young women will come later in the day to wash clothes.

Today is the first day of Navrathri. It begins with puja *to the mother at 9 a.m. and a procession with the idol around the temple. My secular deafness has not achieved the anthropologist's sensitivity yet. On this, my third visit in one year, people reach out to help. Varalakshmi Amma who has been laughing at my need to know, suddenly understands. 'You're so blocked!' she laughs, 'Come out with what you want to say!' This is easier said than done. She is in her late fifties, a woman who came in search of Bhagavan, destitute she says in the beginning, but adopted by a wealthy benefactor whom she assisted in his old age. He left her land when he died, and she instituted a trust in his name, and set up an old-age home, the Ramana Maharshi Old Age Home.*

The puja *to the mother celebrated in the morning at 11 a.m. is extremely beautiful – jasmines and roses and hibiscus fill the sanctum (called Samadhi) of Ramana's large hall. Then the worship shifts to the temple of his mother, an inner sanctum called the Mother's temple dedicated to the Earth Goddess.*

The idol of the goddess is brought out, she is very beautiful and the devotees circle her with prayers and songs. Then the priest and some of the male devotees, including the family members of the Trust, carry her out in a bejewelled procession in a palanquin and return her to the sanctum, where she is placed ceremoniously for all to see during the nine days of Navrathri.

Food at the asramam is always fabulous, a tradition of hospitality passed carefully down, crystallized in Ramana's mother, Alagamma's recipes, cooked by him and his friends.

I return to my room in a gentle drizzle. I listen to Sudha Raghuram singing Ramana Keertanangal (devotional songs) on my tiny recorder, which I carry everywhere. She's excellent. Her voice is rich, young, textured, warm. It oscillates between a classical maturity and a sensual folk idiom. I feel completely happy.

Before lunch, I speak to Michael, a man who was once a Benedictine novitiate in America, but now knows almost completely that at the asramam is where his destiny fulfils itself. We have a quarrel over whether Ramana felt pain in his last days or not – it's the kind of quarrel that intellectuals heedlessly have and we bring in Christological evidence, Cartier Bresson photographs, dialectics and whatever it takes to convince the other. He says Ramana is god, and I argue that he feels pain, whereas Michael says, 'But not like us, he was detached from all experience.' I had met Michael last year, so I know that he was doing a PhD in Sociology before 'the Universe knocked at his door' as he called it. He has no regret about anything; and like other residents, for him, the call of Ramana has been accepted in its entirety. He wonders whether my professionalism, as an inscriber, stands as an obstacle to my devotion or vice-versa. I think not. It seems integrated somehow. I feel after the conflagration, I have experienced what Rajam Viswanathan described in her careful lucid fashion as jwalamukhi (the mouth of fire), that I need no more journeys. I'm here to stay. It's complex to communicate how places can live in the heart. I believe, as devotees do, that Arunachala is mine and there is nothing to prove or disprove.

At lunch I spoke to Sarah who was sitting at the plantain leaf next to mine, so we talked. 'How long are you here for?' I was startled by her reply.

'I live here. I've been living here for two years.'

She's a dress designer who has a business partner in Delhi and another in London.

'Do you go back?'

'I miss my mother and my father. I haven't returned for a year.'

'Are there other English in Tiruvannamalai?'

'I know David Godman, the author, has been here for twenty years, but no, I don't know other English people in Tiruvannamalai. There must be some.'

She is well integrated in the scheme of voluntary duties at the asramam, and I see her very often sweeping yards, washing dishes and organizing festival details.

The French have quite a conclave here. Last summer I met Joelle, a ballet dancer, in her sixties, who teaches at the National School in Paris. She and I grew to be close friends. I was ill, it was my first visit after that preliminary visit in May 1996, and she was very kind, comforting me when I fell ill with fever, and telling me to say Bhagavan's name over and over again, and to walk around the samadhi. In Joelle I discovered a deep tranquility, and acceptance of Bhagavan's grace, and the possibility of surrendering to one's destiny, something which would never have otherwise occurred to me. Surrender arises only from meditational practise. For me, it was always important to say, 'I will. Therefore I am.' I'm still like that, but last summer, following her footsteps around the Bhagavan's sanctum, I learnt to quell my fast beating heart. I learned to accept my fragility.

I am too deeply entrusted to Christianity to break away, although I have never been part of a congregation (other than as an observer compelled to attend by family traditions or in the guise of the anthropologist); nor have I been a tithe payer or decree follower. In Ramana, the Sadguru, I find the clearest evocation of Christian principles, and in his asramam, I find the most successful representation of the virtues of love and compassion. If this is Hinduism, indeed I am a Hindu, and have always been, and my Christianity echoes the principle of Advaita. Ramana's reading of St John's gospel is evident in his teaching, and the linking of theological motifs so wonderfully part of advaitism, and it continues in the life of faith of devotees, who come from different religious backgrounds and are able to co-exist harmoniously.

I spend some hours in the evening with Kanakamma. She is one of the few who are still alive, who lived in Bhagavan's time; in fact, she remembers meeting him when she was eight years old. Her parents were devotees. When I first bungle around, conversationally, she says 'Read my essay, "Cherished moments". Translated into Tamil and English from Telugu,' then, she takes pity on me, because I've shut my notebook, and am staring at her blankly. She starts telling me stories in Tamil. They're about Bhagavan, she's responding to my earliest question, 'What did you feel when you were with him?'

'In those days the asramam was very simple and quiet. There is no resemblance to the asramam as it was then – now you have tourist buses, cameras, lunch parties. In those days, Tiruvannamalai was a very small town, which came alive when there were festivals and after that it would become quiet again. The asramam was in the forest and it was extremely silent. And animals surrounded Bhagavan. Like the pilgrims they came when they wanted. Bhagavan never locked his door – anyone could have access whenever they wanted. He treated everyone the same, whether it was the Mysore Raja or a beggar. They were the same to him, equally important, equally dear. 'Nayandhrishti' – the eyes were his blessing, he only had to gaze, he never gave mantra or tantra, just the meeting of his eyes was everything.

'He used to feed all the animals and they would run around him, the squirrels, the dogs, the monkeys, the peacocks. When he used to keep food out for them, he noticed that one of the peacocks used to turn its face away. He kept trying to feed it gram, but it walked away. So he went to the store, and took out a handful of cashew nuts and fed the bird. The next time, he asked one of his attendants to get more mundriparrupau (cashew nuts) for the peacock, but in the kitchen, they refused, saying it was needed for the payasam for the pilgrims. So Maharshi Ramana said, "How will it matter if we don't have cashew nuts in our payas?" One of the devotees, a Parsi called Framji, who owned a movie theatre, heard this and sent someone to the town, and left one and a half kilograms of cashew nuts, with a note saying "For peacock!"

'On another day, a devotee left a stack of bananas for Bhagavan. There was a monkey with its baby, who used to sit nearby. Bhagavan looked at the monkey and quirked an eyebrow, and then looked at the bananas. The monkey walked over and picked the whole bunch and ate them. When the attendant returned, Bhagavan said, "So I've found someone who does the same work as you. You put them in a basket. She puts it in her stomach (thopae). That's the only difference."'

Kanakkama says that lakshyadhrishti – to have an aim, and to fulfil it is what is significant.

She goes on to exclaim over the queries to Bhagavan. 'A man once asked him, "If I can't meditate all the time, like you can, what can I do? I have a family, a business ... what can I do?"

'To this Bhagavan said, "Set aside some time in the morning for meditation. Then you have your work, you do that, then return to the meditation."

'To another devotee he said, to still the turbulence in what seemed a state of dualism, "You came to see me at the asramam. You set out from home. You met a friend on the way. You spent some time with him, then you sent him on his way – and you continued your journey to see me. So live your life in these parallel spaces, they do not obstruct one another."

'To another devotee who persisted in questioning Bhagavan, saying that he did not receive an answer to "Who am I?"' Bhagavan looked at him for a while and said, "The answer is that you are the one who asks, Who am I? You are the questioner."

'Another devotee wept to Bhagavan, saying "Remove my ignorance. You are a jnani, I am ignorant, and you are a jnani." Bhagavan said, "If I accept that you are Ignorant and I have Knowledge, then I will fall into dualism, so how can I accept that you are ignorant?" To another he said, "If you say that you do not know what consciousness is then it means that you once knew what it was. You can only know that you don't know if you once knew it." We forget because we are human, Kanakamma tells me.

When Ramana lay dying, Kanakamma came reluctantly for the ultimate darshan. She felt that electricity was running out of her body. He merely kept looking at her and she sat with the other devotees and felt peace – the peace that he promised when he said, 'I will always be here. Where can I go?'

7 October 2002

I skipped dinner last night, with some regret since all meals here are so carefully planned. I ate six small bananas brought at a nearby tea-shop and some biscuits, after I had finished writing up my notes, reading a couple of pages of Peter Matthiesen's Far Tortuga, *which is such a brilliant record of Carribean fishermen, that the narrator disappears completely. I've just finished writing a paper on Jean Rhys who was a Caribbean expat living in London from the '60s to the '80s.* Wide Sargasso Sea *is a state of the mind and finishing it at the asramam yesterday (I had brought along a thirty-page draft which needed a conclusion) I realized that home-coming, not home-sickness, is what I'm trying to record through the life of devotees at Ramanasramam. I asked Kanakamma yesterday whether she herself had asked Bhagavan any questions, and she said, 'I listened, and I had no questions because I had accepted what he said.' Her book records some poignant moments in her faith, and also includes her friendship with one of Bhagavan's most loyal devotees.*

Kanakamma told me a few more stories today. There was the time Bhagavan decided to escape from the asramam for a couple of hours. Continually devotees were bringing him food, prasadam as they called it, and he was forced to taste everything. So he thought that at least for one day he should be free of this compulsion to be continually eating. He went for a long walk, but all the people on the wayside kept giving him food. 'Swami, Swami, eat!' and in the fields, the labourers would offer him a little of whatever they had, poor farmers would break off twigs and give these to chew. At last he escaped all of them. He came across seven women in a clearing who asked him if he would help them locate a spring. Then they all took out their lunch baskets and offered him food, one by one they said 'Swami, eat, eat!' He managed to get away, but on his return, it was lunch time and by chance they were again in his path. So again he was fed, each one offering a different item, and so it was a feast invoking all the taste buds. He hid in a bush and waited for afternoon to pass, then came out to see where the sun was, because he felt it was his duty to be available to devotees. To his horror he found one devotee had come looking for him, carrying mango payas*, which he had specially got from his village. Bhagavan laboured back, saying 'Never again will I say that I will escape.'*

After 1928, he stopped circumambulating the mountain. The reason was that whenever he wished to go, droves would follow. None of the food would be prepared because everyone wanted to go with him. So they would come to him and say, 'Let's go.' And he would repeat, 'All right, let's go,' but he would lie back, because someone had to organize the things at the asramam, and he hated to say 'No' to anyone.

Chadwick, known as Sadhu Arunachala, writes,

> One day someone remarked to Bhagavan, there are many things that happen here of which Bhagavan cannot approve. Why does he remain here? He has no ties or desires.
>
> "What can I do?" asked Bhagavan. "If I go off to the forest and try to hide, what will happen? They will soon find me out. Then someone will put up a hut in front of me and another person at the back, and it will not be long before huts will have sprung up on either side. Where can I go? I shall always be a prisoner." (Sadhu Arunachala, 1994: 93)

8 October 2002

I walked up the hill in the morning up to Skandasramam. It has a pretty garden, and a brilliant view of Arunachaleswara temple.

The town looks neat and surprisingly modern, when one looks down from the hill. The breeze is cool though it's a sunny day. I am with Tara, who is from France, but communicates well in English. We've walked silently up the hill, but once having reached the place where Bhagavan lived from 1915-22, we become aware of a very warm and domestic aura in that little house. The mother cooked his meals, and attended to him from a small room that faces the town. She would have been aware of the lights and activity, but the aura of her simplicity is very strong. She would have suffered but she would also have been very proud. We collect some very lovely spring water – the source trickles down from some higher rocks. One of the workers opens the back gate for us and we get to the sheer overhanging rocks where Bhagavan used to meditate. The gardener tells us that 'This is the spot where he sat,' and further up the hill sits a sadhu who has been meditating on a rock for thirteen or fourteen years. The gardener says that this renouncer never comes down; he has only milk and butter which is taken up to him. His legs have become paralysed with sitting in the same posture. Tara and I are unable to climb up to the peak to meet him. We bid farewell to the young swami who keeps the place scrupulously clean, and who has lit the oil lamps in Bhagavan's tiny sleeping room and his meditation chamber, and opened the doors of the room where mother and son cooked and ate decades ago. The simplicity and beauty of the rooms are hard to forget.

We leave the Skandasramam and chatter as we go down the mountain. We become joyous, happy to be alive in a verdant forest, laughing about the smog in Delhi in winter when Tara plans to visit. Lunch is spectacular and I get a little nervous that I'm supposed to be on a strict diet because I had a cerebral stroke, and it's impossible to say No to the sadhya that's served on festival days. The rice, the vegetables, the sambhar, the rasam, the payasam – absolutely heavenly and I realize I'm in serious trouble because I can feel my system heating up. It is dangerous, even fatal, for me to step off my diet. But I decide I'm going to eat this meal, and then tomorrow, my last day here, I shall have rice and butter milk.

Bhagavan was very careful about the preparation of food. He would rise at 2 a.m. and at 2.30 his attendants would assemble to help him. One of them was in charge of handing him salt and water, and the other chopping vegetable or whatever else. By 4 a.m., the meal would be ready, and when the Brahmans came later in the morning, they would find him reclining on his couch (G.V. Subbaramayya, The Mountain Path, *January 1966).*

I went to look for Varalakshmi, my friend, who had told me it would be easy to find her house. 'Ask anybody!' she said. It was not easy. I walked for two kilometres, and no one seemed to know where her house was. It was a road marked by trees and the hill on one side, tea-shops on the other, and there were a surprising number of Ganesh temples (the land mark she had given me) at every turn. Finally, some one seemed to agree that, Yes, there was a house where Varalakshmi lived. So I took the turn as he suggested and found a lovely house. It had a lock outside and a signboard which read, 'Ganesh Iyer is in retreat and cannot meet anyone.' I had no idea what it meant, but since there was a lock, I thought I should see if there was a cottage further down. There were three rooms in an open field, but no sign of Varalakshmi. Then it started to pour, and sheep with no shepherd began crossing my path. So I decided to return to the asram, all of two kilometres in the pouring rain and the red earth, the temple tanks were filling up with opal coloured water, the mountain was hazy with white clouds like smoke and heavy rain – so surreal that I suddenly knew that in Arunachala it was possible to be outstandingly happy. I slushed through puddles, soaking wet, and in a state of bliss – my body cooled at last and hopeful.

There was hot water for a bath from the solar tap, and then I made some tea. I like tea. I always feel as if I'll survive anything – attachment, detachment, cold, cough, fever. So here I am, sitting at a window where some mango trees block the view to Arunachala, but you know it's there. The boys in the garden are repotting flowers, the pilgrims are circumambulating Bhagavan's white marble and black columned memorial, the doctor is laying palmyra leaves to cool the meshed shed where foliage plants are protected, and at 4 p.m. the tea bell will go and the devotees will gather for conversation and tea.

9 October 2002

There is music after dinner, in the Old Hall, which is old with wooden beams and old reddish tiles. The two singers of hymns and their accompanists are brilliant and we all listen completely startled by their ease and virtuosity. The stars crowd the sky. The children in the hall clap their hands in accompaniment. I sleep deeply though there are nights in Arunachala when I see my own ghost smiling at me from outside the window where there is no ledge, only the dark trees and the black and red butterflies. Today, after breakfast, my tongue serrated from sharp pepper corns crushed in snake gourd sambar, I go away up the hill. I see beetles, I've never seen before, a stone craftsman sells me a Mother Mary and Child, last year I bought a Buddha, and on an earlier visit a Ganesha. Yesterday Tara said to me, 'Ramana's is a Universal Religion; it has no dogma – that is why I'm comfortable with it.' Tara is desperately learning Ramana bhajans, and even had a music teacher at Aurobindo Asram in Pondicherry. At home in France she sings Bach, Verdi and Rachmanoff in the chorale at Church.

11 October 2002

The day before I am to leave I meet J. Jayaraman. I'm at the office paying donation towards the maintenance of the asramam. Sri Ramanasramam is always hostile to the idea that donations are solicited. Their website, in fact, carries a note on this! It says 'Anybody who tells you there is a donation to be paid, is not a devotee. Please walk in the opposite direction, and look for some real devotees.'

Devotees are expected to pay what they can, and no more ... and even this information is something which friends inform you about, if you keep pestering them for information. Yet, people are always glad to communicate their gratitude in being guests of the asramam, and surely the costs of maintenance must be very high.

V.S. Mani is teasing me about the notebook I'm carrying. 'Very big book!' He says, laughing.

'That's the anthropologist in me. We never leave our vocation behind.'

He smiles and leaves, knowing that the pilgrim with the camera and the notebooks have always been welcomed at the asramam. (The room I stayed in was donated by K.K. Nambiar's family, who made one of the early documentaries on Ramana, available today on CD and video.)

J. Jayaraman the librarian is at the office and he asks, 'Are you the writer? Can you write a book review for the Mountain Path*?' We walk down to the Library together. He's one of the early computer professionals of the 1970s, but dropped everything when the Ramanasramam asked him to help out with the* Mountain Path*. I had met him on the morning I had fallen into the grassy pit near the water tank, under the lemon tree. I had been overheated, desperate, afflicted with insomnia and had fallen into the cement edge of the temple-tank. I still agonise over that night. Everything I most feared had happened. All my life I've lived so frugally, so cautiously – my greatest fear is of falling into the shaft of elevators, into pits and troughs.*

I had stood by the small pond, thinking how lucky I had not fallen into the water. And then standing there, I had seen a water snake. Then this man, thin and hollow cheeked had appeared from the room facing the tank, and said, 'Snake? There are lots of them. See those holes? They live in them.' It was my first morning at Arunachala where everything seems curiously unreal, and I had said laughingly 'It's come to eat the fishes.' Then he had gone his way to chant in the hall, which he did every morning before going to the library, and I had gone on to eat breakfast with the late comers' batch, having overslept again.

Now here we were, at the end of my visit, walking across to the library, which is on the other side of the main road, past fruit sellers and close to the Seshadhri Asram. Seshadhri was a protector and mentor of Ramana Maharshi, and one of the greatest saints that Tiruvannamalai has produced.

Bharati Mirchandani, the designer who has produced a brilliant illustrated book for Ramanasramam, Heart is thy name, Oh Lord!, *was the conversational link between us. 'Is she still swearing by the Apple?' he asked delightedly and I said, 'She asked me to meet you because she said you knew everything about the books in the library. Do you have anything on Maugham's visit?'*

He did, and he got it out for me – an essay called 'The Saint' which described how Somerset Maugham had fainted on meeting Ramana Maharshi, which according to him he did often, it had nothing to do with mystic encounter, it was a cardiovascular problem, which he had even as a medical student. But he described how Ramana came to see him in the hut where he had lain, and squatted on the ground and meditated on him. The excerpt, describing the event, goes like this,

> We were told that the Maharshi would see us in a little while. We had brought a basket of fruit to present to him, as I was informed was the graceful custom and sat down to the picnic luncheon we had been sensible enough to put in the car. Suddenly I fainted dead away. I was carried into a hut and laid on a pallet bed. I do not know how long I remained unconscious but presently I recovered. I felt however too ill to move. The Maharshi was told what had happened, and that I was not well enough to come into the hall in which he ordinarily sat, so after some time, followed by two or three disciples, he came into the hut into which I had been taken. (Maugham, n.d. in archive text.)

After meditating on Maugham for a while, Maharshi asked if he had any question to ask.

> I was feeling weak and ill, and said so, whereupon he smiled and said, "Silence is also conversation."
>
> Later I heard that my fainting had given rise to fantastic rumours. The news of it was carried through out India. It was ascribed to awe that overcame me at the prospect of going into the presence of the holy man. Some said that his influence acting upon me before I even saw him had caused me to be rapt for a while into the Infinite. When Hindus asked me about it, I was content to smile and shrug my shoulders. In point of fact that was neither the first not the last time that I have fainted. Doctors tell me that it is owing to an irritability of the solar plexus which presses my diaphragm .... (3, 4)

He goes on to say,

> The interest aroused by this incident, unimportant to me, but significant to the Maharshi's devotees has caused them to send me a mass of material

concerned with him, lives, accounts of his daily activities, conversations with him, answers to the questions put to him, expositions of his teaching and what not. (5)

There is nothing that devotees of Sri Ramana like less than someone who withdraws from a mystical moment of revelation in his or her encounter with the Sage, and then retracts the experience. A reader has penciled a line of comment against the last quoted line, (referring to Maugham on receipt of materials) which says, 'Which he asked for!' JJ the asramam librarian, is irritable about Maugham's refusal to acknowledge the grace and attention he received from Ramana Maharshi. Sadhu Arunachala, also known as Major Chadwick in A Sadhu Reminiscences of Ramana Maharshi *(1994) has this to say,*

> In March 1939 Somerset Maugham came to the Ashram. Many accounts have been given of this visit and all of them different. I was the principal person concerned in looking after him. I have decided to give my own version. He was brought to the Ashram by a friend of mine, Mrs Austin, wife of the Collector of Madras. The party had first gone to the Dak bungalow to take their lunch, but finding it full, had come on to the Ashram. They asked me if I could find somewhere for them where they could have the meal they had brought with them. I arranged for one of the small rooms near my own. As I had already had my meal, at their request I sat and talked with them while they ate. Somerset Maugham asked innumerable questions about my life and the Ashram, apologising for his inquisitiveness.
>
> At the end of the meal, which they had taken on the verandah with Somerset Maugham sitting more or less in the sun, he fainted. Many absurd stories were circulated to account for this, that he had seen Bhagavan and this was a state of Samadhi brought on by the meeting and such like. Actually he had not seen Bhagavan at all. It was probably a sunstroke, though he himself said that he had been liable to such black-outs occasionally since birth. We carried him to my room and laid him on my bed. I then went to Bhagavan and told him what had happened and asked him, when he went out for his stroll at about 2 o'clock, to come to my room to see Maugham who was now unfit to come to the Hall, and Bhagavan agreed. (Sadhu Arunachala, 1994: 37, 38)

Chadwick describes as impossible any account of Maugham sitting in the hall,

> But this is untrue, because he could not enter with his boots, he only gazed into the Hall from the outside. He has also tacked a certain amount of philosophy onto Bhagavan, which Bhagavan could never have uttered in his life. But such is the habit of famous authors, to put their own opinions into the mouths of others: (39)

Curiously enough, I was nineteen years old, and studying Sociology at Miranda House, Delhi University in 1976, when I read Maugham's The Razor's Edge, *and my life was transformed by my understanding intuitively what Maugham had fictionalized in the last section of his novel. As a secular academic thirty-five years later, I can only say how much I enjoyed the novelist's sense of biography and space and time, when I first read the book as a young college student, idly reading a novel between classes.*

The 10 a.m. temple bell ran and the library was closing early for navrathri rituals. JJ gave me two books to take to Delhi to review for the asramam's journals: one a collection of Aurobindo's essays, the other a polemic work on Christianity and secularists. We talked amicably about reforestation, quarrelled about some right wing political position, agreed amicably that the future was about choices for freedom. Ramana's path is a strangely encompassing one. As Kanakamma said, 'You have to find your level and fit there.' According to her, Ramana once comforted an aspiring devotee saying that, 'If the other has reached tranquility quicker than you have, it was because he was more prepared than you. And you will reach there in your own time.' Dr Murthy who occasionally comes out of his silence, tells me that one comes onto the path only when one is 'pakka' or ripe.

In the afternoon, I wanted to return to the library, but instead I remembered I had not visited the Arunachaleswara temple. So I took an autorickshaw and reached the heart of the town. The last time I had visited it was in 2000. That visit with Paula Fitzgerald was incredibly vivid in my memory.

Paula and I had set out in an auto, the two drivers saying that they would wait for us and we could leave our shoes with them. We had crossed the large halls, which Somerset Maugham describes so well. Paula and I went into the dark sanctums, and were greeted by priests who took us to inner sanctums because clearly we were people of faith. But then Arunachal Shiva played a trick on us. We were completely lost. We kept coming out from one hall to another, we covered half an acre of corridors and courtyards, a thousand pillars, we ran in and out of gates, lepers and beggars followed us. We walked barefoot, circumambulated the outer walls of the temple – looking for the auto and our shoes. Finally, having seen everything, Shiva released us. The rickshaw drivers were laughing and we drove back exhausted but educated.

This visit was startling – it looked like the influx of pilgrims was much denser. The dirt and garbage was immense. It was sad, because the temple is where the most desperate and the unhappy congregate. They have come from miles away in search of succour and blessing. (However, a lot has changed in the course of these years, and the municipal drives for cleanliness are significant, but still, there are incredible piles of garbage, open drains, and poor workers pick the dense filth out of gutters by hand, without gloves. In Mathura in 2002, I saw scavengers and residents and pilgrims wading through street stench which went directly into the river. There, scavengers cleaning filth were worse off than Tiruvannamalai's workers who wear uniforms and receive wages. Chandan Bose, a JNU scholar, in his unpublished thesis 'The Production and Consumption of Cleanliness' argues that the castes which clean our cities are punished for doing so by the low wages and the insults they receive.)

I shall never forget the face of the young boy of fifteen or sixteen whom I saw clinging to a Shiva lingam at the first gate. He was unobtrusive, he was not begging – but he had lost a world. It is to these people that the fusion of Shiva and Parvati means the world of tenderness and warmth and concern. If Ramana embodied it, in Arunachala and its temple, the perennial promise of a conjugality that clasps the one who returns to the chest is surely clear.

This was not meant to be a Katharine Mayo report, but a cry for civic administrative attention which will benefit the citizens of Tiruvannamalai. They live in a mountain of garbage which will surely erode the sacred city if it is not controlled immediately. The first time I attempted to circle the sacred hill, it happened after a full moon night. I almost collapsed with the sheer visual horror of paper, banana peels, broken bangles, plastic and more plastic. Pilgrimages combine both silence and laughter, but to leave such debris for the residents as the 'return' gift seems horrific to me. I understood the intention of Bhagavan's garden, the peace and carefully crafted order, when I stumbled back after an occasional visit out of the gates of the asramam.

On this visit, I was locked out from the sanctums of the Arunachala temple, because it was lunch time. Fat women rushed out at me saying, 'Buy idlis to feed these poor old people.' They pointed at the vagrants lying near the gate. The starved faces of beggars stared back saying, 'Don't bother! These vultures never give us any of their pickings.' I moved into the courtyard, but the local idli capitalists followed me saying, 'It's not just they who are starving, we are starving too.'

I kept moving. My father was a professional social worker who threatened me once when I was a small girl of seven or eight and wanted to give a charitable coin. 'They will lose the ability to work!' It occurred to me that temple trusts should provide an old people's home, a leper's colony, a hospital, food for work schemes, where for a few hours a day, people can voluntarily or for wages clean tanks and precincts. I remember as a child constructing a street with other children, under the supervision of Prof Mujeeb, the vice chancellor of Jamia Millia Islamia. We were children of faculty on campus (my father taught Social Work and was one of the pioneers of the Rural Development programme) and we carried bricks and laid them out, along with the teachers and the workers. There was a great sense of achievement. I realize that work ethic is very much part of Ramana's theology – it's there in all the accounts published as books or essays. Meditation was a process which led to alertness, and a transcendent understanding which led to the peace of self realization.

I buy some rice crisps from a woman to feed the fishes. I've just come from a barricaded gate, where I can see a golden tower. The thin sadhu won't let me photograph the column arising from one of the courtyards. There's no signboard saying cameras and non-Hindus not allowed. He asks me whether I am Telugu or Tamil. I speak Malayalam, I say in my mother tongue.

He immediately tells me to sit down; he wishes to talk to me. I get nervous – his Malayalam sounds very very correct. So I ask him the forbidden question 'Where is your home?' which is the first question between expat Malayalis when starting a conversation, and then covering my mistake, I say quickly 'Your home is here,' and he nods and says, 'Here. My home is here.'

He tells me again to sit by him on the stone porch, he guards the gate like a medieval figure, his face is narrow and shuttered, but his eyes are suddenly bright and warm and recognizably Malayali. Our language links us. The time is 1:30 p.m., the gates will open at 4 p.m. What shall we speak of till then? I am full of contradictions which sound bizarre – single parent of three daughters, multiple sclerosis is my diagnosed condition, writing is my craft, and teaching is my occupation. Am I here on field-work, or is this a pilgrimage, or am I here to see friends and family? I'm backing nervously from the lean and saturnine sadhu. 'Sit down!' he says again.

'I'm feeling hot. I'm going to sit by the water.'

'The ponds are locked.'

'The fish pond is open. Namaskaram.'

'Namaskaram,' he replies, letting me hurtle off, knowing that I have reasons for disappearing.

I pass by a collection of sadhus, one of them dipping his hands continually in a bag of white powder which looks like arsenic. He has 20 feet of hair knotted on his head, rough like coir rope, and on it sit two grey pigeons. They are his friends. The weight of his hair and the pigeons circling his head don't bother him at all, and then, suddenly, he looks at me and his eyes smile the sweetest and gentlest smile. I am startled by the world of kindness in the look.

I go past him wondering if I will begin to produce flowers and lemons from the sky – he has given me the sudden sense of how magical the world is. However, I am brought back to the stark reality of the paraphernalia surrounding temple life. A swarm of women surround me: One gives me change for ten rupees, for which I pay her one rupee, the second sells me a handful of rice crisps to feed the fish, the fat woman who sells idlis gets five rupees to buy six idlis to give on my behalf to the widows at the gate, and yet another woman gets two rupees because she says she wants it.

Having got the rice crisps finally, I side step carefully over plastic bags which hit my eye, and sit down on the steps near the murky green water. I fling the rice crisps to the middle as far as I can, proving to the couple sitting next to me that I am a novice. The rice disappears in a fraction of a second. They say, 'You should drop it one by one, the way we do, on the first step where the water laps to your feet.' And they showed me how, but I don't want to go back to the mercenaries and money changers at the boundary wall of the pond. I watch the couple and the fat three-bindu fish, who slyly and shyly float up to the transparent water. They are like timid children who run up and accept a slice of cake at grown up parties. They snap up the rice the woman throws in one by one. Those rural lovers could have spent the whole day nudging one another, and laughing at the fish.

I walked out of the gate, thanking the goddess at the portal at whose feet I had placed a country rose in November 2001. She stood there as beautiful as she would have for hundreds of years – I had no idea who she was, but then as an advaitin, for me god lies everywhere, and boundaries disappear in the rapt and fearless gaze of craftsmen's art.

In the summer of 2003, I took my daughters to the asramam.

For me the revealed space at the asramam has been a serene domestic space. When I reach there, one of the first people I meet is Dr Srinivasamurthy and as soon as the first greetings are over I'm full of the wonderful realization that I'm home. Separation is a space of the heart and of the mind, at Tiruvannamalai everything conjoins in a moment of recognition. I'm not sure that biography and travel and faith are a space from which one can actually negotiate with the contours of a book on experienced religion, mine or someone else's. But it certainly is my intention to try.

My daughters have got used to my going to the asramam, and particularly after the cerebral stroke I suffered in 2000, they understand that visits there have magnetized me in such a way that I am better able to carry out my duties at home. This year it has been arranged that they would accompany me. We spend ten days with my mother, my sister and her daughter travelling all over Kerala. It has been tiring but exhilarating, after which we spend a few days in Chennai with my children's father's mother and with my cousins.

We start out from the bus station on 5 June 2003, startled at how ordered and modern it is. The spirit of Tiruvalluvar is the modern accompanying saint of the Tamil Nadu bus system. His world view, so rational and logical, so empathetic, is supposed to guide the driver and conductor as well as the passengers, and indeed they do. One hurtles at a very efficient pace and nothing suggests that the employees of the transport system are maniacs. I do not know then, that I'm on a foreign tourist road, and the road to Puthucherry is similarly served, but what about the rest of Tamil Nadu?

We arrive after lunch is over. My daughters are exhausted, but they are startled by the accessibility of the asramam – it's a courtyard, with trees and ponds and peacocks. After the fort at Gingee, and the first sight of the Arunachala mountain and the Shiva temple, the drowsiness, the lambent sense of order and peace at the Ramanasramam surprises them. 'You never told us it was this beautiful,' one of them says.

'Have you had lunch?' the gentleman holding fort at the reception office says.

'No' I say, disappointed that Dr Murthy is not around.

'Dr Murthy will just come. You take this slip and ask for lunch. It's over, but they will accommodate you.'

Just then, Murthy comes looking amused at the sight of four dishevelled females. I introduce my daughters who are tired and startled by everything.

Srinivasamurthy tells us to carry on for lunch. The girls put on their shoes.

'No shoes, please.' Dr Murthy says quietly. There are signs everywhere saying that shoes must be removed, one must walk bare foot on temple precincts.

In the hall, lunch has long been over and the cooks and servers stare at us, but not unkindly. There is food spilled by overenthusiastic devotees. One of the asramam residents is washing the floor with a hosepipe, watching the waste scattering with a dispassionate gaze. He hasn't recognized me, and looks at all of us with interest. Then, having washed our hands we sit down at the trestle table. My daughters are hungry and lunch is very good. There is *avial* (vegetables cooked in coconut) and rice, and we eat rapidly.

We go back to Dr Murthy's office, and when he gives us the keys, I hand them to Mallika, who loves opening locks. Doc sees Sandhya looking away, because Sandhya always wishes to be treated on equal terms with Malli, so he gives her the printed chart of routines at the asramam. She is pleased and goes off happily. In 2003, Mallika was eleven, Sandhya was thirteen years old, and Meera was nineteen.

'Do you know where the rooms are?' Malli asks me nervously.

'We'll roam around a bit, but we'll find it.' I say, in my usual frivolous way. The girls look anxious. But I do remember, and we pass the shadowed groves of peepul trees and I'm delighted to see that we're in rooms where I can see the mountain when I wake in the morning.

'Who is the I' that speaks?, Ramana would locate this in that great Self, but to get there one must know who one is. The method is one of great clarity. 'Ask yourself, 'Who am I?' and you will receive the answer. Yet there is a certain ambitiousness there. One must be able to believe that the self is significant – or else one will be torn apart and shredded. One is constantly in a state of dread because one will be asked to give up everything. The mystic's resolution is to believe that nothing that's asked of oneself is too much – like Abraham offering Isaac, one should reach a point where the negotiation with that great Self is beyond compensation. But that is the terrifying space from which Ramana Maharshi rescues us, because what he provides is the tenderness of Advaita. A.R. Natarajan writes in his pictorial biography of Ramana, *Timeless in Time* (2006) that an ascetic Amritanatha Yati asked Bhagavan to clarify which incarnation of god he was. 'Ramana replied in the same Malayalam metre, on the same paper ... Ramana was no particular form, nor any of the gods. Who was he then? Arunachala Ramana is the pure intellect shining in the hearts of all. He is the life of lives, the fullness of consciousness in each and every one' (Natarajan 2006: 1).

It is egoism to believe that anything I write will be of use in making the path clearer. One is drawn to the path because one seeks it, and one is flung off because one is not ready to meet the gravity and danger that rests there. Yet bliss is not a hierarchical dispensation. The certitude of *sahaja* or happiness lies in the acceptance of a particular teaching which is applicable to one, and negotiating with different paths, different teachers, and different levels is not the subject of concern here. We are where we are, Ramana would say, because that is our destiny. To obey or to disobey the call or the will to interpret that call – that is our birthright as human beings.

Why do human beings record their actions? Clearly because they feel that what they say or think or do is important to themselves and to others. One cannot deny the impulse to record, it is as primeval as drawing upon sand – a pedagogic practice to be found even today in Kerala where village children are taught their first alphabets by writing on the gravel outside their porches. So I keep this diary for myself, because I have done so every time I've been to the enchanted mountain. I travel through the recurring images that words bring: that sense of heat and light, early morning green and the crawling busy insects which forage for food, living their lives out in the torpor of a constant summer and the promise of shade.

The children and I have two rooms; each room has a distinctive photograph of Ramana Maharshi. Raphael Samuel writes that photography is the space where our different compartmentalization of disciplines, whether of The Science or the Arts would be subverted (Samuel 1994: 333). He discusses the contemporary appeal of old photographs, the grammar of photographs in terms of 'composition, lighting and frame.' He underlines the significance of what is being said, and what is hidden (330). Reading photographs when they are iconic have a greater mystique. The archivist works with photographs as if they are oral testimony. 'Deconstruction, using photographs in conjunction with oral testimony and written documents, splicing together different classes of evidence or using one to expose the silences and absences of the other, is one procedure which historians can bring to bear on the explication and interpretation of old photographs' (332). Here genealogies, family trees, family fortunes are juxtaposed. In the case of Ramana Maharshi, the photographs speak to the believer. Each expression captured by film is therapeutic, even discursive. Nothing is hidden, everything is revealed. We expect photographs to tell a story, sometimes they tell two or more (325).

Raphael Samuel argues that,

> When choosing illustration we are apt to plump for the iconic – the image which will stand for a larger whole. Ideally it should be transparent, an

> objective correlative of truth. We have little patience with pictures which keep their secrets: the whole point of using them is to show history "as it was". (328)

In the archivists' collection the photograph, like oral testimony speaks for itself. Yet, photographs which are read with an eye to contemporaneity are different from those implicated in 'pastness.' 'Here and now' is the transformative moment of *diksha* by glance, where the photograph becomes in mystical accord with the viewer. The Maharshi gazes, the devotee is captured in that gaze. A devotee once remarked on this, on the quality of entranced engagement, which linked the Sage to devotee, and Ramana said, 'What makes you think it is just a photograph?'

I will also argue that reading photographs is like reading narratives, more specifically fiction. The imagination is brought sharply into play – we are told a story, but we also invent parallel structures and planes. For travellers who come to the asramam, have travelled thousands of miles and crossed many boundaries, the act of encountering Ramana has a mythopoetic quality. They have been brought home, they are in the womb of the family, the catacomb of the shrine – and yet, they have the freedom to return to their duties, if they must. Much of modernism is about displacement and loss, about a sense of defilement, and a large morass of emotions which conglomerate in the individual in an odd and untoward fashion. This leads to a loss of self esteem, and that state which Jung called 'Modern Man in Search of his Soul.' Azade Seyhan writes,

> Once we accept the loss of stable communities and the inevitability of exile, then the interdependency of linguistic and cultural experiences both at the local and the global level becomes self-evident. Thus, despite coercively manufactured and enforced national antinomies and fortified borders, history and geography are transfigured in new maps and new types of dialogic links. (Seyhan 2001: 9)

Globalization and pilgrimage together forge new narratives, where individuals bond in situations of commonality which become more real to them as an aspect of the sacred and the mythic than the secular everyday lives they live in their routine worlds of work and survival. Pilgrimage is then a survival mechanism of modernity. It loosens in order to encapsulate in new structures of power and hierarchy, new grammars of belonging or fringe-order negotiation.

Seyhan draws our attention to the ethics of discourse provided by dialogicity. Following Levinas, she writes that forgetting, forgiving, sympathy, and love are made possible, through understanding (6). When one understands a person, one is already speaking to that person. It is here probably that the code of Ramana's preoccupation with silence, which is promoted by residents as the greatest vehicle of divine love, may be understood.

It is in this context that Christopher Pinney demands us to see that religious pictures are not about aesthetics in the conventional sense. He welcomes us into that domain of analyses which is that of 'history made by art' which is not just history of art (Pinney 2004: 21).

The power and the efficacy of the image is located in another dimension, which to my mind is the category of faith. Pinney writes, arguing that there is a sense orientation and psychological transformation of the individual who gazes.

> Within Hindu practice, the enormous stress on visuality endows a great range of images with extraordinary power. A key concept here is the notion of darshan, of "seeing and being seen" by a deity, but which also connotes a whole range of ideas relating to "insight", "knowledge" and "philosophy". (9)

I shall now describe this quality of entrancement more specifically. My room has a black and white picture of Ramana looking extremely skeptical. It's interesting how photographs convey so much of the presence of the Maharshi, the sense of here and now so integral to his philosophy. If there is any deification at the asramam, it is the sense of the photographs functioning as the living image. Devotees plead with Ramana's pictures – understand us, remember us, give us light, salvation, freedom from fear – and the curious miracle of Ramana's presence is that there are visible signs of his hearing prayers. Sociologists have not yet understood the nature of the miracle. Our tools would have to shift from the plane of the material world to negotiation with a spiritual world where the distinctions between the apparent and the known do not matter. Matter in motion does not remain the physicist's preoccupation, but extends itself to the domain of those other realms of reality and of existence. Anthropologists have lost their jobs while handling these debates, so the question of the coalescence of the material and the spiritual world cannot be handled here. It is sufficient to say that for

Ramana it was not important – there was the constant reminder to devotees that strange things might appear from devotion and meditation but they were to be disregarded. Lights, sounds, objects even if they were to materialise should not be an impediment to meditation or the tasks of one's everyday life. That sense of responsibility to the everyday is probably Ramana's greatest grace. Doc (as Srinivasamurthy is called by friends at the asramam) is a devotee who would consider the dualism of this world and the other world a mockery of the search for the real, emotions would be an obstacle to the pursuit of happiness, which is the basis of selfless service to the community. The reasons why one engages in those tasks which bring about one's understanding of the world and our place in it is probably the root of karma – to philosophically understand why one does the work one does.

I sleep in the afternoon of that first day, and then wash clothes while Sandhya slogs at her maths homework. Meera is content and passive soaking in the light and shade of the courtyard, while Malli is chasing butterflies and looking for twigs and stones and leaves. Arunachala, the enchanted mountain, dreams besides us. When I wake up, Malli informs me that the ants have got into the banana chips and dates which we had brought along with us. Ants cram into every crevice of the dry smooth husk of the Moonar dates, a singularly different variety from the thick syrupy fleshy desert dates we are accustomed to. I leave them all for the ants at the foot of the flowering tree, which has delicate white flowers and millions of butterflies swarm at the top. When I go into the room again, and look through the window, I see that one of the boys cleaning the yard is astounded at his find of exotic dates, and he and his young bride collect the lot as if a miracle happened, not bothering to dust off the ants. They have left some for the ants though, enough to propitiate those irate soldiers. In a way I am pleased that I do not have to safeguard anything, the children will now have large meals at fixed times, as is the asramam custom.

The silence, the heat, the inescapable sense of time that has passed – the hill has been the site of the imagination for centuries. Why one chooses to go, or more sharply the idea that one is chosen, is the difficult question for which no answers are sought. Meanwhile the family that runs the Sri Ramanasramam trust has spent valuable time recording the continuity of the method; the dispensation of devotion is to carry out the routine forms of practice associated with the Maharishi. How does one submit to the tranquility of the space of non-thought? Devotees are already aware of the peace that is generated by the hill, so their sense of turmoil is already hushed. Then there is the visible sight of the meditational practice of others which is calming in itself, and the desire to share in that silence and peace by remaining quiet one self. Maharshi Ramana believed in the circumambulation of the hill, and clearly often wished to go on his own, but was always thronged and surrounded by devotees. But he was quick to point out that circumambulation calmed the mind – walk around the hill and all thought would cease. I (in 2003) have not walked around the hill, fourteen kilometres is the distance – I still feel my time has not come – my devotion is not exact enough, my ability to believe in the miracle of good health is limited – I lurk in the clean swept yards at the back under the shade of mango trees, saying to myself, next year I will go around the hill. And then there is the chanting in Sanskrit and Tamil, so soothing that the mind is rendered quiescent.

In a completely different context, with regard to the analyses of narratives of border crossing writers, Seyhan writes that those who live in these existential spaces of overlapping identity have to live in multiple worlds and heteroglossia in the Bakhtinian sense must be readily available without suppression and this border semiotics allows primordial images to surface readily (Seyhan 2001:117). In the asramam one hears a myriad languages – the world appears through the untranslateability of these words to spiralling groups who speak some and not other languages. The experience of tranquility, of magnetism is the common language, and is available in translation through body signs. Mauss argues in *Sociology and Psychology* that the persona is best understood through the medium of the body of which sign language and expressions are symbols to be read. It is there in the smile, the gaze, the silence, the reserve, the sundry ways people use sign language to communicate whether they are available for conversation or not. Experience is what Seyhan would call the original code.

Susan Sontag in *Styles of Radical Will* (1969) has an essay on 'The Aesthetics of Silence', where she says that every period develops its own axes of spirituality, which is the manner contradictions are resolved (Sontag 1969: 4). She sees mysticism and art as similar, in so much that there must not be a self-consciousness, a striving, but that it must be creative and fulfilling.

> Silence is the furthest extension of that reluctance to communicate, that ambivalence about making contact with the audience which is a leading

> motif of modern art, with its tireless commitment to the new and/or the "esoteric". Silence is the artist's ultimate otherworldly gesture: by silence, he frees himself from servile bondage to the world, which appears as patron, client, consumer antagonist, arbiter and distorter of his work. (6)

But as she recognises so well, in mysticism and in art, the market always intrudes. Yet the spiritual, like art, always reinvents itself and it does so by unravelling the thread of thoughts and dispositions, by consuming itself in the moment of narration or some other. Sontag puts it brilliantly, when she believes that language corrupts, dismembers and fixes.

Silence is liberating, but it is also closure, because it subsumes the individual in a blameless world, where no responsibility may be taken because nothing is offered or taken away. That is indeed the text of non-dualism, which most pilgrims understand as a theological space that only some will travel on. Sontag further writes,

> Language is experienced not merely as something shared but as something corrupted, weighed down by historical accumulation. Thus, for each conscious artist, the creation of a work means dealing with two potentially antagonistic domains of meaning and their relationships. One is his own meaning (or lack of it); the other is the set of second-order meanings that both extend his own language and encumber, compromise, and adulterate it. The artist ends by choosing between two inherently limiting alternatives, forced to take a position that is either servile or insolent. Either he flatters or appeases his audience, giving them what they already know, or he commits an aggression against his audience, giving them what they don't want. (15)

How is this call to silence received? Most pilgrims who come to stay at the asramam always communicate that they've come to get away from noise. They look for friends only at fixed hours such as meal times, or at the conclusion of the ceremonies and rituals. Most look for quiet, by fending off enquiries and sociability. For the residents, the milling crowds who come to picnic or to spend the day at the hillside with their families represent the carnival aspect of the monastery which they safeguard. Ramana was a monastic who opened his house for householders, and 'suffered' little children to come to him. This aspect of asramam life is evident in the constant presence of children.

The days pass in an abandon of gladness, my own slow and tranquil pace is not matched by my daughters who throw themselves in a flurry of activity. They have found a potter from Canada, Shailja, who is full of sheer ebullience. She has done everything, everyday, sometimes twice. And she has befriended the aggressive monkey, whom I have not even seen in Skandasramam (the quiet whitewashed home of the Maharishi which is on the higher reaches of the hill). My children go with her to Skandasramam and I am in a panic when they do not return at 11 a.m., just before the lunch time arati. I first ask Sarah who is sweeping the rose and cactus garden, and she laughs and says, 'They will be fine!' Not quite believing this, I ask the doctor who emerges from the office, whether the children will be all right with Shailja. 'Shailja McFarlane? Oh, perfectly.'

I'm not calm; I circle around the asramam wondering if I will ever see them again. Suddenly the place is full of strangers, and all I want is my children safe with me. My obsessive personality is brimming over in a crude terrified cauldron. I have become overheated, I might collapse with fear. It is to overcome persistent anxiety syndrome that I have been visiting the asramam, and each time, I think I have controlled better my predisposition to be as taut as a violin string, a common condition amongst academics.

I am clutching in my sweaty hands the toffee that was given to me as prasadam at the inauguration ritual I have just attended – it is for the air-conditioned archives which will house Ramana Maharshi's letters and photographs and writings. It's an extremely beautiful building – and I have spent the last hour listening to the chantings of the priests and the swirling with water with green mango leaves which is the customary ritual of inauguration. The toffees now begin to melt in my hand, but then the children come happily through the gate. They're pleased, because Shailja's extrovert nature suits their mood completely. Shailja lives in Canada with her husband whose hobby is collecting stones. He polishes them till they gleam, for hours and hours with sandpaper. She comes from a family who has an attachment to Shri Ramana, so she visits the asramam to honour that memory.

Every summer I make new friends – Rupa taught in school till her voice began to give up, and her husband told her she should rest at home. As we exchange details about our lives, it turns out that she was born a road away from where I was born. Her father was the manager of the Thomson Press so they stayed in a lovely bungalow on a road which was called Rouse Avenue. I was born in one of the more proletarian houses on Thompson Road which have now been demolished for the convenience of the metro. But even till last year, whenever I went to catch a train, and passed the Shivaji Park (which was my first playing space, in those days a large open dusty field with no statue and no construction), I would crane my neck to see the little house built for clerks, where my parents and my sister and I had spent such happy years. Rupa and I were stunned that we could have been neighbours, because of course everyone who lived in that enclave, bang next to Minto Bridge ,could have walked across and visited one another.

The odd thing about friends made at the asramam is that they are a constant presence, in memory. The living and the dead merge in a continuity of time – a palimpsest of pilgrims reading about others who had lived in the cottages once. The names of the friends and companions of Ramana live on in the entries about their activities in the *Mountain Path*, and while each case is structurally similar yet the differences, biographically, are substantial. Those who have been invited to stay on in the asramam are marked by the vigourousness of their work style. There is a continuous energy that is poured into the most mundane of tasks. It is as if the concentration at work is a symbol of their *dhyana* – one has heard about the transformation of elite cadres of professionals becoming stone breakers at the Osho asrams in Oregon and Pune, but here, there is a greater quietness, a tranquility and an absence of scandal. A murder and a rape are talked about in hushed whispers but both happened outside the asramam, though the victims were asramam followers. There are notices everywhere, particularly in the women's chambers, which caution devotees not to walk around the hill alone. Now that over the years, the crowds circulating the hill have become an unruly crowd of millions, the problem has become much worse. To step into the constant eddy of people requires some effort, some courage. Residents of Tiruvannamalai who visit the asramam say that they get pinched and pulled by unruly miscreants regardless of their age. It is truly like stepping into the Heraclitus' river.

Shailja, my daughters and I sit on the stone bench after we have had our evening tea. I tell her about the obstacles to my writing a book. 'Everyone here seems to have come to the asram because of a dream or a revelatory experience, or because they read a book, or because someone brought them here or told them about this place. I really don't know how I can structure a book around this.'

She is startlingly logical in her reaction. 'Come and stay here for two years and your book will be written.'

Of course, she is right. The only way to come to terms with the stories people tell the sociologist, is through the intimacy of encounter. Last summer I spoke to a Gujarati gentleman who told me that he had come to the asramam in 1948 because the Maharshi had appeared in a dream. 'I was heart broken after Gandhiji's death. I had only seen Gandhi once, in a crowded hall where I could not even hear what he said clearly, but when he died I wept so much, that my family was worried for my sanity.' Then Ramana appeared in a dream and asked Mr Mehta why he grieved and in the dream taught him verses of benediction and devotion. Sitting at one of the temple windows the old gentleman said he was by Ramana's side, in his last illness and had nursed him while he sat in pain, on the black stone, lion-embossed throne outside the mother's sanctum. Several months later, I met his wife, looking with an expression of certain bliss, while white clouds chased the peaks of Arunachala. I asked her about her husband's visit in 1948, but she did not seem to know of this part of her husband's youth and said that they had come to Tiruvannamalai when their children had grown up and their duties to the temporal world had dwindled. I was baffled but realized these are the crossword puzzles of my profession.

Michel Serres offers us some interesting insights on method in his book *Hermes* (1992). He believes that we must engage with the analyses of systems in a Bergsonian framework.

> Once couched in terms of differences, reservoirs and circulation, energies, power and relations of force, time and motors, deviations, oppositions and dissolution, suddenly this discourse, as if reverting to the conditions of its own practice, begins speaking in terms of open and closed, of isolation and closures. (Serres 1992: 72)

Against this static model of systems, he provides us a key, which is the understanding of the living organism. Living organisms change. Information and thermodynamics become the key symbols in this trajectory. The struggle against death for whatever period is what the human body and the social system are capable of. It is the river, the eddy, the flow that then becomes the metaphor for understanding, what sociologists call process.

> This does not at all mean that it is eternal, but rather that it is an original complex, woven out of all the different times that our intellect subjects to

> analysis or that our habits distinguish or that our spatial environment tolerates. (75)

For him reality is like a star. 'What is an organism? A sheaf of times. What is a living system? A bouquet of times'. We find a similar association of temporality in Gregory Bateson's work, 'Steps to an Ecology of Mind', which beckons us to look at the striations or patterns in shells. Serres says, using the metaphor of the sea and islands, that the 'organism is synchronous for meanings and directions, for the continuous and discontinuous, for the local and the global; it combines memory, invariance, plan, message, loss, redundancy, and so forth. It is old, mortal, and the transmitter of a new cycle'.

Serres also uses the contrast of noise and silence. But for him, while the noise is emphatic, it is the silence which reigns.

> We are submerged to our neck, to our eyes, to our hair, in a furiously raging ocean. We are the voice of this hurricane, this thermal howl, and we do not even know it. It exists but it goes unperceived. The attempt to understand this blindness, this deafness, or as is often said, this unconsciousness thus seems of value to me. We have eyes in order not to see ourselves, ears in order not to hear ourselves. The observer observes nothing, or almost nothing. (77)

A lot of the questions of mysticism as an art form or as science are apparent here. Do we as social scientists engage in the dualism of art and science? In this book, I argue that detachment is the task of social science, and because we are also dialogic in our use of the method of verstehen (subjective interpretation) we cross the chasm between self and other.

What is the process of integration of the individual to the community? First there is information (revelation, or speech acts of committed participants) and then there is enquiry, acceptance and adaptation. If there is no adaptation, either in spatio-temporal terms or in abstract terms of experience and remembrance, then there is departure. Serres puts it for us theoretically.

> These matters are straightforward. Let us imagine a system with two or several elements. In an initial case, these elements are either completely different or identical with one another, repetitive. The information quantity

> is thus either a sum or a reduction to the information of a single element. This is the case of disorganisation, of inoraganisation. If the system is organised the elements are in relation to one another and are therefore different and similar at the same time. Here ambiguity arises. From a point of view within the system, the transmission of information along a given circuit from one element to another subtracts ambiguity because it is a noise, an obstacle to the message. For an observer outside the system, ambiguity must be added, for it increases the system's complexity. It functions in this case as information at the level of the unit's organization. In one case, it covers up, in the other case it expresses. The entire symbolic function is embedded in this process, the entire strategy of free association. (80)

This echoes the basic structural principle that changes in any one element will affect the structure as a whole. Serres works on this point to show us that it is at the boundaries that the most amount of noise is affected. He works with the idea of the unconscious to show that the interlinkages are the vulnerable points, where transformation is most likely to occur. At the core which is isolated there will be competence and stability.

> Each level of information functions as an unconscious for the global level bordering it, as a closed or relatively isolated system in relationship to which the noise- information couple, when it crosses the edge, is reversed and which the subsequent system decodes or deciphers. In each link of the series the question of language is formulated and reformulated by the transformation of the message, the channel, and the noise: by translation. In fact residual background noise is progressively eliminated: what was supposed to interfere begins constructing; obstacles combine to organize; noise becomes dialect.

These transformations are not just part of the linguistic code; they are also transformative in all aspects of the organism, which may be constituted as individual or collective. It is the integration of the individual to the collective that is most sought after. One is alone, but in the company of hundreds of others seeks aloneness as a meaningful space of identity and existence. In the end, the result might be what Serres says is the crushing resolution of being dashed to the shore through the mechanisms of eros and death. But that is what we know to be the just balance which defines our existence as sentient.

The children and I climb the hill everyday, not very far, and only once upto Skandasramam. We quarrel bitterly over something or the other at the door of the sacred abode where Ramana stayed with his mother, probably over where the shoes have to be left behind 'Here, not there' says the sign, and we differ over what that sign means. Maybe the sign says 'There, not here.' I'm near tears, I'm like those mother hens who run around trying to protect my children, and they playfully scatter while I try my hardest to round them up. They're now too old for me to brood over. I must give them more space and autonomy. I meditate in the inner sanctum, and a translucent green caterpillar appears on my sari – it must have climbed on board while I sat on a bench under the trees. It's a curious creature, but I suppress a scream, even so disturbing the person meditating on an adjacent cushion. I come out, and we all go into Ramana's mother's room where a Japanese gentleman is reciting his prayers, he nods at us, he has a prayer book and he recites from it in a Buddhist drone in which we recognize the word Shiva continuously, but nothing else. I think we are calm again, all of us, but suddenly as we go down the mountain, one of my daughters weeps, for her father who had disappeared into work and had forgotten what sociologists call 'the habit of loving' (a book which thus titled, he had once laughingly bought us from the Sunday book bazaar in Delhi); his work schedule has now created an unresolvable indivisible chasm. The post-modern demands of parents' careers don't apply to the needs of childhood. I try to explain that I had brought them here so that they would always feel that they had a home to go to, and that Ramana's hill and his home would be theirs. But I myself oscillate between the sense of being a devotee and being an anthropologist. How will I help them with their difficulties? I don't try to find a way. Time will heal.

6
TSUNAMI NEW YEAR

27 December 2004 to 2 January 2005

Somewhere, every anthropologist knows the futility of subjectivities, and yet we continue with our work! This embarrassment that we are tainted with our short-term drives, which is recording events, emotions, words, and yet our subconscious carries with it a whole submerged iceberg of the epiphenomena of events … we know of no way of handling this, except to write. The tsunami has just occurred, and yet our lives run routinely on track. For someone who has chronicled the struggle of artisan fishers, from 1994 onwards, this is a horrifying moment, personally. The detachment of the observer can never drown out the cries of dying people, and yet I understood what Fr James Stuart, a friend and chronicler of Swami Abhishiktananda, once said laughingly to me. 'You anthropologists are like shifting cultivators … slash, burn, hoe, reap, and move on! And do you know what the word translator comes from? Tradiottore … which means betrayer or traitor.' He was in his eighties, and we understood each other perfectly.

I have no working notes for this trip to Ramanasramam, because it passed in a sunny haze of being safe in the shadow of the mountain – the calm glow of an unquestioning love, an unspoken love. I've been recording this for years now, and it shocks me that such a place exists which quietens all desire, and leaves the mind a calm and lambent pool of fulfillment. My children feel the same way, but they make no fuss about it, are never surprised … perhaps happiness is an unquestioned part of childhood. My eldest daughter Meera thanked me for bringing all of them to Ramanasramam, and then I realized she is now an adult, who can be startled by pleasure and happiness. When we got off the taxi at the Ramanasramam, it was only 1.30 p.m., since the driver got a cell phone request from a client at Ooty, and he was desperate to get back to Bangalore and cater to the next business. So we reached in four hours, at suicidal speed, instead of the conventional five or six hours. I was nervous, because Doc had said, 'Come at 4 o'clock, otherwise you will be stranded with your luggage.' After that the three children trooped off to find food across the road, because I said when Doc said something he meant it, so we weren't to look for him and ask for keys till 4 o'clock. They trooped off happily and came back a little disappointedly with small bananas and biscuits and *khatta-meetha* mixture, which we contentedly polished off sitting on the cement ledge just adjacent to the old tree and the square where lepers and beggars are fed.

I was so tired that I lay down on the concrete platform, on my red and blue Naga shawl. A flock of pilgrims all dressed in red have arrived from some *mutt*. They were journeying all over the South on a pilgrimage. Everyone was wearing red in various hues and shapes. They were like hibiscus gone on a rampage, but were clearly having a wonderful time. Just as anthropologists and photographers see the world by inventing intellectual reasons, a lot of people in India just go on a pilgrimage. I suddenly get up because there are cartloads of people getting out of vans and going to the office.

The Doctor has arrived. We speak perfect and short sentences to each other; we are formal to a painful degree. I try to hide the happiness from my face, I sign the guest register and say, 'We have no idea about Brojo's whereabouts!' Part of me is nervous about the arrival of my nephews, Zul and Brojo Pillai. They are subversive by nature, one never knows what they will do and say. But that's true for the entire family ... it can get quite taxing, because we always say what we mean, and we always mean what we say. The problem is that it can be quite eccentric and threatening sometimes. Doc asks me where we are sitting, and that as soon as the rooms are ready, he will give us the keys. I fall asleep on my rug, and then Meera nudges me, and I wake up, looking short-sighted and vague, Doc is holding our keys. I run up to get them, and then my eyes fall on the most beautiful flower I have ever seen. It's reddish pink, a deep thick colour, the petals are like satin and in the centre is a frond of the most amazing strands, which are hellbent on warring with one another. It is a water lily. I pick it up.

Doc says, 'I will send a boy to help you with the suitcases.' But that awful feminist slant surfaces, and the four of us struggle with our suitcases, with me yelling, 'We'll manage!' All so untidy, and at odds and ends, and we have as usual far too many things. There is one suitcase whose zip has snapped ... it fell down from the porter's load at the beginning of our journey. It could not be repaired and it's still with us. In it, are all the clothes that we wore when setting out from Delhi: so many woollens and coats and scarves, it amazes us, for now we are in land where the sun shines bright and hot. Doc watches us impassively. I have to choose between the red flower and my rug, and I choose my rug ... but Sandhya picks up the flower and puts it in one of the bags. A youth has appeared with a bicycle and has strapped one of the suitcases on a bicycle. Meera carries the other ... but then she gets irritable with the weight, and flounces off faster than the rest of us, and we go down the main road, looking like we don't have a man to control and govern us ... unruly women, the bane of all societies everywhere.

We're so tired, the room seems like heaven, cool and with two beds, on which the three girls cram ... and I as usual, have a bath and wash clothes ... then lie on the ground on a rug. Then we go down to tea, and Meera makes awful faces, because you can smell the fresh cow milk, and we all laugh at her expressions. I think it's also because Meera's fetish for a clear light brew with very little milk and sugar is something that we have got used to over the years. The usual thing follows, that is we let the asramam take over us ... the lovely sense of being taken care of, and of being loved without reason ... it's the aura of the mountain and the cultural logic of Ramana's own personality, which is sharply tended, sharply because indiscipline is not welcome. The calm of the asramam, the quiet of others' meditation ... these are valuable things, and protected against everything else.

The surge of the tsunami follows us everywhere. It happened when we were in Bangalore with my sister's family. We are never free of its shadow. Yet the asramam protects one from every possible upheaval ... from sorrow and tomorrow, and that is why one longs to return. What was Thomas Mann's *Magic Mountain* about? It was about a sanatorium where the heated up and the despised go for a while, and the young man tormented by his desires, finds good company with a Jesuit. Here too, one knows that everyone who is here is here because they have been in crises. So many of the books written on Ramana are unashamed accounts of great love for the sage, descriptions of his life, of friendship and love that blazons the pages ... what shame is there in loving? That's the interesting thing about Ramana's life and his work ... we have no veils to hide the quality of our feelings when we are on the mountain, yet we are asked to don these veils, so that the light on our faces will not dim our recognition of routine tasks. Those routine tasks must continue, and we become known by the work we do. Mine is, I fear, only to appear and look around and be startled by the Annamalais, and particularly Arunachala ... clouds, plants, creatures which inhabit these green hills and sudden shadows. The rest is locked in history and the sameness of things which is what mythology is about.

Whenever I read the chronicles of devotees, I'm startled by the tactile nature of these records. A. Devaraja Mudaliar describes how Skandasramam was built. The entry is for 9 December 1945.

> Bhagavan said that the old disciple Kandswami was anxious to build a separate Asramam for Bhagavan. He inspected various places on the hill and in the forests to select a site, and finally suggested the present Skandasramam site and then Bhagavan also approved of it. There upon Kandaswami bagan converting what was a thick forest of prickly pear on the mountain slope. The result of his labours unaided by any at the time is the Asramam we see now. He added, "You cannot imagine the site was in originally. Kandaswami worked with almost superhuman effort, achieved by his own hands what even four people together could not have done. He removed all the prickly pear, reduced stone and boulder to level ground, created a garden and raised the Asramam. We got four coconut trees for planting. To plant them properly Kandaswami dug huge square pits about ten feet deep. That would give you an idea of the amount of labour he put into the work he took on hand. He was a strong, well-built man." (Mudaliar 2002: 66)

Publishing as Creation of Community: The Narratives of Three Women Writers

Stuart Blackburn has shown how much print has affected the cultures and traditions of South India. As he sees it, following the pioneering work of Natalie Zemon Davis and others, 'books are cultural objects, and readers are 'textual communities' and 'consumers of popular culture' (Blackburn 2003: 7). The Ramanasramam has a strong publishing history, where the president of the asramam is a publisher, and authors augment through interpretation or memoirs the story of Bhagavan, friends and devotees. There is a circular structure at work: by reading these works and remembering them, present day circumstances are re-established within previous wisdom.

One of the most revered devotees is T.R. Kanakammal. Her *Cherished Memories* have been read over and over again. One of the startling themes of her work is that of companionship. She handles the friendship between men in the community (it was truly a fraternity, with women allowed to be present as witnesses) with a grace and laughter that is truly unique. One of her most common themes is Murgunar's friendship with Ramana. Murgunar was a brilliant and eminent Tamil poet, who was introduced to the Maharishi by his father-in-law. He was a school teacher who caught the train to Tiruvannamalai at every possible opportunity, but because of the illness of his mother he could not shift to the asramam. His devotion was such that he had eyes only for Ramana, and his wife would complain to the sage of her husband's neglect of her. Kanakammal, who was a close associate of the poet, writes of him,

> Murgunar was one of the greatest Tamil poets of this century. In fact, Thanigaimani Sengalvaraaya Pillai said that Murgunar is to be considered an equal to any of the Tamil poets of the Sangam Era (the period, a few thousand years ago, which is acknowledged as the Golden Age of Tamil poetry.)
>
> Murgunar's extraordinary poetic gifts became apparent while he was still very young. After his meeting with Bhagavan, his entire personality underwent a change. Not only did the pattern of his external life change; his spiritual awakening is also to be attributed to his meeting with Bhagavan. (Kanakammal 2002: 142)

After his mother's death, Murgunar came to live at the asramam. His devotion was so palpable that Maharishi was often amused by it. Murgunar would listen to the Maharshi, and swallow him with his eyes, with his mouth falling open. He so desperately desired to eat from Bhagavan's left-over leaf (the plate from which Bhagavan had eaten), that he wrote the following verse,

> Lord Brahma, the Creator of the Universe is very good at chanting all the four Vedas; but when it comes to fashioning suitable dwellings for all the souls entering the world, He is obviously incompetent. Let us consider my case. I have the body of a man. Maybe, my actions in previous lives had entitled me to a human body. But the soul that resides in this body is undoubtedly that of a dog. That is why I have developed the desire to eat from your used plate. O Noble Ramana! I prostrate myself at your feet and beg you to grant me Real Knowledge. (142)

Ramana Maharshi found his adulation amusing and was at some trouble to communicate how important detachment was for non-dualism. But for fifty years, from 1923 to 1973, Murgunar devoted himself to Sri

Ramanasramam singing the joy of having found the Lord. 'His Sri Ramana Sannidhi Murai contains 1,851 poems in praise of Bhagavan' (129). He was also the author of numerous other works. While he forgot his food, his belongings, even his conjugal responsibilities, his friendship with Bhagavan remained one of the lasting testimonies of a truly startling relationship between two erudite men. It verged on the simple and the surreal.

Once, Meenakshi Ammal, Murgunar's wife who loved Ramana equally, complained that her husband never noticed her. At this Ramana asked her to substitute Murgunar's name for his own, when she sang her usual hymn of praise in the hall.

> Meenakshi Ammal was a simple soul and her faith in Bhagavan was total. So she agreed to do exactly as Bhagavan said, even though she had no idea why he should want her to do it. Now, the verses selected by Bhagavan were very well suited to the occasion because they presented the picture of a love-lorn lady chiding her lover for his cruel neglect. In these verses, Murgunar portrays himself as a love-lorn lady and entreats Bhagavan to favour him with his grace. To be precise, the lady describes the happy times she had shared with her Lord, and the promises that he had made to her. ... Each of the verses ends with the phrase, "Ramana Mayavan" (the term mayavan can be translated as the "great deluder"). The lady is accusing her lover of misleading her with false promises. Yet, her language is far from abusive. In fact her words are full of affection and reflect the remembered joy of happier times. Each of the poems in this section is exquisite in the beauty of expression and the delicacy of feeling. (149)

Murgunar entered the hall and heard his wife singing. He presumed that she was referring to Lord Murrugan.

> Bhagavan glanced at him with eyes full of mischief. Then he directed a look of approval and encouragement at Meenakshi Ammal. This repeated substitution of "Muruga Mayavan" for "Ramana Mayavane" now appeared highly significant to Murgunar. He was finally convinced that Bhagavan was deliberately teasing him, using Meenakshi Ammal as an innocent, yet effective agent! (150)

Murgunar fled the room, but Bhagavan stopped him, saying 'Hey! Why are you leaving the hall now? Is it not because she sang about her

"Muruga Mayavan"? Well, does that mean that whenever somebody sings about "Ramana Mayavan", I should immediately walk out of the hall?' (150).

On another occasion, Meenakshi Ammal, did not stretch out her hand for *prasadam*, hoping her husband would notice her, but he merely passed her by. She complained to Bhagavan who again laughingly mediated between the couple (151).

One of the most amusing accounts that Kanakamma gives us is of Murgunar being asked to officiate at pujas. He was a perfectionist, but then, he started to mumble to himself,

> "I wonder how others manage to recite the mantras, ring the bell with one hand, and keep up the circular motion of the Arati plate with the other hand, all at the same time. It requires such perfect synchronization of activities! I suppose it is a gift that other people possess. I can never master this art!" ... Bhagavan started to tease him, and Murgunar said he could not possibly continue with this ritual duty, so Bhagavan said, "That is good. Now you have granted liberation to puja!" (157, 158)

When Bhagavan's teasing became too much to bear, Murgunar would retaliate in verse. Once he was helping Maharshi to clean the greens for cooking. The Master began to describe the various medicinal qualities of herbs.

> Murgunar was fascinated by Bhagavan's words and completely forgot the work at hand. Bhagavan finished his portion of the job and with the intention of stacking all the greens together, and gathering all the roots into one single heap, he looked at Murgunar's work spot and remarked, "Look at him! He is really very smart! Murgunar, your skill in chopping greens is as striking as your success in running a household!" (Murgunar's extraordinary "domestic skills" are, of course, well known to all of us!)
>
> Bhagavan's remark jolted Murgunar out of his trance like state. He looked down at his handiwork. The few stalks he had managed to chop were lying scattered all over the place. The roots were in an even messier state, lying like wounded soldiers on a battlefield! Then he looked at Bhagavan's portion of the work and saw the chopped greens piled up neatly in one place, with the roots in a separate pile! Not a scrap had been wasted; nothing was out of place. Murgunar was quite ashamed of himself. He could think of only one form of retaliation. (160)

Murgunar wrote a poem which Bhagavan summarized to the devotees gathered there:

> In reply to my remarks, he has written this poem. The gist of the poem is, "O Ramana! You are an extraordinarily efficient person. Why don't you marry an equally efficient young lady and set up house? Why should you be wandering around as a mendicant in loin cloth, begging food when you could so easily have set up an ideal household?" (160)

What Kanakamma brings to our attention is the joy and laughter between equals, the first text of non-dualism. If hierarchy is to be established it may appear in many ways, in many nuances. What Murgunar established in another work was the significance of words, of hymns, and the unashamed expression of love for the Master.

I turn now to another narrative, which is Monica Bose's *The Hill of Fire* (2002). In this very exquisitely crafted book, which I have referred to in a later chapter as well, we find the uses of biography in the telling of history, which has been the main theme of this work. These are indeed hagiographies, but they are neither canonical nor apocryphal. They are memoirs of lives lived in proximity to the Master. I have used the same methodology in an earlier work, *The Christians of Kerala* where I have argued that one can understand the Christ better by looking at those who were close to him, or in a related fashion one can understand canonical rituals better if one can examine the paraphernalia of rituals and cults associated with satellite figures. There are many who were close to Bhagavan. Since he refused to take disciples, it was understood that they were seekers and that self-realization was so close at hand, each individual only had to accept the nature of being. What was that state of mind that allowed one to ask in the first place 'Who am I?' What was the concomitant state that allowed one to accept Maharshi's teaching culminating in *sahaja* in being what one was? In the life of Suzanne Curtil Sen, or Sujata Sen, as she came to be known, we shall find some disturbing revelations about the nature of the quest, and the suffering therein. It seemed almost a truism that those who suffered found Bhagavan. It is in this context that his teaching of *prarabdh* (karma leading to rebirth) and destiny may be interlinked.

Suzanne Curtil was born on 13 December 1896 to a Parisian called Jeanne Curtil, and Gabriel Sursock who came from a banking family in Beirut. She grew up to be an acclaimed dancer, a Theosophist and a trained medical doctor. In her biography, *The Hill of Fire*, her granddaughter writes,

> Whilst a student at the medical faculty of the Sorbonne, Suzanne seems to have been quite a firebrand, siding with the anti-vivisectionist students who protested often and vociferously against the appallingly cruel experiments and demonstrations that were carried out on live animals in the classroom. She became something of a feminist, too, after seeing how some of the authorities were prejudiced against women wanting to enter medicine, and were not above failing them to keep them out. Once her studies were over she would retain a combative attitude towards unfair treatment whomsoever it was directed against: women, the poor, or people of a different race. (Bose 2002: 24)

During this period she joined the Esoteric Section of the Theosophical Society, which was a sub-society, for those who believed that they would, through the path of spirituality, come in contact with a great Master. Following five years of apprenticeship, she came to India. She became friends with George Arundale and Rukmini Devi, who gave her the support she needed. While she listened to Jiddu Krishnamurti, her spiritual path took her onwards to Theravada Buddhism.

> Suzanne met Sri Jinwansaswami, sometimes called Prince-Priest because of his aristocratic descent, but generally known as the Swamiji on 30 December 1925, when he came to inaugurate the small Buddhist temple the construction of which had just been completed in the compound of the Theosophical Society. He was a Maha thera, a High Priest of the Theravada or Southern Buddhist Church, who had received the higher ordination from the Head of the famous Abhinawarama Temple in Wakaduwa kalutara in Ceylon. (42)

Meeting him Suzanne felt that she had met a realized being, and in turn the Swamiji felt that Suzanne could be a nun, or in fact a priestess.

> This was a very bold idea because no woman had entered the Theravada Order in Ceylon for over eight hundred years. However, the Swamiji hoped to persuade the Chief High Priests there to admit her since, as a medical doctor, she had proved she possessed qualities of intellect and character at least equal to a man. (43)

The Swamiji believed that if Suzanne were to join the order as a nun, since she was a European, many doors in the colonial hierarchy would perhaps open for Theravada Buddhism. It would also prove to the world that there was no discrimination of caste, race or sex in Buddhism. This dream was realized, and her going forth (pabbaja) ceremony was performed where she renounced objects of sense, and also the very thought of sensuality (45). She was given the name of Sujata after the woman who gave the Buddha milk and rice, which revived him and set him on the final path of Buddhahood (47). Suzanne went on to Tibet.

> After Phari-Jung, they traversed still more desolate country. A tropical sun shone in the deep blue sky but at altitudes nearing, 4,600 metres, the cold was intense. By afternoon, strong winds arose making the cold still hard to bear. Suzanne, inadequately clad and equipped for such conditions, tried to keep warm by stuffing paper in her boots and between the body and her clothes. They passed mountains which were so steep that it was a wonder how the monasteries perched on their slopes were not swept away by the onslaughts of the wind and rain. Suzanne visited a monastery that was inaccessible to outsiders for nine months of the year. She would report that within the limits of those lonely eyries the monk far from suffering any sense of isolation enjoyed the widest communion possible. (71)

In Tibet she discovered communities of nuns.

> The size of the religious communities varied greatly, from small groups of four or five women living in isolated retreats to highly organized, well-known convents of three hundred nuns or more. There were also women ascetics who led a Yogi's life alone in mountain caves or forests, and there were itinerant nuns who fearlessly trod the lonely and dangerous pilgrim paths. With the flexibility characteristic of the Buddhist religion, another alternative was countenanced, especially in southern Tibet. This was for the priestesses to be married women who lived in convents and performed the religious ceremonies for the community that were usually the function of priests, while their husbands stayed at home and cultivated the land; an arrangement that was said to work well. (72)

Suzanne never reached Lhasa because she fell very ill. She returned via Sikkim to India. In Egmore maternity hospital, where she enrolled to take an obstetrics course, she met Dr Ranjit Sen, an anglicized soldier, who courted her and married her.

> Suzanne let herself be persuaded. Perhaps she wanted to prove to herself that she was capable of loving, and in her eyes he had all the qualities that made it possible for her to love. (75)

However, having led a monk's life she had no idea that he was an accomplished philanderer, who could not understand why Suzanne resented these liaisons or was humiliated by them ... And heartbroken she returned to her Buddhist preoccupations.

> Adding to her sense of disappointment was that she had not been able to start her medical work since the military authorities had turned down her request for permission to start a charitable dispensary. Nor had she succeeded in starting a new Buddhist centre. In fact, her work for the Dharma had been reduced to writing a few letters to prospective donors. The situation had become unbearable for her, yet she did not tell Ranjit that she wanted to leave him. Instead, she asked him to release her so that she might go and fulfil her mission of service to humanity to which she had long ago dedicated herself. Ranjit reluctantly accepted that reason and agreed to let her go. (75)

This time Suzanne went back to a more purist Buddhist practice, and also returned to the stage as a dancer. It was 1936, and she brought to the stage, in Brighton, dramatic and dance enactments of her experiences in Tibet. Fourteen such secular and sacred dances were performed (85). Yet, there were major differences now, with her patron Jinararadasa.

> It was at this juncture in her life, when she felt baffled, distressed and uncertain as to what to do next, that she came across a newspaper article about Bhagavan Sri Ramana Maharshi ... Suzanne felt a great desire to go and see him, and so, accompanied by two European ladies from the Theosophical Society who also wished to visit him, she set off for Tiruvannamalai on a day in December 1936. (85)

It is Sujata Sen who by her wilfullness brought about dramatic changes in the attitude of asramam administration to women. She who had fought for equality all her life, flatly refused to believe that she would be sent away at dusk from the presence of Ramana Maharshi because she was a woman. I have referred to this incident in a later chapter.

> The two ladies from the Theosophical Society who had come to Tiruvannamalai with Suzanne returned to Adyar after a couple of days. Like several other Theosophists who visited the Maharshi, they were disappointed by his attitude towards altruistic service. They believed that it was through service to others that one developed one's Divine potential. The Maharshi, however, did not teach that service was to be deliberately used as a means of Self-Realization, but rather that Self-Realization was to be sought so as to be able to render the greatest service to others. (112)

Suzanne stayed for a decade at the asramam, but fell victim to rumour and gossip, and further longed for initiation from Ramana, which he refused to give.

On 20 December 1945 she came to the asramam to take her leave of the Maharshi. Sorrowfully, she told him that she was going away. The Maharshi did not reply. But then something very strange and wonderful happened for she saw the Maharshi as Dakshinamurti, the Divine Inner Guru who teaches the unutterable truth in the silence of the Spirit. As she would write, 'When I was talking to him his appearance changed and I thought that Dakshinamurti was sitting before me. In the silence I heard, "There is no separation, for all gurus are one. They are the indwelling Self of everyone. I shall ever remain as the Jewel shining in the lotus of your heart"' (134). She went to Anandasramam, on the Canara coast, and stayed there till Ranjit Sen turned up in her life again. She thought they could practice medicine in the villages of South India together. Monica Bose writes:

> He had not yet made up his mind how and where to spend the years of his retirement. My mother suggested that he stay on in India and that they practice medicine there together ... My father told her that he had to attend to various matters in Europe, but that he would return by the end of the year. In the event, he never did return. He settled happily in Menton in the south of France, and would remain there for twenty-seven years until his death in 1974, a popular and respected resident of that little town. (138)

Sujata Sen would return to Ramanasramam, believing that the isolation and hardship of the path that Arunachala offered would be her refuge.

Monica Bose writes, 'There were people – I was one of them – who found happiness and peace with the Maharshi. For Suzanne, the experience of being with the Maharshi was like going through the fire' (141). Coincidentally, I have personally exactly the same feeling at Ramanasramam as Monica did, but my friend Joelle Mazet, a ballet teacher in Paris, speaks of labour and silence and love as the path that she has experienced at Ramanasramam for decades.

Let me now turn to my third descriptive narrative, which describes the experience of Ramanasramam and encountering Ramana Maharshi through the songs of Mahalakshmi Suryanandan. Her songs set to ragas have been extolled for congregational worship by many including the *Hindu* of 21 May 1996. The author of these songs is now in her eighties, and is still invited by the asramam to sing her compositions on every birth commemoration of Ramana Maharshi. She was fifteen years old when she first came to Ramanasramam. Her father K. Swaminathan was a loyal devotee, and also a staunch Gandhian as many Ramana devotees very naturally were.

K. Swaminathan was invited by the Government of India, to edit the *Collected Works of Mahatma Gandhi*, which he proceeded to do in the decades after his retirement. His wife was perturbed, that in spite of a long and dedicated work life, he had to start a monumental new work which would displace them from Chennai where they were so happy. They had to start life again in Delhi, but he reminded his wife that when he was a young boy, Gandhiji had come to Chennai. He was a volunteer who had been deputized to take Gandhi from place to place. He asked Gandhi to let him join him, but Gandhi said, 'I'll call you later.'

Now that he was old, he saw this as a fulfillment of the promise that Gandhi had made to him so long ago. Often he was ill and asthma troubled him all his life, but he always told his wife, 'I won't die yet. I still have the index to do.'

He worked with a very dedicated team of writers and translators and editors, who all called him Appa (Father). Maggie (as Mahalakshmi is called by her friends) said that his greatest assets were that he had a lot of able sons who assisted him, and one of them was her husband Suryanandan. Swaminathan's eagerness to be with Ramana Maharishi is recorded in many places, and at any given opportunity he would rush to Tiruvannamalai. So his three daughters, of whom Maggie is the eldest, were constantly, in their childhood, finishing their homework as fast as they could in order to rush to Tiruvannamalai.

Mahalakshmi and her husband Suryanandan have a house facing Arunachala directly across the street from Ramanasramam. They speak of K. Swaminathan with joy. He was ninety-three years old when he died, and the legacy he left for Maggie was a love for Ramana and Gandhi.

During the years of the freedom struggle, K. Swaminathan, his wife and three daughters would spin together as a family. Each had a charkha. These were available for sale at the Gandhi Bhandar, and every nationalist family had them. She said K.S. was not very good at spinning, but the girls were. When each had a sufficient amount of counts the weaver would make saris for them. She showed me the saris her sister Dr Dharma Chatterjee and she had made as young girls. Suryanandan remembers his father-in-law, K. Swaminathan with great pride and protectiveness. There is in old age, a startling physical similarity between K. Swaminathan and Suryanandan. Maggie says that their marriage was arranged between their families who were known to each other. K Natesan, the compiler of the poems of *Kavya Ganapathi*, was Suryanandan's sister's husband. When Maggie was very young and her marriage was being arranged, one of the suitors was a wealthy young man who asked her, 'Who on earth is this naked fakir on your walls?' She was very disturbed since she had been brought up to revere Mahatma Gandhi and adore Ramana. She refused to be in the house after that for any prospective suitor. She prayed to Bhagavan, 'If at all I must marry let it be to someone who loves Bhagavan like my father does.' Her prayer was answered, and Mahalakshmi and Suryanandan live at the foot of the mountain, in a lovely house, with a pretty garden. Her earliest memory of seeing Ramana was that she thought he was Lord Rama himself.

Out of her many songs, I shall present only one: *The Story of Ramana*,

O brothers and sister,
Come running hither,
Let us sing Ramana's story
Let us become like Ramana.
In the holy town of Tiruchuzhi
Under the sacred star punarvasu
Was born Venkatarman.
To father Sundaram Iyer
And mother Azhagammal

The boy grew up fast,
Charming all who saw him,
Greatly interested in sports he was,
Running, jumping, swimming,
Always surrounded by friends,
Happy times they had together,
Deeply would he sleep at night
Nothing could shake him awake.
When he was studying in Dindigul
Suddenly his father passed away.
He made the move then to Madurai
To continue his schooling there.
He was in class ten then
But studies did not hold his interest.
To discover what death meant
He acted dead and gained realization.
In Madurai to the temple he would go
To pay obeisance to goddess Meenakshi
To the sixty-three Saiva saints, too,
Asking that he become like them.

One day, there came a guest,
'I am from Tiruvannamalai.' He said.
Hearing this, Venkatraman was overjoyed
And longed to go to that holy place.
He left a letter for his brother,
And set out for Annamalai.
In Ariyainallur, when he arrived,
He saw a wondrous, luminous light.
On Krishna's birthday, he reached Kizhur.
The Brahmin's wife thought he was Krishna in person.
She gave him the Prasad meant for Krishna,
And the boy Krishna appeased his hunger.
No money in hand, tired of walking,
He pledged the rings on his ears.
Four rupees he got in exchange
And went on his journey by train.
Early in the morning he reached Annamalai,
Swiftly he went into the temple.

He stood praying to Lord Annamalai,
'Father Annamalai, I have come to you.'
On the banks of Ayyankulam,
he discarded all that he had,
tore away his dhoti, shaved his head,
girt in a loin-cloth he remained.
Fully drenched in pouring rain,
In ecstasy he entered the temple,
Sat in the Hall of Thousand Pillars,
And was immersed in deep meditation.
As little boys threw stones at him,
He sought refuge in the padala lingam
It was the mahan Seshadri
Who took care of the young ascetic.
In Gurumurtham where he went next,
Surrounded he was by devotees.
His mother Azhagammal, in distress,
Approached him later in Pavazhakundru.
She requested the silent swami to speak,
And asked him to return home with her.
Wrote the silent sage on paper,
'What has been ordained will take place.'
Sadly his mother returned home.
While in Virupaksha cave the swami took residence,
There came Ganapathi Muni to see him,
Fell at his feet, cleared of his worries.
'O, my countrymen, know you this,
He is Bhagavan Maharshi Ramana,' the muni proclaimed.
When to Skandsramam Ramana moved,
His compassionate mother returned to his side.
His younger brother Nagaswami joined him,
Assumed the name Niranjananda,
Took over the running of the asramam,
And the mother cooked for the devotees.
The happy mother suddenly fell ill,
The Maharshi released her from repeated births,
Her Samadhi was at the foot of the hill,
Where arose the temple of Matrubhuteswara.

At that spot, stayed Guru Ramana.
Ramana Asramam grew around it.
Rare and great poet Murgunar and bhaktas
From world-over thronged the place.
Ramana is the personification of ahimsa,
Squirrels, monkeys, peacock, played about
Cows and dogs and cats, too,
Some have samadhis in the asram.
Singing the Akshara Manamalai,
Ramana, with his devotees, went round the hill.
He composed Ulladu Narpadu
And Upadesa Undhiyar too.
Playfully, he wrote the appalam song.
sang that Self-knowledge is simple indeed.
Enquire deeply into 'who am I?'
That is the path of self-realisation.
A growth was noticed on the Master's hand
Alas! The doctors pronounced sarcoma.
'It is the false body that is destroyed,
the atman lives forever,' Ramana consoled.
To the strains of Arunachal Siva sung by devotees,
A brilliant light emanating
Mingled with the Annamalai hill.
Ramana became Arunachal Siva himself.
Arunachala Siva Ramana, namo, namo!
Arunachala Siva Ramana, namo, namo!
Arunachala Siva Raman, namo.namo!

The poem describes every detail of Bhagavan's life. What is interesting is the weave of the verses where each stanza communicates biography and faith .... Yet, what Mahalakshmi's life communicates is the survival of the narrative as an embodiment of faith. Stories are told for a purpose, chroniclers appear because so much of life is really a description in words.

A lot of the functions of words, I have argued consistently in this book are to create community. But community also implies a sense of well being, of feeling at home in the world, even if the avowed sentiment is to transcend the world! There is a pragmatic quality to asramites, which is heart warming for outsiders to witness and the anthropologist is always the outsider. No amount of camouflage can take away the quality of duty which is the return to the university and to the discipline which demands that objectivity prevail. And yet, as Joseph Brodsky writes, shadows change the way we look at sculptures, or the expressions we read in those empty bronze eyes. The tragedy of writing history, according to him, is that it is a one-way street:

> It is a one-way affair, and you recognize its Platonic nature in this city instantly. The closer you get to the object of your desire, the more marble or bronze it gets, as the natives' fabled profiles scatter around like animated coins escaped from some broken terra-cotta jar. It is as though here time puts, between bedsheets and mattress, its own carbon paper – since time mints as much as it types. (Brodsky 1994: 47)

The historian's anguish is that he did not inhabit 'that' past, and yet, for the anthropologist, nostalgia serves well as an essential tool for recording, comparison and analyses.

In this context it is interesting for me to look at the work of Gaston Bachelard who lives in two worlds simultaneously as a laboratory scientist and as a humanist. Bachelard argues that the cosmos is domesticated not just by our dwellings, but also the words that writers use to describe these dwellings, and this includes gardens and seasons, so perhaps logically even the absence of these. In marked contrast to Corbussier's world, Bachelard recreates for us how cosmos and microcosm intertwine through a process of intertextuality, through a process of invention and memory, by loving and living. This world that Bachelard describes is a collage of many poets and novelists, writing in French, and the universality of emotions is made manifest through the act of translation.

Ramanasramam can only be understood in the domain and metaphor of nature. It is the hinterland of the Annamalais that give it the scenic splendour of the mornings which are associated with Brahma, a time of meditation and quiet, and the redness of the sunrise turns the mountain into the aura of Aruna or the glow of dawn. With the day's heat it would become tejolingam. The grandeur of heat transforms pilgrimage into a suffering which, however, is often and quite startlingly made glad and comforting with the rustling of leaves in the garden, and the falling of rain, as the hill is now green and cool with a band of new and young trees.

A lot of the procedures of housekeeping is what asramam life is about, effecting the transformation of the wild and the virile to the calm of a domestic aura. It seems paradoxical that this should happen, but the symbol of Shiva and Shakti in union are always brought to mind. So also is the love of Ramana's mother Alagamma for her husband and the transformation of Ramana into Vishnu as the keeper of peacocks. It is because Ramana is desired by men and women equally that the androgyny of work actually proceeds. Cooking, cleaning, dusting, polishing, shopping for provisions are all as much male dominions as well as women's. Because it is a monastery open to householders, the axes of work begin to diversify. It is in the routines of the householder as manager, and both householders and monastics as workers (there being indeed a thin line that divides them) that this androgyny begins to surface. Work means to worship and to belong! Visitors often long to contribute their labour, but may do so only with permission from the workers and trustees.

For feminist writers, androgyny is not hermaphroditism. It is the integration of anima and animus in the most creative Jungian fashion. All the dusting, polishing and cleaning which goes on endlessly in the Ramanasramam is about fulfiling and maintaining the asramam as both home and museum.

Bachelard writes,

> The minute we apply a glimmer of consciousness to a mechanical gesture, or practice phenomenology while polishing a piece of old furniture, we sense new impressions come into being, beneath this familiar domestic duty. For consciousness rejuvenates everything, giving a quality of beginning to the most everyday actions! And so, when a poet rubs a piece of furniture – even vicariously – when he puts a little fragrant wax on his table with the woollen cloth that lends warmth to everything it touches, he creates a new object, he increases the object's human dignity; he registers this object officially as a member of the human household. (Bachelard 1969: 67)

Bachelard then quotes from Henri Bosco's *Le jardin d'Hyacinthe*,

> The soft wax entered into the polished substance under the pressure of hands and the effective warmth of a woollen cloth. Slowly the tray took on a dull lustre. It was though the radiance induced by magnetic rubbing emanated from the hundred year old sapwood, from the very heart of the dead tree, and

> spread gradually, in the form of light, over the tray. The old fingers possessed of every virtue, the broad palm, drew from the solid block with its inanimate fibers, the latent powers of life itself. This was creation of an object, a real act of faith, taking place before my enchanted eyes. (Henri Bosco cited in Bachelard 1969: 68)

Either characteristic of the labours of housewife or of servant, the descriptions of this alternate consciousness is about the 'wax' civilization, which Bachelard argues men usually know very little about.

> If we attain to the limit at which dream becomes exaggerated, we experience a sort of consciousness of constructing the house, in the very pains we take to keep it alive, to give it all its essential clarity. A house that shines from the care it receives appears to have been rebuilt from the inside; it is as though it were new inside. In the intimate harmony of walls and furniture, it may be said that we become conscious of a house that is built by women, since men only know how to build a house from the outside .... (Bachelard 1967: 66)

It is interesting that Alagamma's spirit of cooking and cleaning are so archetypical of asramam life, and that Bhagavan extolled these virtues to the greatest extent. Bachelard quotes Bosco's work again to underline the spiritual imagery underlying servitude.

> Indeed figures from this land appeared to her familiarly, however commonplace the work she was doing, without in the least seeming to dream, she washed dusted and swept in the company of angels. (68)

He then suggests that we do not psychoanalyse these motifs.

> We should need, then, purer "reagents" than those of psychoanalysis to determine the "composition" of a poetic image. The fine determinations required by poetry bring us into the field of microchemistry, and a reagent that had been adulterated by the ready-made interpretations of a psychoanalyst could cloud the solution. No phenomenologist re-living Supervielle's invitation to the mountains to come in through the window would see in it a sexual monstrosity. This is rather the poetic phenomenon of pure liberation, of absolute sublimation. The image is no longer under the domination of things, nor is it subject to the pressures of the unconscious. It floats and soars, immense, in the free atmosphere of a great poem. Through

> the poet's window the house converses about immensity with the world. And as metaphysicians would say, it too, the house of men, opens its doors to the world. (68)

This world of polishing and maintaining is for Bachelard where women's work and the tasks of creativity converge, where poets are born, and where mysticism flourishes. He quotes Rilke to prove his point:

> Politeness tinged with mischief was my reaction to the friendliness of these objects, which seemed happy to be so well treated, so meticulously renovated. And even today, I must confess that, while everything about me grew brighter and the immense black surface of my work table which dominated its surroundings ... became newly aware, somehow, of the size of the room, reflecting it more and more clearly: pale gray and almost square ... well, yes, I felt moved, as though something were happening, something to tell the truth, which was not purely superficial but immense, and which touched my very soul: I was an emperor washing the feet of the poor, or Saint Bonaventure, washing dishes in his convent. (70)

Rilke's memoir cited above is about polishing his piano as a child, which releases then other memories of cleaning ... whether by obligation or force in childhood, the nostalgia which an act brings about is for Bachelard the significant point:

> The nostalgia for work that emanates from this fragment by Rilke, or realizing that this is an accumulation of psychological documents from different mental ages, since to the joy of helping his mother is added the glory of being one of the great of the earth, washing the feet of the poor. The whole thing is a complex of sentiments, with its association of politeness and mischief, of humility and action. (71)

For Bachelard, the nest, the chrysalis, and the garment are all examples of dwelling places. For Ramana the body is the site of consciousness. We inhabit our body in the manner that the universe inhabits itself in us. We are consciousness and when we realize this we share in the natural bliss of the universe. For those who are practitioners this is not a dream or an abstraction, it is the reality that they constantly try to achieve. Bachelard draws us to the practice of rhythmanalysis, rather than psychoanalyses, to understand such images, where the rhythms of the universe echo in the finer rhythms of human sensibility. In this scheme alternating daydreams cease to be rivals.

> To sleep well we do not need to sleep in a large room, and to work well we do not have to work in a den. But to dream of a poem, then write it, we need both. It is the creative psyche that benefits from rhythmanalysis. (65)

Ramanasramam provides these networks of communication, sleep, food and work, to those who are claimants of a legacy ... from Ramana Maharshi they learn that the fabric of life consists of being in the world and making sense of it. This practical wisdom is what made it the finest point of equilibrium, which allowed even rich men and women to live in simplicity and silence, and find happiness in the routines of ritual and hospitality. But the world is an anvil, and new shapes are hammered by the day. In the name of development, new metaphors come into existence, and those who are suspected to be lotus-eaters are always besieged with enquiry about the life they have chosen away from the crowds. Around such magnetic personas the crowds begin to circle and isolation is no longer a possibility. In protection of a chosen norm, aggressiveness and egoism may become natural protective skins and the house indeed gives way to rules, regulations and museumization. But Ramana's spirit pervades and there is no discrimination as to who may worship at the shrines of Ramanasramam.

The archives are the most treasured of the asramam's new developments. Its architecture and aesthetics are typical of the best scientific imagination. Everything is carefully guarded and monitored. The air conditioning plant is itself as big as the Virupaksha cave. Television screens monitor all comings and goings. The objects of veneration, which were once Ramana's belongings, are guarded under glass. Kanakamma writes that once Bhagavan said to Venkatratnam,

> You said that the garland was huge, you said so much about the intricate patterns on the flower umbrella, you said the carriage was drawn by bulls and you even described the garlands around the bulls' necks. But you have not talked about Arunachala at all! That is why I asked. Maybe you feel that it is not necessary to talk about Him. After all, He is always the same, is He not? Perhaps that is why you did not mention Him at all! (Kanakkamal 2002: 170)

This then is the crux of the problem, whether it is biographies of Ramanamaharshi and Arunachala, such as the one I write as a collage of other work (using the concept of refraction and light as other writers have) or museums and loving momentos: that risk of objectification is the paradox of faith, where the laughter of Ramana is an anchor that always brings us back to earth.

7
RETURN TO THE SOURCE

20 August 2004

There is so much happening in the asramam ... it is the culmination of the 125th year celebrations. The excitement wells out of the halls and the corridors and the gardens. Ramana's teachings of solitude, silence and simplicity are momentarily quite forgotten in the conflagration of chanting and burning ghee ... the people are waiting for his idol to return after it has been carried in an open carriage all over South India, a silver statue, where the god has been tamed and miniaturized. 'Who can say that god has a form?' Ramana's question is thus answered with certitude ... yes, there is Bhagavan and the cult of Bhagavan which is now louder than the quest, louder than the path!

This is the summer that I decide to read Osborne more closely. I am struck by the clarity of his collected essays which the asramam has published. I ask many people if they know anything about him since I find his work interesting. Joelle, my friend from Paris who has been visiting the asramam since 1994 (she first came here in 1987) goes into the adjoining room where she has been living for the last two months and loans me her copy of Osborne's autobiography. These were notes, completely lucid in Osborne's typical style, his daughter Kitty had found in an old suitcase a long time after his death. How useful this book is for me ... it is the language of doubt that has resolved itself, a traveller's notes about mistakes and discoveries.

Last summer Christopher Quilkey had told me that he had been assistant to Osborne and that after his death he stayed on with the family. He said that Osborne's son developed a motor neuron degeneracy which left him completely handicapped. One of the saddest details in the story was how this young man had once been a brilliant inventor and made millions which he then proceeded to lose. And then the shock and the illness, and that his mother had said that her son had always been moving too swiftly all the time, and this was Bhagavan's way of tying him down to Arunachala.

I find the texts of illness and destiny hard to follow ... after all, Bhagavan's arthritis and finally his death by a fatal cancer would also in these terms be the consequence of past life and *prarabdha* ... transcendence seemed much beyond the questions of affliction and mortality. Yet, I suppose the lesson was really one of detachment, to detach from pleasure and pain and to understand the space of bliss which went far beyond these. Osborne records Bhagavan's response to his mother's death in 1922, that he helped her to die, by keeping his hand on her heart and the other hand on her forehead, and experienced the end of her mortal life as an absorption in the divine, after which he persuaded everyone to eat their food, saying, 'There is no pollution.'

The question arose of the disposal of the body. There was the testimony of Bhagavan himself that she had been absorbed into the Self and not remained to be reborn to the illusion of ego, but some doubt was felt whether the body of a woman saint should be given burial instead of being cremated. Then it was recalled that in 1917 this very point had formed part of a series of questions put to Sri Bhagavan by Ganapati Sastri and his party and that he had answered affirmatively, 'Since *jnana* (knowledge) and *mukti* (deliverance) do not differ with the difference of sex, the body of a woman Saint also need not be burnt. Her body also is the abode of God' (Osborne 2004: 88).

The relationship with the mother, who is a subject of worship at the asramam, is one of the most interesting pivots on which Ramanine theology lies. She was an orthodox Tamil Brahmin and her taboos were, very often, the source of joking for her son. From a relationship of avoidance in the early years, to a carefully crafted relationship of joking, a lot was said which became the sub-text of Bhagavan's relationship with the world in general and devotees in particular.

The interesting thing about Osborne's work is, of course, that he vehemently felt that Bhagavan taught that one could remain in one's own religion and follow his teachings. In some senses this is the most emphatic note in his memoirs ... that those who felt themselves to be in the quest could not be distracted by theologies and dogmas. Further, that Ramana Maharshi's teaching and interpretation was sufficient to this body of received wisdom either through revelation or through meditational practice, to the quest called self-realization.

The crowds are immense; everyone is headed for the rituals commemorating the rededication of the temple which had been Ramana's sanctuary. It is a hot day, much ghee is burnt in *yagyas* sponsored by the asramam and the cooks are cooking gargantuan meals for devotees. Words cannot describe the intensity of cultic feeling.

A young child called Annamalai follows me around asking for chocolates. Brojo Pillai, my sister's son who has accompanied me, laughs saying that we obviously look like people who eat and carry chocolates with us. I meet her again, she is begging with a sweetness which is hard to describe, so I ask her what is in her lunch-box, and she brings me something, hard and black which I think is tamarind or some berry, so I hold it in my hand, ugh! It is a snail in a shell. I scream and drop it, and she looks embarrassed and apologetic. I feel rotten because I think she is going to boil snails for lunch, (not culturally acceptable as food in my community) but she tells me that it is for the peacocks … she collects them and sells them to the asramam. A couple of days later she is begging from Doc … he seems impervious to her, but she is dancing around a pole saying something in her seriously charming way. She is dressed like a boy, but that particular way of speaking and looking … I presume Annamalai must be a girl! It reminds me of the riddle that The Queen of Sheba (also called Makadeya, a form of Arachne the weaver of webs perhaps) asks King Solomon, when she dresses boys and girls equally in boys' clothes, and he guesses that the children, who roll up their sleeves when drinking from the river, are girls! I ask Dr Murthy later when he is busy collecting cold water to serve to the guests who are waiting, what he said to her … he can't remember who I'm talking about … I keep pestering him, he says he doesn't know anyone called Annamalai, but then finally he recollects and laughs and says, 'That child wanted sweets so I gave some.' The answer to my question … why was it so urgent to have an answer? Perhaps because there is so much food that's eaten by us as visitors to the asramam and the worker's families still seem so dreadfully poor. This child told me her aunt worked in the asramam, and that her parents were dead, and that she had stopped going to school after her mother had died. Later, I discovered that Annamalai is a boy. With his long hair and thin frame and piquant face, I had been mistaken regarding his identity. My former teacher of sociology at JNU, emeritus Professor Yogendra Singh, once told us during his annual lecture at our centre in 2007 that in sociology, Othello's occular proof is not sufficient.

One is always confounded by the facts and therefore, 'seeing is not believing'.

Elimination of poverty is not the asramam's concern, but sometimes I wish they would put back the clock and produce the meals described in reminiscences of Bhagavan's interactions in the kitchens … *sambhar*, rice, *pappads*. It was all so frugal, there are descriptions of women who bring forest greens (*cheerai*) and evidence that Ramana hated even the peels of vegetables to be wasted. He demanded that they be used as organic manure and when one day someone forgot (or the Lord was disobeyed) he was so upset that he never went back into the kitchen again. Yet, every day now is a feast day and devotees apparently come from hundreds of miles to eat the wonderfully cooked food in the asramam. There is a reason and a rationale … the space of the heart and of quietitude is assured in spite of the tendency to culinary excess.

It is on this visit that I first see the young Frenchman who is later found dead in a cave. Dr Murthy says subsequently, when I enquire, that the French embassy had been informed, that the young man had gone away for psychoanalytical treatment, but kept returning whenever he could.

A few days after we arrive Brojo decides that we should climb the mountain. He will be leaving the next day. I agree to accompany him to Skandasramam, which is half way up the hill. I am carrying my turquoise-coloured umbrella, my keys are tied to the end of my dupatta and we set out after breakfast. The day is perfect, cool, windy, and not too hot. I remember my promise to tell him about my father, his grandfather. We sit on a rock and I tell Brojo everything I remember about my father and his father and his father's father. It is not much, since my father always fobbed off questions about family history with the lapsed Marxist's question, 'How is it relevant?' But grandchildren are always curious.

After we reach Skandasramam and drink water and absorb the peace, we climb on. Brojo has persuaded me that climbing the mountain is what I've always wanted to do and this is my chance. I enjoy climbing, and indeed, I'm good with heights, but after a while I figure out that it's getting hot, I have multiple sclerosis, I'm slowing down my nephew … so I tell him to go on ahead, and that I will wait for him. He hands me the bottle of water, and leaps off like a mountain goat at an alarming speed. I accept the benefits of middle age, which is to stop whenever one thinks fit, and look at the city lying below me. From here, one can still hear sounds … religious music on megaphones and the insistent blaring of drivers' horns. After half an hour of staring down at the town of Tiruvannamalai, I figure out that the order and clarity is an illusion of distance and realize the necessity of starting the descent. It will take me an hour to go down, it is only 10 a.m. but it is three hours since we set out. While devotees are free to follow their persuasion, punctuality at meal times is the only real claim that the asramam management makes on the devotees' attention. So I start going down, realizing with a qualm that now I have a bottle in one hand and an umbrella in the other. However, since I have an excellent balance, this does not bother me. I edge my way down the crags and crevices very slowly, holding on to my belongings, my heavy room key clanking against my knee. Suddenly a famished little boy appears from nowhere. He offers me a stick which he is carrying. He looks ragged and hungry but is friendly and concerned. He says that he has seen me from very far and that he can see that I am walking down very slowly, so he has come to help me. I say I do not need any help. But he is charmingly insistent. I refuse to relinquish my water bottle and my umbrella, but he just wants to be my friend, so I ask him his name. He is aptly called Shravana, but his father and mother are dead and he lives with his grandparents. He has an oozing ear, which he tells me causes him great pain. I tell him to go to the Ramanasramam clinic, there is a doctor who comes every evening at 4 p.m. and free services are provided. He tells me he will have it treated. He is very tiny and malnourished, and I ask him if he is eight years old, but he says he is fourteen. When we reach close to Skandasramam, he asks me if I am all right now. I say 'Yes', and he runs off for lunch to his grandfather's house. Of course, before he leaves, he asks me if I have any money. I show him that I have none. He says, 'Does the Anna (elder brother) who went up the hill with you have any money?' I say, 'No' and Shravana nods sadly and runs off to eat rice and nothing with his grandparents. He does not, in spite of his poverty see himself as either a mendicant or a beggar or a vagrant.

I drink some more of the water, thanking god that Brojo remembered to leave the water with me. I should now turn to get to Skandasramam and I see a young sadhu dressed in saffron, washing clothes at the small pool of water. I feel I should not disturb him, so I take the next turn left. The arrows painted on the rocks by someone wishing to help clueless climbers are still there, so it seems a viable option. The rock ahead of me now seems a little steeper that any so far, but it is small and not terrifying, a little like a washing stone, where people beat clothes. I think I can climb it. I take one step and fall backwards, headlong into a trough which rolls me four rocks down into a pit. I yell with surprise, but luckily my fall is broken, nothing is sprained, twisted or wrenched. I manage to pull myself out of the pit, noticing while struggling out that there is *bel* (a wild and nutritious fruit associated with cooling properties) and clean white strip of cloth on the bush overhanging the pit. I, typical of devotees, see this as a sign that I shall have food and clothing, water I'm carrying anyway! My umbrella is lying on its cone, its cloak outstretched, and its ribs are unbroken, my glasses are also intact. As I emerge, I look mad and shocked and dishevelled; someone rushes past, but I act as if all this is in the day's work. It is. Even now, I tragically think of one of my favourite writers, Michelle Rosaldo, falling to her death from a ravine, in the pursuit of anthropological knowledge. (She was studying the Ilongot, and after her death, her husband Renato Rosaldo wrote a compelling account on head-hunting and rage and funeral practices among this particular tribe in the Phillippines.)

It's not the first time I've fallen or stubbed my toe. I thank Ramana that I survived the fall ... more specifically I think, the mountain hates me, I'm never going to return, I don't like being knocked off like this! Did anyone see me fall? I have no idea. I go into Skandasramam, I wash my face and comb down my hair with the chill sweet mountain water. I eat some *tulsi* and place some chewed *tulsi* on my much bruised knee. My shoulder seems stiff but not alarmingly so. I refill the bottle with water and go down to the asramam. There everyone has gathered for lunch. I am just in time. I don't tell any one I have fallen. Later, when Joelle hears she is aghast. She says, 'But no one climbs the hill in summer.' She even seems to suggest that going beyond Skandasramam is unusual for women in general ... 'No one climbs a lingam!' But I'm not sure of that, there must be many women who do climb the hill.

Brojo returns looking pleased and successful. He says he almost climbed to the peak, but then said 'There is no peak really, there are many peaks, every time you think you've reached a peak, another one rises before you and sets itself as the goal.'

I return to Delhi a week later after the procession, which was due to arrive, culminates at the asramam in an abundance of crowds, *rangolis* drawn by the women, good food and spiritual talks. I am more convinced than ever that anthropologizing would be a difficult and treacherous task. It is my belief that the work one does should have the integrity of insight and the fearsome quality of knowing that one's life is at stake.

The method, as Michel Maffesoli dramatically pointed out, is to forage within the cults of individualism to discover the manner in which communitas is forged. This is not a critique of objectivity, but it is the knowledge that as sociologists we are free to ask the right questions and to be startled by the answers. Many texts of sociology have reinstated the faith in paradigms rather than in paradigm shifts, and much of what is considered the casualty rate of the disciplinarian sociologist lies in the publication of experiential accounts of experiments in the field!

The women are excited about the decorations for the asramam. They have coloured rice powder, a complex design book and a great deal of enthusiasm. They start at 2.30 p.m. ... first there are two women at separate spots, outside the office, near the large ancient tree. But then more and more women join in to give comments and advice and to watch. The circle grows along with the design pattern ... and the women grow more and more articulate and involved. It takes two hours to complete, and there are at the end of it about five or six women participating, filling in colours and laughing and talking. It's very much women's work, and once it is done, the striking colours and the lucidity of the design are breathtaking. However, the speaker for the evening's discourse, a venerable old exegete, does not notice the patterns, walks past the ornamented courtyard, since these are extraneous to the real world of spiritual realms of male power. However, the women do not feel slighted since there are many people, both men and women, who stop to admire the *rangoli* as the day goes on. There is a guard who is posted to stop the children from stepping on the design, and there is only one unruly girl who races past and leaps through the pattern, but luckily it is not disturbed. She stops to look at the work, and then finds a peacock feather with which she dances dreamily with. The children are always happy with the crowds and the food and the excitement. There is, however, one set of children, all boys who are hard at work. These are the boys from the *pathshala*. They wake up very early and by 5 a.m. they are bathed and combed and ready! Their ability to chant *shlokas* undergoes various stages. Early in their career, they are loud and raucous, by the time they are fifteen or sixteen, they are almost musical. However what is required from the Brahmin priests is incredible amounts of energy and commitment to the cult. At the moment, there is an old priest who dominates the show. He is so methodical and concentrated in his work that he stands out for the piety and intensity of a particular way of thinking and being. Yet, he is now old and tiring out, and poor, like everyone who has given up everything for the asramam. It is, as Edward Said writes, that in translation we must understand that sometimes the cultural maps of two places do not approximate each other. While looking at the realms of spirituality and its organizational forms, it is not always possible to use the measuring stick of trade unions and workers rights.

The old priest washes the lingam with a concentration that any housewife could well emulate while going about her daily chores … it is tenderness and manual labour that only women are associated with. The old priest uses his concentrated energy to make all the menial tasks of a priest's servitude a celebration of his personal loyalty to Ramana. On the other hand, the younger priests have not yet taken over from him. They are more passive and peripheral, carrying out their duties as he directs them. The day he is ill and cannot appear, they are amazingly volatile, almost as if at last their chance has come, no longer acolytes, but men of power.

I have sat in the hall now, at sporadic intervals for over five years, and each time I see that the day is divided according to ritual hours interspersed by cleaning hours and closure times.

There are seasons of intense activity, as during Navrathri Puja, when the goddess is taken out and the intensity of reverence is like a flood of desire. Devotees desire the goddess for what she is and what she can give them. The advaitic principle appears in Ramana's ability to be all things and nothing at the same time, divine and beggarly on Shiva's hill. In the recording of faith, several questions are posed by us and others of the validity of anthropological recording. How do we straddle the line between faith and reason? Perhaps the only reason for such exercises is that, today, the anthropologist is not the interrogator of the informants, but has become with the tools of post-modernism a player of the game, a pawn within the very fabric of interaction. Let us presume that mortal life continues within the trajectory of all that is stated or claimed as having truth-value. It is possible that we fetishise the ideal even today, and yet as observers, we discover what social reality is … that the most pious of devotees, striving for detachment, suffer from love and hate and disappointments.

In a sense the Trust family is now under strain. Will there be a new generation of sarvadhikaris or managers? Routinization of charisma seems necessary, since it is not always that hereditary lines can conform to the expectations made of them. One of the potential heirs to the trust once said quite loudly that at the moment it would be impossible to leave his temporal obligation, 'But this could be a retirement option perhaps!' What does it take to continue a cult, and how can one imagine the routinization of charisma? Bhagavan made it very clear that if he was god, then everyone was god as well! Yet, he was not against the idea of people treating him as divine and as he said it is easier to submit to people's wishes than to assert oneself against them when it comes to rituals.

The excitement of the coming of the image of Maharshi, the murthi as it is called, the sacred embodiment, or manifestation as idol, the carnivalesque procession is palpable! The women want to go to the farthest point where they can greet the padayatris. The procession has wended itself around the main towns of Bhagavan's birth and hermitage. The culmination is the vortex of a year of waiting and watching and planning. What people love is the sense of communitas ... everything and everybody mingles in a fervour of dust and lights and colours and joy. And the sense of homecoming. Not of the idol, but the god, is manifest to all in that it is believed. But where *did* god go? I have no idea. The machineries of accolade and triumph are too obvious for me to analyse. Who am I anyway to ask questions about the existence and manifestation of god?

Maffesoli argues, following Simmel, that god is 'coincidentia opposoitorum' a centre where 'the antimonies of life blend together.'

> It is no less true that these gatherings and the interdependence they imply are a heady mixture of communication and conflict. To quote Simmel once again, the 'side-by-side' experience, the living together and the 'all for one and one for all' can go hand in hand with a 'one against the other. (Maffesoli 1996: 113)

Maffesoli further goes on to argue that because monasteries are the keepers of relics and the personal belongings of the sage, they become the hub of memory.

> It is mainly thanks to this that the monasteries became havens of peace; that they were able on the one hand, to extend this function of preservation to the liberal arts, to agriculture and technology, and on the other hand, to expand and build up a close network of houses that became sanctuaries of culture. (131)

The place of Ramana centres or kendras are of great importance to the movement, since it unites the body of believers wherever they may be in hymns, music, discourse, books and congregation.

While there may be differences of opinion, of how to read Ramana's life and work, against the axes of austerity or extravagance, cult or asceticism, one cannot posit these as opposite logic. Certainly the latent tension between Brahmin and ritual oriented cultic worship, and austere and transcendent modes will always be present, in fact it was characteristic even of the asramam when the sage was alive. Stuart Hampshire writes that:

> Any actual choice between two ways of life, which comes to a head in a particular conflict of duties, arises from dense personal experience, and as a consequence of a man's particular conditions of life, and his philosophical beliefs. No more can be said in general terms, except that morality does unalterably have this aspect of commitment to a way of life, even though many persons may never consciously confront such an ultimate choice. They are ready to recognize the possibility of an ultimate conflict. They are aware of openness at the margin of morality and in their own way of life. There is some willfulness, as well as naturalness, in the structure of practice and belief that they have accepted or imposed, and they recognize this, when they reflect. They know that they may be confronted with a conflict of duties which expresses a point of divergence between two ways of life, both of which have a nobility and worth, but which cannot under actual conditions be combined. The problem then has for them no rational solution. They will be guided by intuition, which entails reflecting on the two possibilities as fully as possible and then coming to a conclusion for reasons which they cannot arrange in a conclusive argument. A decision in an ultimate conflict may commit the agent to a way of life, which will extend in time indefinitely as far as he knows, and, as far as he know, it will close certain possibilities to him for ever, even though they are possibilities that he had thought of as being very highly desirable and valuable. (Hampshire 1980: 47)

Very often asramites leave to find new paths, to return to their roots, to re-negotiate their membership in the community. Sometimes they write works of biography or autobiography which the trustees find distasteful, sometimes they gossip among themselves, sometimes they are warmly welcomed, or rebuked, or coldly avoided. All these are signaling systems which informs the observer that while there is tranquillity, there is also order and regulation. In non-dualism, the force of two competing ways of life is sometimes found side by side: success in business and conspicuous consumption, along with detachment. These need not, however, be in conflict, though there might be steadfast gossip about accumulation of private property versus the ritual observances of asceticism.

Hampshire writes,

> Every reflective person has had the experience of oscillating between two possible descriptions of his conduct, whether it is actual conduct or only envisaged conduct; one correct description makes the conduct acceptable and not despised, and the other correct description mentions features of the conduct which make it morally questionable and regrettable. Two competing ways of life, between which a man chooses, explicitly or implicitly, may impose different descriptions on the same envisaged conduct, which may emerge as prohibited in virtue of the descriptions relevant to one way of life and as positively required in another way of life. It is not only that the priorities to be aimed at are different in the two ways of life, both in respect of moral claims and of disposition; but also the questions that one asks about a course of conduct, before evaluating it, will tend to be different. (48)

In these two theoretical excerpts we find that Stuart Hampshire takes away the sting of hypocrisy, allegations often made against spiritualists and ecologists, by positing how conflicting or competing claims coexist in every day worlds. Abstract logic competes with varieties of rationalizing. But are competing ideologies really a problem for the sociologist of religion? Much of the discipline rests around why being poor is the fruit of karma, and why the attitude of the rich to the poor is also part of an ongoing karma that will result in a new capital of events in one's next life! Not surprisingly, 'poor feeding' is one of the greatest contributions of Ramanasramam which always defends philanthropy and charity as the back bone of asramam life ... no one can be sent away hungry.

Mr Mehta, who is a frequent visitor at the asramam, is not at all pleased by the noise and excitement. He is complaining to all who will hear him, that the indiscipline in this asramam is hard to accept. No other asram, he says, is as noisy as this one! But everyone is in an effervescence of joy and anticipation. For the Durkheimian sociologist this is the culminating moment ... the integration of community, faith and ritual. When the small truck arrives with Bhagavan's image everyone abandons themselves to euphoria ... there is shouting and crying, fire dancers, and attempts by individuals to get onto the vehicle. Everyone who wants to get on is allowed, but in the melee only the most devout attempt to do so. The rest stand on verandahs and some climb the ancient tree and slowly people are heading to queue for food.

I ask V.S. Mani if I can return for New Year with my three daughters, and he says 'If you book in advance ....' From being an anthropologist, I discover, startled, that now I am up front, puzzled and ecstatic like others before me. I shall never suffer from certainty.

Clifford Geertz, the greatest exponent of the subjective moment in field work, describes what happens to secular anthropologists like me when they are studying rituals:

> Religion is never merely metaphysics. For all peoples the forms, vehicles, and objects or worship are suffused with an aura of deep moral seriousness. The holy bears within it everywhere as sense of intrinsic obligation, it not only encourages devotion, it demands it; it not only induces intellectual assent, it enforces emotional commitment. Whether it be formulated as mana, as Brahma or as the Holy Trinity, that which is set apart as more than mundane is inevitably considered to have far-reaching implications for the direction of human conduct. Never merely metaphysics, religion is never merely ethics either. The source of its moral vitality is conceived to lie in the fidelity with which it expresses the fundamental nature of reality. The powerfully coercive 'ought' is felt to grow out of a comprehensive factual 'is', and in such a way religion grounds the most specific requirements of human action in the most general contexts of human existence. (Geertz 1973: 126)

Much of the dialogue of religions has premised the understanding of other religions in a mode which emphasizes standing and watching and learning. This is the method of comparative religions as well.

One of the most interesting of theoretical arguments on what is isolation and community and evolution, in fact, comes from an ecologist, David Quammen. In his discussion of insularity, Quammen drawing from a host of scientists shows how island topography creates its own life, which is markedly different from that of the mainland. When there is a disruption, due to the increase of numbers, due to varieties of invasions, the possibility of 'obligatory mutualism' which is typical of one type of species becomes chronically mutated. What results is the loss, if not extinction, of that which existed previously. This was the popular view, but dissent came from other quarters .... Life and biology cannot according to them be reduced to simple bi-polar explanations, reality is much more complex (Quammen 2004: 349). In Tiruvannamalai, one way of life has given way to another, from quietness to noise, from mendicancy to monastery, but is this necessarily a problem? Those who live there will probably have to accept the magnitude of changes that come as a result of pilgrimage and tourism. Quammen summarizes the questions of ecologists pertaining to vanishing resources and structure of ecological communities. When with the influx of floating population of tourists, reserves are created, what is the consequence?

> What exactly happens when a sample of habitat, newly isolated, relaxes to equilibrium? Species are lost, yes, but which species?
>
> Are the losses random, or are they determined by aspects of the community structure of the ecosystem?
>
> Will a particular nature reserve give long-term protection to those species in greatest jeopardy? Or will the reserve lose its jeopardised species over a short span of time while maintaining its population of species that don't badly need protecting?
>
> Will several small reserves, offering similar habitat, all lose the same species and save the same species? Or will they vary randomly from each other preserving assemblages of species that are different and complementary. (463)

That David Quammen is interested in questions of human community as well is abundantly clear in his discussion of the sole Tasmanian aboriginal who survives the colonial sweep of sheep farmers in the nineteenth century. We might well ask what happened to the cattle market which was such a dominant theme of carnival life in 2004 for the winter festival of Deepam, but curiously by the winter of 2006, there were hardly any sellers of cows or the fodder that accompanies cattle markets. As Tiruvannamalai becomes larger and larger, welcoming tourists from all parts of India and the world, the ability to keep the green paddy and agricultural lands will diminish.

8
ONE HOT SUMMER

In the summer of 2005, my younger daughters and I arrive at the asramam and find that life has its even tenor, for the routines are given and are ably followed. It is therapeutic because the day is punctuated by meal times; and by the ringing of temple bells we know that the people have gathered and are at worship. There are no demands of any kind made on anyone, we are all left to our predispositions, but as the days go by we fall into the customary rituals and find them oddly liberating – to be unnoticed and part of a crowd, one among many, is to experience freedom. It is normal for a Durkheimian sociologist to understand this perfectly; the euphoria of ritual and the symmetry of collectivity. Bees have it, so do humans.

However, most days when I'm at the asramam, I turn up at meal-times, rather like Pavlov's dog, exactly as one of the residents clangs an ancient scrap of metal with a gong. I always enjoy meal-times because when I'm in the hall there is so much to see. There are the photographs of Bhagavan, each so large and evocative, and one's concentration is on the food, yet one feels that Ramana is overlooking the procedures. Then there are the families, particularly the children, for whom a day's outing to Ramanasramam is so important. One can feel the excitement in the air, and the cross-cultural exchanges, often tacit, sometimes verbal. Most 'outsiders' tend to find sitting cross-legged very difficult, so do old people and Westerners. Yet every one, unless severely arthritic, tries. There was one Japanese woman whom I had noticed sitting in translucent meditation ... I say translucent, because some of them begin to gleam like polished seashells while sitting in the prayer hall. However, she found eating food while sitting on the floor impossible. She had to constantly change position, finally almost kneeling on the floor and eating with her head bowed. Then, she tore a piece of her banana leaf, and used that to scoop up the *payasam*. The old Tamilian lady sitting next to her looked stunned, and then made round sweeping gestures on her leaf, showing the Japanese girl how to eat her food. The girl ignored her, blank-faced and desperate. She then got up with both hands really messy. That was difficult too, because she had to pick up her water-bottle, and from her fastidious displeasure, one could suddenly imagine her in a kimono, pouring tea in delicate cups, rather than swimming about in curd and *payasam*, which are finally difficult to scoop for anyone new, if they are using their hands!

A similar sentiment is described by Mouni Sadhu, the courteous secretary to the sarvadhikari, while he ate with a spoon at an asramam in the presence of some honoured guest.

> It seemed to me that the Maharajah's family were casting somewhat envious glances at my spoon which was so comfortable to use, especially when dealing with liquids, for out of courtesy, they had to follow the common custom of eating with the hand, whereas when at home they had probably long ago forsaken it. (Mouni Sadhu 2002: 90)

The other thing one can really mess up, if one is not used to it, is the *kum-kumam*, the red vermillion, and the grey ash (which, I suppose, stand for love and death, those constants in life, love, literature and religion). There are times when I've looked in the mirror in the bungalow in the backyard, and thought 'Oh my god! How fearsome!' for the vermillion put on the brow, with a generous and unsteady hand (mine), has smeared in a blood chilling way. After many such blunders, I've learnt to wear a stick-on bindi, and carefully touch it with red *kum kumam*. In the South, caste and religion markers are very vivid. Wearing a chain around one's neck, a vermillion dot on one's brow, bangles, a nose-ring, jasmine flowers in one's hair, these are the typical motifs of everyday attire for women. Those not adhering to these are outsiders or foreigners. Men do not have strictures of this kind and are dressed in white *veshti*, or trousers with shirts or kurtas. While the asramam has not decreed any rules of dress, most visitors dress inconspicuously, though some western women do wear 'Indian dress' as typified by export-import companies which provide them with flowing skirts and linen loose-sleeved garments.

One of the most interesting problems in the study of the Ramana asramam is the understanding of the substantial work that has been done by its residents. This has included everything from clearing land, building and the more routine tasks of cooking, cleaning and keeping accounts. Mouni Sadhu spent some weeks at a Catholic monastery in the heart of Paris and spoke to the brothers of this order.

> They accepted everything without question. Then I understood the meaning of 'renunciation of one's own will' and it's place in spiritual progress. It was but another form of extinguishing the so-called ego … When I asked them which they preferred, prayers or work for the community, they told me simply that their work was only another form of prayer. (Mouni Sadhu 2001: 57)

The superiority of the rational method can only be an aid to the institutionalization of the cult, and the family has sustained its sense of virtue and integrity. Nagamma, one of the many interesting women who lived close to Bhagavan, has left us a wonderful record of the asramam, as have many others. She attained a startling degree of closeness and was valued for her intelligence and her loyalty. She was also fearless and devout and left behind her writings in a diary. These were so brilliant and evocative that Bhagavan himself was eager to have them read out.

> Brother, you have asked me to write to you from time to time, whatever striking thing happens in Sri Bhagavan's presence and what Shri Bhagavan says on such occasions. But am I capable of doing so? Anyway I will make an attempt and am beginning this very day. The attempt will succeed only if Bhagavan's Grace is on it.

This entry for 21 November starts an interesting collation which records in very clear and evocative language the manner in which one woman saw the world and her life as someone who spent each day in the proximity of Bhagavan.

The entry for 15 June 1948 is typical of Nagamma's style which is not merely descriptive, but essentially communicates a writer's abandonment.

> As the summer has set in, Bhagavan has started staying all the time in the Jubilee Hall only. At mid-day, when it is hot, the attendants shift the sofa to the north where there is a bower with crotons on either side and sprinkle water on khus-khus tatties that are tied around. This afternoon I happened to go there at about 2 o'clock. Bhagavan was seated there with a matty cloth

> over his body and his head. There was no one there except Krishnaswami. He was standing behind Bhagavan with sprinkler on his hand, which appeared to be full of rose water. He opened the screw-cap. From that sprinkler the rose water was sprayed on to Bhagavan like a light shower of rain and Bhagavan was rubbing his body with evident satisfaction. When he saw me coming, he said, "Look! They are doing Abhishekam to me (sprinkling holy water)." So saying he covered his face with that matty cloth and said, "They have covered me with this wet cloth. They have tied tatties all round and are sprinkling water there on. This place is now cool like Ootacamund."
>
> I went a little closer to the sofa, and found it was cool. "Coming from the hot atmosphere outside, this seems very cool," I said, and came back to my usual place. (Nagamma 1992: 326)

Hundreds of people mill around in the asramam every day. They are visitors, who live in Tiruvannamalai or outside and come every day for a couple of hours. The most famous of these is perhaps David Godman, whom everyone admires, but he is reclusive and reticent.

Many of the white visitors form cliques and spend time together at the tea-shop outside the asramam, where they sit smoking cigarettes with the sadhus and watching the traffic, the beggars, and the grand and silent mountain. There are some who wear dread locks and communicate visually that for them Saivism is the idea of excess. Visitors to the asramam, however, are encouraged to be circumspect and properly clad. One glance from one of the trustees is enough to communicate that someone is disorderly, and even children are disciplined regularly if they chase peacocks, pluck flowers and fruit or play too loudly in the hall.

There is an elderly man, a frequent visitor to the asramam, who looks like a spare actor in an American film on the Ancient Romans. He is large and heavily built, bare-chested and wears only a lungi. However, there is a certain animal magnetism, an ease, brought about by many years of living in Tiruvannamalai. He has many friends and many foreigners coming to Tiruvannamalai find an immediate friend. He provides advice on the shortest way to getting to Tiruvannamalai and its many sacred shrines to those who are unaccustomed to journeying in South India. People tend to form communities and know one another. One day I sit outside the large hall, in my usual self-effacing manner (which comes with my trade, as a trained observer, as Primo Levi might say), on the steps where a collection of sadhus and young people sit, all at ease with one another. The young people are with their families, and the sadhus congregate together, in a state of calm and slumber, and alertness, which is so paradoxical. The man comes with a woman, who is from Scandinavia, and he sits down near me saying, 'We can sit here; there are no negative vibrations here.' I'm careful not to say anything, though we smile at one another, and say Hello. He proceeds to ask her why she has come here. She says she is suffering from intense pain in her spine, unbearable pain. He tells her that if she were to come to his room he will explain to her the source of the pain (anger) and that he will massage the pain out. She does not seem to suspect any base intentions, he is elderly and kind. They go off together happily. She has told him that she was at Puducherry and came at the invitation of Polish friends, who told her that Bhagavan would heal her. Voyeurism and information, espionage and informant, psychoanalyses and dialogue, power and extraction ... these are the many facets of the social anthropologist's work. The current preoccupation we have is with the term respondent, implying a non-subjective and questioning attitude, involving mutual engagement.

I speak to a young woman from Moscow. There was one occasion when she held the wrist of a young woman, and said, 'I am a grandmaster, trust me, there are places we travel, things we see, we will meditate.' The woman was with her friend, and laughingly agreed. They both shut their eyes and held hands, and after about five minutes, tears started rolling down the woman's face, while the 'grandmaster' looked serene and beatific. The weeping woman's friend looked entirely stunned and helpless, then finally she released her friend from the trance by nudging her and the woman from Moscow laughed a great deal and said, 'Whatever there is in us, begins to come out when we meditate.' The woman's friend scolded her, saying, 'Why did you do that?' and the woman wiping her tears, said, 'How was I to know?' Then the two friends went off together to the routines of the evening, startled by the velocity of feeling aroused by a moment's acceptance of another's powers.

The grandmaster agrees to speak with me. She says she was living in Moscow, a normal and undistinguished life. She was bored, lonely, alienated and then one day she had a mystical experience. She cannot describe it, but she says it changed her life. The world began to look different, it was full of light and she felt indescribably happy! She thought that every one felt like that, but then it turned out that no one understood what she was talking about. So she began to read on Indian mysticism and she discovered Osho. So she came to Pune, but she fled from Pune because it was 'a merchandise of spirituality' that she could not adjust to. So to Pondicherry, and then to Tiruvannamalai and in Bhagavan she found her Sadguru. There is laughter about her and a conceitedness that I find disconcerting. I ask her questions, which she answers with a startling wit and a profound quality of having thought it all out previously. Space is empty for her and meditation puts us in touch with it. The things which exist are constructions within that empty space .... meditation is as healing as being in that space, empty, the sky is blue, but it's not blue, it's not even there and so on. In the end, she says, 'You think I'm your victim' and she laughs and laughs till tears roll down her beautiful oval face, 'But, maybe, it is you who is my victim!' she says. I begin to feel like the woman whose hand she held last October, and was reduced to weeping over nothing. Quick to respond, I say, 'I resent that, I think friendship and dialogue are possible, and we need neither be a victim. I think it's arrogant to say what you did.' She wipes her tears of laughter and says, 'You are right...' But then laughs a lot more! I panic, a bee has bitten me on the back of my neck and I can feel it swelling up. It's a sharp searing bite, but I don't want to tell her about it, because she will say 'Brahma has appeared or Periyavan (Siva Arunachala), the big one is here' or something like that!

I leave her laughing in the dark, and go and sit next to my daughters, relieved to have them with me. They seem so innocent and child-like, Mallika is reading *Jane Eyre* and Sandhya is peacefully listening to the evening pranayam. It begins to rain, it pours so heavily one cannot see anyone in the rain, but there are people still waiting in the courtyard, under the thatch shelter. One of them is an impassive, brown-gold skinned man. He is in a wheel chair and he waits out the rain with a calm that I find startling.

Sometimes, when people ask me, 'How does Ramana manifest himself in your life?' I think for a moment, and then I say, 'By giving me the courage to accept danger and distress and be calm about it.' I'm not particularly interested in detachment as an end in itself, but I'm happy for the peacefulness which now seems to be my birthright. I pick up a fallen leaf and I show it to Mallika, for the colours are my favourite, a kind of burnt orange, and she yells and says, 'Look, there are bees in it!'

And indeed there are a whole lot of bees, drowsy and compacted, the storm shook them from the tree and there are some silken cobweb strands which have kept them lightly trussed. They're alive and moving, and I run and put them in a flowerpot. I don't want to be stung again this evening! In Nagamma's diary there is a section on Bhagavan's conversation with her on bees. A large banyan leaf had drifted down on his path, so Bhagavan went looking for the tree:

> When I saw that leaf I was reminded of the sloka in the Arunachala Puranam where there was a description of the banyan tree under which Arunagiri Yogi was living ...
>
> As soon as I was reminded of the Sloka, I thought that leaf must be from that banyan tree and so felt that I could see that tree if I went along the direction from which the leaf came. I started climbing up further and soon saw a tree on an elevated spot. As I was going along to it, my thigh hit against a bush. On account of the disturbance, the bees in the bush came out and began stinging me. I thereupon thought that I had committed an offence and that was the punishment. So thinking, I stood still. The bees did not sting me at any other place than the one that touched the bush. They bit me to their fullest satisfaction. After they left me, I began walking. Curiously enough, I forgot all about the banyan tree and wanted to reach the place of the seven springs. But there were three big streams in between, which were very deep. The thigh too had swollen and was paining. I somehow crossed the three streams and reached the seven springs. From there I began to descend the hill and reached the cave of Jatawame by the evening. Till then I had no food, nothing whatsoever. There they gave me a tumbler full of milk which I drank and then took a little fruit. After some time I went to the Virupaksha cave, and stayed there for that night. The leg got still more swollen. Jataswami and others did not notice it, but Palaniswami saw it and said, "What is it?" and I told him all that had happened. Next day, he applied some gingelly oil to it. When he smeared it with the oil, he found that in every place I was stung, there was a spike as strong as a wire nail. With great effort he took out every one of them and gave some treatment. The swelling subsided after two or three days."
>
> "Did not Bhagavan make any effort afterwards to trace the place where the banyan tree was?" I asked.
>
> "No. That thought never came to my mind again," replied Bhagavan.
>
> I said "It seems that some time later, Venkatramayya, Murgunar, Kunjuswami and others went in search of the place and came back disappointed."
>
> "Yes, yes, that was a tamasha. You were also here at that time and you have heard about it, haven't you?" questioned Bhagavan.

> "I did hear about it but I do not know the details." I said.
>
> "If that is so, you had better ask any one of them. They would tell you. It would be good if the people who had experienced these troubles told you about them," said Bhagavan.

Another version drawn from Mudaliar's *Day by Day* (dated 2 May 1946) is given in A.R. Natarajan's biography. One line is constant in both.

> "When I saw for the first time a remarkable banyan tree on a huge and precipitous boulder, I was prompted by curiosity to have a look at it. Meanwhile the hornets stung me and I forgot all about the tree!" Maharshi Ramana composes a song *Apology to Hornets*
>
> When I was strung by hornets in revenge
> Upon the leg until it was inflamed
> Although it was by chance I stepped upon
> Their nest, constructed in a leafy bush,
> What kind of mind is his if he does not
> At least repent for doing such a wrong?
> (Natarajan, *The Mountain Path* 2006: 30)

Shalini Saran, the photographer meets me next morning. She says she has seen me somewhere and I say mine's a typically Malayali face, or something trite, and she says, 'No, we have definitely met.' I tell her that one of her photographs was used by Oxford University Press on the cover of my book *The Christians of Kerala*. She has never been to Ramanasramam before, though she has planned to for many years. We meet after breakfast and go up the hill together. It's peaceful and green. Suddenly school children throng the path. Shalini is a quiet dense person, she photographs the Skandasramam. The swami gives us some lemons from the tree, for I pick up a ripe one from the ground and then ask permission to keep it. He speaks Malayalam, and asks me if I want more. I nod and he gives us two more. We climb the steep rock and then descend some stairs to the Virupaksha cave. I tell her about the little boy who helped me last year, when I had climbed so high, half-way towards the top. Suddenly, Shravana is there again. Such a coincidence! He is happy to see me, I give him some money, he pesters me for more. He becomes febrile and persistent. Then we go into Virupaksha cave, which has a lovely white-washed exterior and inside it is post-modern and lovely in it's colours – those bright reds and yellows on the floor, with a geometric pattern of flowers, like what very young children do in space-work class. Shalini is deeply happy and she photographs the young priest who takes care of the gardens. We go back, Shravana is waiting for us, his beggary forgotten, he is just my friend from last year, eager to say goodbye and run home! He looks in better health this year.

The librarian, J. Jayaraman, and I discuss Nagamma, standing in the hot and busy street. He enacts a story where a woman devotee writes romantic letters to Bhagavan and this enrages Nagamma who feels it is very misplaced and licentious on the woman's part to address Bhagavan in this manner. But Bhagavan is quiet and accepting of this undisciplined and tumultuous love. Nagamma classifies this episode under the title 'Anger and Resentment':

> A lady devotee from Andhra Pradesh came to the Asram and stayed for some time. Her devotion was of a peculiar nature. Her conception of Bhagavan was that he was Lord Sri Krishna and she was a Gopika (shepherdess). The devotees here however felt that such a concept had no place here as Bhagavan was a brahmachari from birth and a Jivan mukta. But then, she would not keep her view to herself but publicized it and even wrote to Bhagavan accordingly.

Nagamma rebukes the lady, who turns nasty, but then goes through a period of derangement. Bhagavan is non-judgemental and looks towards the lady's well being by remarking, 'Somebody must take pity on her and do something; otherwise how she can get on?' Much later, the lady recovers from her misplaced infatuation and writes to Nagamma asking about Bhagavan. Since Nagamma mistrusts her (since besides her inappropriate behaviour, she had also brought a lawyer to the asramam during that turbulent time, to slap a case on asramam members) Bhagavan communicates his displeasure at Nagamma's unforgiving attitude (Nagamma 1992: 165).

It seems interesting to me that the palimpsest of these published narratives is constantly being evoked in everyday conversations. The codes of conduct are reinvigorated by remembering Bhagavan and his conversations with friends and visitors. Reincarnation is a pleasurable theme in such recollections ... most frequent visitors are associated with Ramanasramam and here the nature/culture boundaries sometimes blur. The cow Ramana loved most is thought to be Cheera Patti, so also the dog who has appeared from nowhere and befriended one of the asramam office staff is thought to be an asramite in his previous incarnation. The dog knows the office well and is more at home than any one else. It is a matter of laughter, but also of the understanding that nature is a continuum and all life is to be valued.

II

I leave Delhi on 1 October 2005 and am scheduled to stay for ten days from 3 to 13 October at Ramanasramam. On 28 September, I meet my friend Chandrika Grover's father. He is ninety-two years old. He met Ramana Maharshi in 1939. He had read Paul Brunton and set out for what he called Thiruvanmalli. He said he asked Bhagavan a question, which made Bhagavan laugh a lot. He doesn't remember the question, but does not think it was important.

Grover shared the sense of his calm joy at having met Ramana so long ago that he had never forgotten him and had believed that He was God. This sense of dualism is something which is continually dispelled in Advaita as well as the devotee's conversations. To recite the name of Bhagavan is the first step, to be constantly aware of one's breathing, the second, and the third is self-enquiry. In this last exercise of meditation, the understanding that 'I am He' pervades the sense. What is the answer that you receive? Mr Grover asks me, when I say honestly that I am comfortable with peacefulness and don't proceed to a uni-focused awareness. That 'I am a fool', I say quite unselfconsciously and, 'That I am Ramana'. He smiles and says as a blessing, 'Whatever your needs are, they will be met.'

He brushes past my own excuses for not following the path of meditation to it's logical conclusion and tells me that it takes years, and that simple though it is, in actual practice it takes time.

Mouni Sadhu says, 'It is so much easier to write books than to achieve realization of the self' (72).

Grover speaks of two spiritual experiences he has had, one of levitation after meditation, when he was a boy where his body was flung out of the door and travelled and the other when he had an indescribably sweet experience after meditating upon Krishna, but that feeling never returned. The meeting with Ramana Maharishi took place many years later. He said that after the meeting with Ramana, he felt that Ramana was always with him, that he had never left him and that whenever there was any crisis, he would hear Bhagavan's voice. Bhagavan would say, 'Why do you worry?' He never went back to the asramam, because Bhagavan never asked him to.

A.R. Natarajan chronicles many such experiences of devotees where the Maharshi spoke to them, and assured them:

> That he was not bound by time or space. They could feel his presence in their hearts wherever they were. Eleanor Noye writes while travelling in Kashmir and North India under unimaginable conditions could hear Ramana Maharshi's assurance "I am always with you wherever you go." (Natarajan 2006: 1)

Mr Grover tells me that he is happy to have met me and that he has been wondering what the reason for his coming to Delhi was, but now he knows, it was to meet me. He says that all these years he could not communicate with anyone what it meant to love Bhagavan, but with me he could. He says, 'We are brother and sister!' and I agree.

In Devaraja Mudaliar's account of 24 December 1945 there is a reference to an interrogator 'who pursued the question of pranayama'. Bhagavan said:

> The aim is to make the mind one-pointed. For the pranayama is a help. A means. Not only for dhyana but in every case where we have to make the mind one-pointed, it may be even for a purely secular or material purpose, it is good to make pranayama and then start the other work. The mind and the prana are the same, having the same source. If one is controlled the other is also controlled at the same time. If one is able to make the mind one-pointed without the help of pranayama, he need not bother about prananyama. But one who cannot at once control the mind, may control the breath and that will lead to control of the mind. It is something like pulling a horse by the reins and making it go in one direction. (Mudaliar 2003: 76)

Devotees even now remember Mudaliar as a man who was able to speak his mind to Ramana Maharshi and even scolded him on occasion (Suryanandan, personal communication, May 2006).

Madame Taleyarkhan, a great devotee of Bhagavan, said of Mudaliar 'with all my great affection for him, I consider him a rather dangerous person, as he could never be expected to keep anything confidential. He would reveal it to the next person he met on his way – so frank, sincere and clean is he.'

It was Shri Devaraja Mudaliar, the author of three famous books *Day by Day with Bhagavan*, *Gems from Bhagavan* and *Recollections of Bhagavan* who asked Madame Taleyarkhan to write her memoirs. She says,

> He was quite uninhibited with Bhagavan. One day he remarked, "Bhagavan, what have you done for me?" Bhagavan turning his kindly gaze on him replied, "Oh, Oh, with a veritable flood around, one seeks water. Is that not so with you?" (Taleyarkhan 1970: 216)

For Ramana Maharshi, the moment was of significance, each visitor was significant and to each he answered in a manner that was appropriate for the understanding of that person.

In Days of Great Peace, Mouni Sadhu writes,

> Maharshi has a strange power to awaken love for himself in the hearts of all; this devotion uplifts his pupil, incalculably raising the level of their lives, enabling them to touch the purest form of this power energy that is perhaps the creator of the Universe. Love and devotion for the Saint have none of the ugly qualities of an ordinary love, like jealousy, possessiveness, exclusiveness, and delusiveness, and last, but not least, the pain of separation from the object of love. Here the love devotion for the Master does not ask for anything in return. It asks only for the grace of utterly giving oneself to him, to enter into unity with the perfect and all-pervading object. (46)

A lot of the conventional questions raised in the theology of inter-religious dialogue are surpassed in non-dualism with the eternal resolution of existence sans boundaries. This might raise existential problems for those of us who are situated in mundane or profane worlds, but to those who enter the realm of the boundless sacred, it is a given (Veena Das 1975). It is for this reason that Mouni Sadhu writes, 'It is so much easier to write books than to achieve realization of the self' (72).

To one man, Maharshi replied to his question, 'I am told that according to your school I must find out the source of my thoughts,' with the answer, 'I have no school' (Mudaliar 2003: 267). Looking for the source meant simply understanding who 'I am', the rest was the seed and tree story (268).

The Self is real, and further 'All this is Brahman', therefore Shakti and Shakta are conjoined. Bhagavan argued that different paths developed 'to meet the needs of different minds dissimilarly constituted, but they all reveal the same Truth' (270).

Sometimes he would ask visitors questions posed to him. When someone asked him what one ought to do for the betterment of the atma, Maharshi posed the question back, 'What do you mean by atma and by betterment?' To this the visitor said, 'We don't know all that, which is why we come here' (273).

Maharshi goes on to say, 'Questions are always about things that you don't know and will be endless unless you find out who the questioner is. Though the things about which the questions are asked are unknown, there can be no doubt that a questioner exists to ask the questions, and if you ask who he is, all doubts will be set at rest' (273).

It is understood that the contemplative path is chosen by seekers because they need to, whether they be householders or others. It is a path that is voluntary, and does not offer riches or physical apparatus of any particular convenience. What it does offer is stillness of the mind, which we call tranquility, and the ceasing of the apparent struggle that goes into the fulfillment of duties. Maharshi's teaching were immensely practical in the carrying out of duties, so that they no longer felt burdensome, but filled the doer with a sense of that happiness which Ramana called *sahaja*. There were devotees who looked for visions and palapable evidence of their years of meditation. 'Visions are not a necessary stage. To some they come and to others they don't but whether they come or not you always exist and you must stick to that' (275).

In his book *The Power of the Presence: Transforming Encounters with Ramana Maharshi*, David Godman gives us several case studies of individuals who came very close to Bhagavan. N.R. Krishnamurti Aiyer speaks of Bhagavan putting his foot on Ranga Aiyer's head as the latter sang, 'Let me place your soft, holy feet on my head ...'.

The narrative continues:

> As this line was being chanted one of Sri Bhagavan's feet descended, came into contact with the top of Ranga Aiyer's head and stayed there for quite some time. The whole group, including Ranga Aiyer, was more or less hypnotized by this act and went on repeating the same stanza over and over again. It seems that they were quite incapable of proceeding any further. Only when Shri Bhagavan withdrew his foot and resumed his former sukhasana posture was the group able to continue and complete the chanting. The devotees all viewed this as a rare example of pada diksha (initiation by being touched by the Gurus's foot). I have spoken to Ramaswami Pillai about this incident, since he was present when it happened, and his own account agrees in every detail with Ranga Aiyer's. (Godman 2000: 148)

N.R. Krishnamurti Aiyer goes on to describe his own visions, while reading with a group the eighteenth chapter of Sri Ramana Gita, which is a book of Sri Ramana's teachings by Kavayakantha Ganapati Muni. He says he:

> ... experienced a coiled, luminous serpent moving upwards from the base of my spinal column. It flashed upwards to my cranium, spreading out as a canopy of lightening streaks that were gathered into a bright, roseate spot of light at the base of my nose, between the eyebrows. It returned immediately as a luminous coil, winding a reverse cycle around the spinal column down to its starting point at the base of the vertebrae... (148, 149)

The author of this reminiscence did not stop having visions, there were many of these. However, he says that Bhagavan reiterated that he was a householder, 'that salvation you want to gain as a sannyasin in the forest you will have even as a householder in your profession!' I say, 'Return home!' (157). Bhagavan was completely supportive to N.R.K. Aiyer, both as householder and academic, and when on 14 April 1950, a sudden blinding flash of lightning had enveloped him at about 8 p.m. further compounding itself in the heart, 'However much I tried, I could not stop that powerful reverberation. Fortunately, by the time the following day dawned, the throbbing had subsided of its own accord' (174). At daybreak, the faithful devotee came to know that the moment of his tumultuous experience was the time of Bhagavan's death.

III

My journey to the asramam for Navrathri begins, as scheduled, on 1 October 2005. I'm sick and nervous, I have suffered insomnia for several weeks, and the previous three months have not been easy. There were unedited student theses to correct, submitted by scholars at the last moment. Each scholar had insurmountable problems (deaths in the family or illness) and as a result I was put under more pressure than I was used to. My children coped through these exigencies having difficulties and tests of their own. Meanwhile I got badly bitten by a friend's dog and suffered, simultaneously, a racking cough. My homeopath who had been treating me for five continuous years for active multiple sclerosis was optimistic, but I myself knew by the end of September that my resources had reached rock bottom. I set out, hoping to recover at Ramanasramam.

The ladies coupe on the train heading South was interesting to begin with. There were some school teachers returning home, after a successful training programme in Delhi, and a pair of deaf and dumb women who were endlessly talkative kept gesturing in sign language to each other. They had recently discovered one another and there were life stories to tell one another. It was interesting to watch them, because the conditions of friendship are attention and listening to one another. However, our peace was disrupted by the appearance of three large alcoholic and boisterous old men, who took over our seats and our privacy, illegal though it was on their part … these 'unreserved' passengers were compellingly nasty and sulphurous of breath and looked offended whenever anyone tried to edge them off.

However, none of these tribulations, irritating though they were and disruptive of calm, approximate the descriptions of journeys made by Claude Levi-Strauss, which he describes in *Tristes Tropiques*. Levi-Strauss is bitten by maggots and mosquitoes, eats the most astounding fare of insects and animals and survives infections and rafting accidents. It has been an arduous journey for me, fear overriding the pleasure of travel, because we have travelled through monsoon country, but the railways provided a detour, so that we went by Warangal instead of Vijayawada, which was under water. My sister had given me a mobile phone as a birthday present and it takes a lot of the panic out of travelling … It's a miracle of modernism to be telephoning from a moving bus or some obscure station, telling friends and family that one is safe.

This visit allows me to talk to Dolly who is one of the most popular of visitors to the asramam. She tells me that first one has to learn everything, then 'One must unlearn everything. Which is very hard to do'. I know that I could not probably write a book on Hinduism, I'm too secular for that, although hundreds of prostrations on festive days at rural Jacobite and orthodox churches in Kerala, with due respect to Jesus and the saints, led me to write a competent work on Orthodox Christianity in Kerala. I am perfectly able to understand divine experience; I have no psychological explanations, only sociological ones … catharsis, effervescence, integration. I come back from each trip to Sri Ramanasramam healed.

Dr Srinivasamurthy, 'who greets visitors when they first come to the asramam' (his official designation on the Ramanasramam website), has put me in K-16.

'It has a bathroom, but it's shared. If there is a problem, there is another room …'

I'm grateful to be back at the asramam.

'I never mind anything' I said, and it's true since I was brought up very strictly by a socialist father who was a trained social worker. I race off with my keys. I count the number of visits by the rooms I have lived in and this is my tenth visit!

A woman who looks strangely dreamy in a silk coat stops me on my way near the gardens where the peacocks gather, there is elephant grass, overlooks water, and these tame birds can hide from the monkeys under the lemon trees. We become good friends, Apeetha Arunagiri and I. She is acclimatizing to her old home (Arunachala and the Ramanasramam where she lived for thirty years), after spending a year in Australia, where she is originally from. We spend quite a lot of time together and she tells me that she lived in Tiruvannamalai for thirty years, during which time she adopted a daughter and participated in the ecology movement, in the greening of the Annamalais. Her daughter grew up and married the man who owns the internet café on the main road opposite the asramam. Aruna and her daughter and the two grandchildren live in Australia now and when she showed the father of the children pictures of his family, he called every one and showed them how well the children were growing with their foreign grandmother.

There is something ethereal about Aruna. She came to Ramanasram at the same time as David Godman. He comes to the asramam every evening, and has written very scholarly and well accepted books. I now realize, after a very heavy lunch as I write my notes, that the pleasure principle has overcome me ... but then what about Verrier Elwin? There is always a precedent. I set out into the hot afternoon to read a book in the shade.

Aruna arranges an interview with Captain Narayanan, who spends an hour with us and since his schedule is so tight, it is difficult for him to give us this time. He tells us all about the Arunachala court case, but alas, he now feels that the struggle has been in vain. The case has been squashed; later another acquaintance tells me that the asramam withdrew the case because there was so much opposition from the town to the environmental concerns of the devotees. They want the town to be a prosperous bustling town and all the interdictions are seen by them to be corrosive to their real estate interests. Enmity to the asramam is expressed by a hostile hinterland, which sees protection and greening as antagonistic to vested commercial interest. Aruna invites me to have tea with her at Bose's courtyard. There is a nice restaurant, set up by a descendant of a devotee. He lives in Bangalore and runs the café on weekdays. The ambience is nice, cool, earthy, with film music playing and a self-service counter.

Aruna's interests over the last thirty years have ranged from forest cover, engendering protection from forest fires, community participation, informal and formal education for children and adults alike, water harvesting and theatre. The Arunachal Kadu Siva Plantation is her creation, with help from an Australian NGO and resource base. She writes in one of her newsletters, the AKSP report (at *my newsletterbuilder.com)*

> We have not had an appreciable fire for two summers, thanks to the community participation fostered very largely by our two District Forest Officers, who have recently been transferred. These gentlemen were tremendously encouraging and helpful to all of us engaged in the Greening of Arunachala, in fact we of the AKSP owe our very existence to them and have only recently realised the auspiciousness of their term.
>
> The AKSP has permission to plant on the hill within the area designated Reserve Forest, this area is off-limits to other than Forestry Department personnel unless special permission is given. Very good reasons promote this structure. Within this special permission which we have been given, we in turn honour the original, cognitively competent considerations behind it. AKSP is very happy to be planting on Reserve Forest because in this way we are enabled to work without disturbance.

In another report (*saranam.com*) Aruna writes:

> The past two monsoons have given sinking rain and a new lease of life to the parched landscape of the denuded mountain, Arunachala, the embodiment of Lord Siva. Luxurious waterfalls have resulted in overflowing tanks for two consecutive years so we have enormous optimism for our task of greening of Arunachala.
>
> During this 2006 season, members of the Village Forest Committee of Arunachal Kattu Siva Plantation realized that eleven streams flow down from the slopes within the areas allocated for our responsibility. After nearly twenty five years engaged in fostering the return of a forested natural lingam, I feel confident that the Greening process will surmount all difficulties, it is too strong for defeat now.
>
> A sure sign of an awakening within the community to the value of the forest is in progress presently near to our site; the renovation of three

previously neglected Vediyappan shrines, carried out by the Panchayats of two adjacent villages and by ourselves.

This indicates that the wilderness is being recognized as valuable once again, as it was in antiquity. Vediyappan is the god of wilderness.

This means it is much more likely that the plantation on the mountain will be respected, now it will be protected by the psychological involvement of the community at large. Moreover, our Forest Department Conservator in Vellore and the Principal Chief Conservator in Chennai are determined to put a stop to the illegal grazing, wood cutting and burning which have so far thwarted our efforts until recently. We have not had a fire for two seasons now.

She writes in detail, from Sri Ramanasramam, where the greening programme has had its greatest support,

The town of Tiruvannamalai on the east side of the mountain became District Headquarters some twenty years ago, causing an unprecedented increase in population, now around two hundred thousand. Over-exploitation of water is endemic. During these years a growing awareness of environmental mismanagement has contributed towards the present day upsurge in intention to reforest the potentially resourceful monolith.

Arunachal Kadu Siva Plantation is linked to Rainforest Information Centre in Lismore, Australia and has taken responsibility for six hundred hectares of denuded Reserve Forest Lands on the lower slopes of the mountain. The thrust of this project is social ecology. Twelve rural people, most illiterate, are engaged in water conservation strategies, seed collection and nursery work, and the plantation, maintenance and protection of saplings on the slopes. Day to day decisions are made on the basis of dialogue reaching consensus.

The primary objective of the greening of Arunachala is the rejuvenation of our artesan system. However, the Arunachal Kadu Siva Plantation has a wider social ecological import.

a. to undertake responsibility for solutions to civic needs

b. to participate in making decisions about these responsibilities

c. to utilize and regenerate indigenous knowledge

d. to follow through the work beyond the call of duty

e. to communicate about its meaning on every opportunity with members of their own villages and in the wider community.

The reforestation of Arunachala will furnish Tamil Nadu with a perfect environmental precedent site

> Because a mountain in the centre of a plain is such a conspicuous advantage in water management.
>
> Because the terrain has been so obviously ravaged in recent centuries that a return to health will be spectacularly dramatic.
>
> The transformation will be witnessed regularly by a vast number of persons from all over India since Arunachala has become an extremely popular pilgrimage place with an estimated six to eight million visitors every year.
>
> The upsurge to reforest the mountain manifests in the educated culture. The Tiruvannamalai Greening Society, formed a few years ago by community members and administrative officers, has still not been formally recognized by the state government. A recent move on the part of devotees of the mountain to seek legal protection for the sacred mountain has recently failed entirely in the Supreme Court, paving the way for the building of hotels and tourist facilities on private lands adjacent to the mountain.

Apeetha Arunagiri's work is formidable in terms of its consistently 'local base' stability, integrating peasants, housewives and school children.

Tea at 4 p.m. at the dining hall has thick milk-brewed tea and yes, I've got used to the sheer joy of being at the asramam and responding to its bells! Four o'clock tea is a time when the devotees sit alone or in groups, depending on temperaments. The workers come in from the gardens and sometimes the devotees can be seen recovering from their heavy lunches and their afternoon naps, in strong contrast. The food at the asramam is always delicious and heavy, because it is understood that the devotees will want to do the fourteen kilometre perambulation of the hill. It is curious to me that Ramana left behind such a legacy of wonderful recipes: clearly it is the food that his mother cooked for him! On the other hand, the apocrypha is always about how the shepherds, cowherds and the old widows and pilgrims on the hill wanted him to share their food. As a mendicant, he spent many years either eating nothing, or waiting to be fed. Families have proud histories of how they fed Ramana when he clapped his hands outside their house. Much later, in his old age, there would be old women who still cooked for him. He would eat the food they sent though it was unpalatable, and though he himself had already cooked with his friends and companions the wonderful food which was to be served at the dining hall. Food and the body were central to his cosmology, and his remembrances were always marked by laughter and understanding. Lakshmi, the cow, was for him the reincarnation of an old woman who cooked wild greens for him when he was living on the mountain. One of the most important rituals of the day is the sanctification of the image of Lakshmi at six o'clock in the morning, when the idol is bathed in milk and garlanded with flowers. The rituals of the mother become grounded in the understanding that the moon, the mother, the cow are all linked, and no one understood better than Chadwick, who instituted the tantric pujas in the mother's sanctum.

I quote from Chadwick's book, *A Sadhu Reminiscences of Ramana Maharshi*:

> Bhagavan was deeply interested in the construction of the Shrine built over his Mother's tomb. He attended every function in connection with it, placing his hands in blessing on the various objects that were to be enclosed in the walls. At night when no one was about he would walk round and round the construction consecrating it. That he should take such a demonstrative part in anything has a very deep significance. It was extremely rare and has been doubted by many but I myself was an eye-witness to these things and can vouch for their truth.
>
> He took a personal interest in the cutting of the Sri Chakara Meru in granite which was installed in the completed temple and is regularly worshipped. This is about one and a half feet square and proportionately high. At the time of the kumbhabhishekam on the penultimate night before the sacred water was poured over the images, he personally superintended the installation in the inner shrine. It was an extremely hot night and with three charcoal retorts for melting the cement adding to the heat, it must have been intolerable inside the airless cave of the inner shrine, but for about an hour and a half Bhagavan sat there telling the workmen what to do.
>
> On the last night of the function he went in procession, opening the doors of the new Hall and temple and passing straight up into the Inner Shrine, where he stood for some five minutes with both hands laid on the Shri Chakra in blessing. I happened that night to be at his side the whole time. This was unusual as I deliberately avoided taking prominent part in such things, preferring to watch from the back. Strangely, something made me keep by him on this occasion and on account of this I was instrumental after Bhagavan's passing, in persuading the asramam authorities to institute the Sri Chakra Poojas six times a month. The explanation for this unusual action on Bhagavan's part may be found in the necessity that Shiva must be always accompanied by Shakti. The world would stop otherwise. On the

> only occasion when such a pooja was performed shortly after the dedication of the Temple during the life of Bhagavan, he refused to go for his evening meal but insisted on remaining a witness of it until the end. When someone remarked how magnificent it had been and it would be a good thing if such Poojas could be performed regularly, "Yes," replies Bhagavan, "But who will take the trouble?" The trouble is being taken now and it undoubtedly has the blessings of Bhagavan.
>
> I do not think that anyone who has written about Bhagavan and the asramam has remarked on the extraordinary fact that we have a temple dedicated by a jani. (Chadwick 1994: 59, 60)

However, I am told that the Kanchipuram *mutt* heads cannot visit Ramanasramam because there is a woman buried on its precincts (Alagamma, the saintly mother of Bhagavan Ramana Maharshi).

Madame Taleyarkhan, the dazzling socialite and author of *Sages, Saints and Arunachala Raman* (1970) who became very close to Bhagavan, was at Chadwick's bedside, when he was dying.

> We both stood by his side. All the doctors and nurses were doing their best. At last I asked them to leave him alone. Meanwhile he said, "Look, look, someone is standing in that corner and wants to shake hands with me." So Hugo said, "No, it is the glucose bottle." He turned to me and said, "See, ma, what he is saying? This man in white clothes is extending his hand." I at once knew it was Lord Jesus, though he was Ramana Maharshi. Yet, in his graciousness he had come to take him. Immediately his terrible breathing became silent and smooth, his eyes became so soft and nice, and early in the morning at 4 o'clock he left his body. (Taleyarkhan 1970: 75)

Taleyarkhan records her observations about Sri Chakra Puja, which many consider the signature of Chadwick's participation in asramam life:

> It is well known that, after Bhagavan's Maharanirvana, asramam affairs were a headache to all concerned. We reached a crisis in these affairs when we had seriously to consider the closing down of the dining hall. The late Shri T.K. Sundaresa Iyer, who combined in him great devotion to Bhagavan and to Sri Ganapathi Muni and was for a very long number of years closely associated with Bhagavan and the asramam, approached me with the suggestion of instituting the weekly Sri Chakra Puja at the asramam so as to invoke the

> blessings of Goddess Sri Lakshmi for the prosperity of the asramam, but I was not inclined to agree. Shri Sundaresa Iyer broached the subject to Major Chadwick and together they tried to persuade me to approve of the idea as also to take steps for the revival of the Veda Patasala at the asramam. I made the first contribution of Rs 20 for the first month's expenses of the puja, then fixed at Rs 5 per puja. At our request, Major Chadwick took charge of the puja and until ill health obliged him to hand over to the asramam. The puja became popular with the asramam devotees who had many a material want to pray for; thus it considerably augmented the revenues of the asram and the fee for the puja came to be raised subsequently to Rs 10. Major Chadwick, as in all things he undertook, took a deep personal interest in the proper performance of the puja at the shrine every Friday, the first of the Tamil month and on full moon days. He could be seen sitting before the shrine when the puja was going on in the shrine and his very presence there acted as a tonic to the priests, six in number, to perform the puja with deep faith and interest and in a solemn and impressive manner. (Taleyarkhan 1970: 76-77)

Of Taleyarkhan's own death, Nathakiamma (who knew her well and was loved in return, and was attentive to Madame) remembers it as a lonely and painful death. 'Yet she was far removed from her body, and between lasting unconsciousness she would have visions (personal communication July 2006). She would say, 'Nathakiamma, I see Bhagavan.'

Nathakiamma herself is one of the most interesting residents at the asramam. Her story combines both devotion to Bhagavan, and the recognition of his grace. Her foster father was Chellam, one of Andhra's most revolutionary writers. My associates at JNU, Ravindra Karnena and Dr G. Srinivas, to whom I told the story of Nathakiamma, said that Chellam's attraction to Ramana Maharshi was the catalyst for many Telugus turning to Ramana, from Marx. Chellam was so powerful a writer that his word was sacred to many readers. Nathakiamma was brought up in Chellam's house. She told me,

'When I was very very young my mother died and my father married again to a non-Brahmin woman. My grandmother was very worried that I would be brought up in non-Brahmin ways and given in marriage to someone outside our caste. She took my brother and me away. But when I was five she died. My aunt gave me to an orphanage and kept all my grandmother's land and wealth. My brother went to my father. From the age of eight to fourteen I kept hoping that I would be adopted like the other children were. But they kept telling me, "Not now, not now. You are needed here." So from the age of five I was fetching and carrying and looking after other children. Then the lady doctor who ran the hospital for destitute women and abandoned babies – there was no contraception and no abortions in those days – died. Her brother-in-law, the great Telugu poet Chellam adopted me and another girl. He had lost a son, and had three daughters, so now he and his wife had five daughters. He was the greatest father any one could have ever had, and the love I received from Chellam and his wife is difficult to describe. But I had developed a great hatred against men, not only because of my father's abandonment of me, but because of all the women who had been seduced and impregnated whose suffering I witnessed. I hated men and I would scream from early childhood that I would chop them up. And Chellam would laugh and say "No chillies on their wounds?""

Nathakiamma continued her narrative,

'Then when I was a girl, very young, I came to know of Bhagavan Ramana. Chellam's family were Ramana's devotees. I loved Ramana. He fulfilled every emotional need. I felt secure and safe in my love for Ramana. Chellam used to tease me that Ramana is a man and I would say, "He is not a man, he is not a woman, He is Bhagavan." In 1948, we came to know through newspapers that he was ill. I wept so much that Chellam shifted all of us to Tiruvannamalai. We stayed very close to the asramam on rent, and later we bought two flats. When I saw Ramana tears flowed down my face. I was fourteen, but I wept so much that I had to lift the hem of my skirt and wipe my face. I don't know why I cried so much."

'Because his compassion drew out your agony,' I said. To this she replied,

'Ramana's glance was gentle. We continued the hospital work in Tiruvannamalai with abandoned mothers and I helped Chellam with his publishing work and after his death, I came to stay at the asramam, to help at the hospital we run here.'

She showed me the photographs of her own father (an astonishingly handsome man in a romantic way typified by the '30s and the actor Valentino) photographs also of Chellam and her foster mother smiling back at her, Chellam's eldest daughter, who at the time of the interview (October 2002) was ill and old, a picture of herself when she was in her twenties and in the employ of an English woman. Nathakiamma looks full of vitality and confidence and even today, she has an almost unnerving sense of peace and joy. She has adopted children who come to visit her with their children, and the radiance of faith is a generous and loving presence in her being. We embrace one another because her sharing of her life is for her a witnessing to Ramana. The quietest people in the asramam have sometimes told me everything about themselves without being inquisitive about my own circumstances, and I find this startling. The interview, unlike dialogic conversation is sometimes a hindrance to friendship. In Nathakiamma's case, however, it is not. She gives me *vibhuthi* (the sacred ash) when I leave and then says, 'Why *vibhuthi* alone, take *kum-kumam* as well', and thanking her for her blessing, I leave.

In 2003, an abandoned child was found at the asramam, and Nathakiamma took on the responsibility of caring for her. She was in her seventies and working as a nurse in the asramam dispensary. The obligations of child care were joyous for her, but age and asramam rules being what they were, she had to shift out of the room she had stayed in for so many years in 2006. The child grew very well, a dark, beautiful, fat, curly haired child of extraordinary intelligence, with great charm. Nathakiamma asked her adopted son and his wife to take over from her, but they had obligations of their own. So she shifted with her new daughter to Sai Baba's Puttaparthi asramam, where the child was assured free schooling.

There are two women who befriend me on this visit during Durga Puja. They are always bright and cheerful, dressed in beautiful silks and proud of who they are. One of them sings every day at the prayers. She lost her husband forty years ago, and has brought up her sons on her own. She tells me that early in her marriage her husband made her promise that she would not watch films or read novels, since they gave a false impression of the world. And she kept her promise. The night before he died he told her that she was the star by which he had charted his course, and she asked him if he was going to leave her, to which he said nothing. A major heart attack cut his life short leaving her with the boys to look after. She learnt to run the office and had a trusted staff who helped her till the boys grew up and were able to take over. Her friend shared her sense of joy at being in the asramam and they both explain to me the various rituals, where women are foregrounded during these nine days, each day embodying the goddess in a different manifestation.

Varalakshmi, who has been a devotee of Maharshi for many years, assists the priests in the changing of costumes and jewellery.

Each day the goddess is bathed and dressed in the most beautiful silks, the young priests are initiated into the task by the eldest priest, who is called Appachi Mama (mother's brother) by most. Mama was a young boy of ten or eleven when he was called by Ramana to serve him *rasam* (pepper water). The veneration the old man carries on his face, his demeanor is hard to describe as he goes about his daily tasks of bathing and purifying the emblems of worship.

He was once a school teacher, but took on the job as head priest when he was requested. He is famous for his artistic arrangement of flowers and is careful with each and every jasmine flower that goes in the arrangements in the temple. For Appachi Mama each flower is a prayer, an offering to god. Over the years he is learning to delegate, but it is always understood that he is the chief priest, and the others, though old or young always defer to him.

Two of my informants, have discovered from their own queries that I am a single parent, and they are very upset on my behalf, and I am put in the idiotic position every anthropologist faces, which is the sudden desire to run away and hide. Instead, I pass on past the whirling brown bees who have colonized the cactus plant outside Chadwick's room, beside where his mortal remains lie. Three others lie there too, the graves are of different sizes and I sometimes imagine them interlacing their skeletal fingers in friendship. There is an aura of calm there, in spite of the terrifying bees. I feel peaceful again, remembering that in the cactus grove behind converge the butterflies, thousands of them all resting peacefully together on afternoons when it is summer, and my children settle to watch them. In October, the cactus has actually flowered, and they are extremely beautiful, a pale yellow silken mass of flowers with red centres, open at dawn and closed when the sun rises up to the skies.

It rains a lot, and the hills are green and very beautiful. There has been a major tree-planting programme, and the young saplings look as if they might survive. There are music recitals every night, and the old dining hall is crowded with devotees. The old father of the asramam president moves around confidently and people remark on his good health! He is in his nineties and still communicates a certain authority, and people give him a wide berth. He greets some with ostentatious cries of joy, most he ignores.

There are specific rituals during navrathri for the women, each day an old woman, a young woman and a girl are singled out for ritual ceremonies and gifts. They look beautiful in their silks and their finery; navrathri is definitely a time when the women are marked out for their life giving, protective, creative and fertile powers. To look upon rituals one must believe, one cannot merely be an observer. On the tenth day when the goddess is bathed and her finery is packed away, the old priest and the young priest look desolate. But she has not gone away, she merely returns to the world, and engages in her duties.

II

Apeetha Arunagiri and I have spent some time talking with Captain Narayanan about the greening of the Holy Mountain. He tells us that he has spent many years fighting for the ecological survival of the hill, and has been a participant and witness to the court cases which have centred around the environmental protection of the mountain. They were successful in some things, like making sure that the construction of the administrative officer and the commissioner's bungalow did not take place on the *pradeekshana* (circumambulation route) but the residents of Tiruvannamalai are hostile to the suggestion that no building of commercial interest takes place on this route. Over the years the asramam has lost its ability to hold out, and has taken a more submissive position, apparently. It is well known that the town has attracted millions of people over millennia. Its magnetism is both mythic and therapeutic. I believe this is one of the great sites of Indian religious and cultural heritage and should have the status of a World Heritage site. As Captain Narayanan, a retired ship's commander, hopes their plea that Arunachala will receive this status will in time be heard, so do I.

Commerce and tourism are the catch-words of the twenty-first century. We cannot deny the impulse to prosperity that the people of a small town feel. How to safeguard the interests of the people is the task of sociologists and policy makers. My suggestions are that all small towns which have benefited from commerce and tourism have actually merged with the ecological patterns of the terrain. Hotels and shops should be concentrated in a new quarter away from the site of antiquity and conservation. The temple and the mountain itself can allow for the cohabitation of ASI and local merchants (as in the case of Rome and Delhi). The fourteen kilometre walk around the sacred hill may be kept free as a trust site for present day ritual purposes, as well as for travellers and tourists of future generations. The percolation of the benefit from tourism should be made visible to the people by way of jobs, schools, medical facilities and small town necessities for recreation and learning. Garbage collection is better organized, but workers still do not have gloves to scoop up the muck from open drains.

Banking is easier now, with SBI banking; I do not hear complaints from foreigners, whereas earlier they had to go to Puducherry for complex financial matters. The search for the mysteriousness of God goes side by side with the mundane aspects of survival. The class and comfort interests of foreigners seem palpably the new aspect of trade in Tiruvannamalai. From being a small town, quiet almost rural, it is now a bustling tourist town.

Captain Narayanan while speaking about the mountain, in whose shadow he has been living for many years now, told Apeetha Arunagiri and me that the asramam was a quiet place in Maharshi's time, and women were requested to leave in the evening. 'There was an English woman, Mrs Sen, who changed all that, however!'

As mentioned earlier, Sujata Sen (Suzanne) had left her home to become a Buddhist monk, then had received permission from her order to marry, in the hope that the order would be strengthened by their combined work. Her husband, however, was a charming womanizer, and she opted to start her life again without him, to which he had no objection. He continued to support her and her daughter while he lived apart. Sujata went back to her mystical search, and found the resolution of her dilemma in Maharshi Ramana.

> Suzanne saw a slender, golden-skinned man in his late fifties. Except for a loincloth, he was completely bare .... There was about him a certain indefinable quality; the splendour of Realization perhaps described it best. She saw how the psychological labels which the modern mind tended to affix to spiritual experience turned out to be irrelevant and unworthy when one was confronted with true achievement....
>
> When Raja Iyer introduced them to the Maharshi, he nodded in acknowledgement and for a moment gave them his attention, but did not speak. Suzanne was so engrossed in her contemplation of the Maharshi that at first she did not hear when one of the attendants told them that they should take their place among the women, who sat on his left. The men, who were more numerous, sat facing him down the length of the hall. (Bose 2002: 105)

Suzanne was so happy to be there. Then, to her distress, she noticed at some point that all the women were leaving. When she did not get up to go, two men came to her and,

> explained to her that the Asram Management had made the rule that women must leave the Asram before 6.30 p.m. so that they could safely return home before dark. She protested that she was not afraid of the dark and asked to be allowed to stay as long as the men. The Sarvadhikari, alerted that there was some trouble in the hall, arrived and told her himself that the Asram rules must be respected. The Maharshi did not intervene at any time during this incident.
>
> Very upset, Suzanne left the hall. She found her two friends from Adyar waiting for her outside. They looked dejected because they had just found out that there was no guesthouse for women at the Asram and they would have to find some accommodation in town. They tried to persuade her to go with them, but since she refused they left without her. Suzanne declared to the small group of Advaitins who were trying to pacify her, that since she could not stay at the Asram she would go and spend the night on the hill.
>
> She climbed some way up the Hill and without difficulty found a cave in which to shelter. She entered its dark interior and in spite of her bravado a little afraid of finding herself confronted by some wild animal. But she was alone. She had meant to spend the night in meditation, but it was impossible for her to meditate, so great was her feeling of indignation at what had happened ... Meeting a true Master had been the event she had longed for and she had hoped so much to receive some indication from him that he had accepted her as his disciple. Instead, at what had been the most significant moment of the day for her, she had been made to leave his presence because she was a woman which in this society obviously meant someone local and inferior. The incident aroused in her an old impulse to revolt against exclusion because of arbitrarily determined inferiority, a reaction which went back to her student days when more than once she had been indignant at the unfair discrimination against women ...
>
> Her anger drove all other thoughts from her mind. It was then that she had a vision of Arunachala as a Hill of Fire. In its many caves, siddhas or Realized beings in their pure and invulnerable bodies sat or moved unharmed in the flames. In her vision she was taken into the Hill, and passed through its fire, but felt no fear, no pain. And she saw many worlds existing within the Hill, in a series of extraordinary revelations. (108, 109)

In this sensitive account of her mother's battle for equality, Monica Das has outlined some of the chief principles of conformity. Women may gaze at the masculine spaces of privilege and power, but they may not partake of them. Her mother was trained as a medical doctor, was a professional dancer and had performed modern and mystical dances on religious themes for public audiences, had walked in the mountains of the North to travel to Buddhist sites of worship. She was a seeker who would not be dissuaded from her path.

> While Suzanne was on the Hill that night, the Maharshi knowing that there were wild animals such as cheetahs, leopards and jackals on its slopes, asked Mr Cohen, a former Theosophist who had known her at Adyar, to go and persuade her to come down. When Mr Cohen and his party found her she was calm, being still under the influence of her wondrous visions. Without further protest she agreed to spend the rest of the night in a hotel. (110)
>
> The Maharshi did not want the devotees to go against the rules made by the Management. He, himself, observed them although he could not always have been in favour of them He did not engage in debate, since he knew that it only inflamed passion and led to endless argument. In controversial issues he preferred to keep silent or to convey the truth through symbols. But sometimes he set an example, as he did by instructing women on a par with men, thereby establishing that they were as capable as men of reaching the highest levels of achievement. Indeed, his mother had been the first of his pupils to attain self-realization. (131)

The play of orthodoxy is always evident in traditional structures steeped in antiquity. What Ramana Maharshi was able to do was to negotiate past these structures and provide his faithful followers with a sense of their own self-worth. It is a space of both righteousness and grace. Suzanne's story is set in the '30s and '40s. She is French by birth, and all the agony of her seeking has been sharply outlined by her daughter, who in her growing years had lived with her grandmother. As she grew up, she spent her holidays in Tiruvannamalai, and records with charm the great and joyous aspects of these visits.

A poem written by me in 2003 goes like this, I'm clearly desperate to be going to that hot landscape where the stars are always visible:

Departure
Frangipani cast aside,
Hrshingar is here
Crows fly in battalions
Far away the Sun rises
Here the globe rotates in singular fashion
Scattering stars
The earth is sullen with too much rain
Winter edges closer
With threat of fog.

And there is another poem I wrote in November 2007:

In the span
Of a God's
Body conjoined
The Goddess
In the span
Of time we
Call the flutter
Of an eyelash
Love was found.
Trees, grass, water
Fell from the sky,
Insects, birds, animals
And all of us whom we describe as human
Gathered
At the feet
Of this ancient hill.
The winds rushed and seeds scattered
The stones were bronzed under sunlight
And waiting becomes
A sign in the soul
Quieter than absence
More still then dead
More willful than living
And nothing is achieved
Except the sound of hidden waterfall
And a lost stream.

Gary Snyder has an interesting poem on this grand love:

The Voice of the Dharma
The voice
now
A shimmering bell
Through all
Every hill, still
Every tree alive, Every leaf.
All the slopes flow
Old woods, new seedlings
Tall grasses plumes
Dark hollows, peaks of lights
Wind stirs the cool side each leaf living.
All the hills
The voice
Is a wife
To him still.

(*The Mountain Path*, April 1968, Vol V, No 2)

In conclusion, one returns to the statements made by Chadwick, a foreigner who made himself at home in the asramam. He was the original mind behind the Tantric Srichakra Pujas at the asramam which was a mesmerizing catalyst for householders as pilgrims, to come to Ramanasramam (just as the *rath yatra* of 2005, whose aim was to make Ramana known to the local people of the hinterland brought in millions of peasants and traders from the countryside).

> His purely rational arguments and the lack of sentiment in his teachings had a great appeal. He never preached or laid down the law, but always concentrated on turning the seeker back on himself and pointing out to him that it was entirely up to him; the Guru could only indicate and guide, for no one could give self-realisation to another. (Chadwick 1994: 16, 17)

9
MID-SUMMER

The room K-25 is dark and cool with a large tree shadowing it from the front, and at the other window there are more trees and a tank where all day, sadhus and children bathe, splash and shout. The photograph which hangs in my room is a blurred one. Bhagavan is sitting on his couch, and the verse below says that the mind more restless than a monkey should be controlled and that one must detach oneself from worldly possessions. The photograph has been donated by the Kappa Electrical Company ... I wonder if Kappa means a bishop's cope or whether it means tapioca. With a differing intonation in Malayalam it could mean either ....

I spend the first ten days sleeping a great deal, but do follow all the rigorous time observances of the asramam. I eat large meals, all the courses, just like all the devotees who come for a couple of days and walk fourteen kilometres around the hill as soon as they can, or two kilometres uphill. The food is wonderful; the rice is soft and cooked perfectly, never pasty or coagulated. The vegetables are as Ramana would wish, and the *payasams* appear everyday, each fragrant with different seasonings.

On full moon night I go for the *pradakshanam* with a woman who I've met at dinner. She is a widow with a grown up daughter. Her husband was a doctor, who when they got married insisted that she pursue a career. She is with the Allied Services and is at the top of the professional ladder. Her room is next to mine. We pass the lime tree (where once I had taken a toss, and landed on the muddy embankment of the water tank) and just then a snake looks at us. It slithers up the wall. I say Jesus! My voice is guttural with fear. We cross over while it is perched precariously on the steep stone side of the wall. It is probably more terrified than us, but we don't ask after its well being. We scurry past like fearful well-fed rats, glad that it has not bitten us!

I have often at the asramam tried to garner support to chase away snakes, but no one listens. As devotees, they are perhaps in tune with Mudaliar's account for 10 December 1945,

> Yesterday or the day before, in the morning a snake was seen by Chinnaswami and others in the Asramam premises somewhere near Bhagavan's hall. We heard the cries, "What kind of snake is it?" "Beat it! Beat it!" When we heard the noise of actual beating, Bhagavan cried out, "Who is beating it?" Apparently the remonstrance of Bhagavan was not heard by the party, and the snake was killed. Bhagavan added, "If these persons are beaten like that, then they will know what it means." (Mudaliar 2002: 7)

Suri Nagamma writes:

> There is no need to mention the love and affection Bhagavan has towards the peacocks. Not only is he especially considerate towards mild animals like these: he is equally considerate towards beings like snakes which are also given shelter in the asramam. (Suri Nagamma 1979: 75)

It must be admitted though, from old-timers' reports, that Bhagavan hated cats. They ate up his squirrels, and pursued his peacocks and peahens.

A few days after I had arrived, I saw a snake-skin, which I thought was a dead snake, or maybe a sleeping snake, little frogs jumped over it, on the grassy edge of the lotus tank. I told the guard who nodded his head and thought that my plea, to check if it was sleeping, dead, moulting or alive, was eccentric. I then reported it to Dr Chandramouli, who helps run the office, at tea-time, and he replied,

'We see many snakes.'

'It's stretched against the grass. It crossed our path and climbed the wall two nights ago.'

'It must be sleeping.'

'It might be dead.'

'They sit coiled up for days. They are water snakes. They live in the water.'

He was generally unimpressed. The man who guards the cottages at the back, Sundaramurthy, laughed when I asked him if he was afraid of snakes.

'They come and go.'

Salamma, who sweeps courtyards and waters the plants and trees, said comfortingly, after throwing pebbles at it, 'It's only its skin.'

My point was that the skin was an index that there was a snake about. And what I ought to do?

Clearly the snake was an inhabitant of the sacred mountain, and no one was going to be nervous! I started to take the main road to go to the main part of the buildings for evening rituals, coming back through the well-lit main road. I did not want to see the snake again, even though it was a harmless water snake.

And then Neeraj and I, after seeing the snake, decide we will go for the circumambulation of the hill that evening itself, the evening on which we saw the snake climbing the cactus ornamented wall near Chadwick's bungalow. As soon as we step out at 9 p.m., we are in a surge of people. The crowds are as I remember them, so full of love and laughter and that sense of jubilation which crowds at a festival always give to one. The beggars have lined up, and there are carnival shops and the monsters and the magicians and the jugglers and the sellers of sweets, music, fruit, cereals, particularly corn. An elderly French woman is in the crowds, she is getting pushed around in a jocular fashion because she is white skinned, dressed in a sleeveless shirt and there is something elderly and charming and sophisticated and vulnerable, all at the same time. She is holding a motley set of parcels which keeps slipping. I have just bought a vegetable shopping bag for my mother from a young woman who has a stall, so I give this to her to put her things into and we ask her if she would like to walk with us. She says, 'Yes' gratefully, for she cannot find her friend, who had stopped to take photographs. They have come from Auroville in a taxi, and they have parked the cab outside the asramam, and will return at dawn to Pondicherry.

We walk slowly while the crowd rushes past us. The French woman is a retired school teacher. She loves India, and spends six months in Pondicherry and six months in Paris. Her daughter and family have never been to India, but will hopefully visit her at Auroville next year. She is excited about that, because she wants her grandchildren to discover the beauty and intimacy of India. The mountain is silhouetted against the bright lights and we stop to sit on an empty bullock cart in a field and look at the moon which hangs in the sky as it has done for millions of years. There is a sense of eternity and the three of us are pleased by it. We buy rice puffs and peanuts which have been roasted by a family that has travelled from a neighbouring village. There are mountains of different kinds of cereal, some raw, some roasted, some fried, and in the darkness of the night, the light and colours shine in a variability which is very beautiful.

Two of us are middle aged and one of us is elderly, so occasionally we sit on cement ledges and watch parents carrying their children and coaxing them to walk a little more. For the rest, they are all hurrying to fulfil a dream or to ask for one. We walk and walk. It seems interminably long; the moon is up, the lights of the wayside shops were so bright that the hill is obscured. And yet there it is, growing larger and more abstract and never ending. Finally when we reach the town and the temple it seems that the citizens have no intention of sleeping. They are all out in the streets selling camphor, coconuts, puffed rice, toys, ribbons. Beggars and lepers abound. There is a parallel city of beggars quite visually and horribly characteristic of Bakhtin's work on carnivals in medievalism – armless, headless, handless, speechless, some writhe, some call, some in spite of being bandaged from head to toe with flailing stumps for arms have the most resounding voices. To tell the truth I felt quite sick – they sat in rows and rows, half a mile long in the city, while on the fourteen kilometre mountain path their chants of Om Shiva and Arunachala are cries which follow us lap upon lap of the walk. In the city along with the lights and the food, they provide a valorization of disjunction. There they sit together, scratching, unwashed, ill; and facing them, quite out of reach are mounds of exotic fruit piled for sale, pineapples, varieties of bananas, mangoes and melons.

One of the interesting things that Frantz Fanon wrote about in the *Wretched of the Earth* was about the seduction of colonialism. His hypothesis was that the colonized were as engaged in the act of becoming a colony as were those who imposed on them the rule of power wealth and canon. These thousands of beggars, this displaced peasantry, what can one say of them except that they have no say in their fate. Yet, V.S. Mani, one of the trustees says that many of these beggars live in and around Tiruvannamalai and they make a 'good packet of three-hundred rupees or so every night'. It haunts me though, this self merchandise of mutilated bodies, this display of the most tremendous personal squalour. Whatever the accumulation of coins, the old, the handicapped, the widowed, the abandoned, each will have a story to tell.

My foot is sore, not from the walking, but from an insect bite. It could have been a snake or a scorpion, except that I did not feel anything clammy or creepy on my foot. It bit me as soon as I had my dinner, that first night (7 April 2006) as I walked back to my room. It was dark outside the meditation hall and that is when I felt a sharp bite. I felt very miserable, fearing the worst, went to my room, squeezed out the poison and applied the turmeric-sandalwood paste which I carry with me when I travel. I slept like most people who are ill do, heavily with many dreams, many times waking up and thinking, as if it were a theoretical proposition, 'At last I'm safe, at last I can rest.' My foot was badly swollen in the morning, but I went about the usual details of arrival, visiting all the shrines, and that included visiting the office where I discover the central ritual which I wish to observe is to take place on 25 April. This is *aradhna* or new beginnings. Being secular, I had forgotten that the ritual calendar is lunar, and had arrived in order to understand the commemorations of 14th April, the day on the Gregorian calendar on which Bhagavan had died. That is Samadhi day, where in fact there is a solemnity and an unnerving quietness. This year, 14 April is Tamil New Year, Vishu and Good Friday. I'm a Christian by birth, from a lineage of Christian families which go back to 2000 years, and like Kamerer's toad we carry some cultural traits and so there is a genetic predisposition that arouses cultural symptoms of sorrow on Good Friday and joy on Easter, so I accepted the quietness in my heart and the synchrony of Christ's death and Ramana Bhagavan's death being commemorated on the same day. Devotees are dressed in new clothes, and I presume that since they are believers they will not accept death as an ending. Ramanine theology, in fact does not believe in death at all.

Walking around the mountain does not cause me any visible distress, so it is difficult to remember the morning when I am horrified to see that the swelling has started climbing up my foot. It is beginning to look like a stigmata, a pinprick of pus and reddish festering. I run around trying to find a homeopath. I have seen a sign board just in front of Agni Lingam, as the mountain is called on the asramam road. The asramam trustee, Mr Mani and his wife, who are passing by, and to whom I disclose my problem are immediately concerned. There is an eminent heart surgeon from Chennai and his physician son who are coincidentally there. The surgeon, a kindly, heavy built, dark man touches it and says, 'Infection has set in.' They look horrified at my sore, and my idiotic joke that it is probably a stigmata and I should go to see my relatives in Vellore for Easter. I go on rambling idiotically and feverishly that we are Syrian Christians, and the Resurrection is more significant than Christmas. They insist I should take antibiotics. Since I suffered a stroke six years ago, I am adamant that I will only consult a homeopath, to which the younger man says that he seriously feels that I should take something that will work immediately.

'I never take antibiotics.'

'But you need to take it for this. I strongly recommend it. What do you do when you get into trouble?'

'I tend to stay out of trouble.'

'Well, when trouble follows you, then what?'

'I ask the advice of friends.'

He nods, looking worried. The asramam trustee sends for someone who can take me to a homeopath whom he says he knows. His clinic is right behind the asramam (the same one which I had seen on a previous walk) and he is a man with much influence among the Germans in the town. We go there, walking through the cow fields, where a monkey is irritating a puppy by rolling him over and over familiarly, and I keep worrying whether the *chanagam* (cow dung) will give me tetanus. My town-mouse identity is always in the forefront when it comes to illness. Alas, the homeopath has gone with his family to his home-town. I am beginning to feel mildly feverish with fear. Field work is always over-run with tremors; people can fall sick, go insane, suffer marital discord, fall in love and even die. The bite is of no consequence.

The most frightening story is of Michelle Rosaldo, whose work all feminists love, fell to her death while travelling with her husband Renato Rosaldo, who then out of the spirit of mourning wrote a brilliant interrogative text called *Culture and Truth*. Studying Tiruvannamalai is one of the unintended consequences of my having a cerebral stroke in 2000. I went to the asramam to heal, and then over the next five years became immersed in the writings of devotees and the material culture of the asramam, and the rituals which I observed. They were always interesting and life giving, full of a certain continuous sense of biography and memory. Ramana Maharshi gave to those who understood his life and work the benediction of tranquility and the grace of detachment. Nothing severed us really from our mortal passions, but as members of a cult there is a schooling of emotion, a cultivation of demeanour. Sometimes the façade crumbles, but long discipline and the understanding of *sahaja*, as the certitude of happiness is one of the paths to eternity.

I call my cousin Geeta. She and her husband are professors at the Christian Medical College, Vellore. They are much younger than me, but we are great friends, since we share a love for books and travel. Her mother is my father's sister, and her father is the theologian Mathai Zachariah, who invited me to read Swami Abhishiktananda in 1989, when this particular journey in inter-religious dialogue first began.

'Geeta, this is an SOS. I've got bitten by something, I think a tree spider. Can you suggest something for me to take?' I describe the foot, which is looking worse by the moment. She calls up the specialist whose forte is insect bites and who recognizes my sclerotic condition, and prescribes accordingly. Yerramalai, one of Dr Murthy's assistants has already been with me to several medical shops, all open on Sunday, to get Dettol and bandages, so I ring up one of the shops, which delivers the required antibiotics in half an hour. I now have to take twenty pills in five days. So I came here to recover from routine stress, but alas, I am afflicted. Anyway, after all the running around is over, Mr Mani says it is probably an ant-bite and there are these vicious red-ants which make the area bitten swell, for three days, and then it calms down. Doc helps read the prescription for me impassively, while I tremble and think I'll pass out with terror at taking so many pills! I'm not afraid of dying, just afraid of how long it can take!

While I am waiting for the swelling on my foot to subside, and waiting for Easter so that my resolve to be with family on 'our community's most important feast day' is met, I write up my field notes sitting outside Viswanatha Swami's memorial. There are hierarchies of command. The president and his younger brother are the benevolent presences. Dr Murthy takes care of many of the day-to-day chores, 'a whirlwind worker' as one old friend described him. He did once say he would tell me his story, but I liked him too much to ask, since writers never keep anything to themselves. Secrecy is unknown to them. Virginia Woolf, according to the writer Ashok Srinivasan, never believed anything was real until she saw it in print. I suffer from the same delusion, and often people take me by the hand in the asramam and say, 'I'm afraid to talk to you, because then I'll see my words in the *Hindu*!' I'm often introduced as a journalist; and once Doc was asked by a mutual friend whether he had revealed all his secrets to me, to which he replied, 'I told her to improve her sadhana.' Indeed, he offered to educate me on the Vashishta Yoga, which I quickly went to read in the library – it was all about Prince Rama's boredom and the solutions thereof. I do admit that secular can mean scurrilous sometimes, and to keep my friends in the real sense, I have to understand how much the things they value mean to them before I ride rough shod over everything. It's a hard task to remain true to one's discipline and to love one's neighbour, not to speak of one's own family. Like all academics I try very hard to be in many different places at the same time, and am always grateful for the kindness and hospitality of those who harbour us.

Besides the trinity of managers at the top, there are a whole array of men who head a variety of functions: accounts, books, (publication and sale) music, website, library, the byre of cows, gardens, medicines and community care, kitchen. Everything is routinized and runs calmly. Women workers are everywhere, dealing with the most significant chore of cleaning and decorating the temple and its environs. Then there are the priests, of which there is a head, other dominant males, lesser and younger priests learning on the job. Very often the children of the kitchen staff and the priests come for worship and run around happily, playing with each other. It is a family trust in more ways than one, since with the joy of children a new generation of devotees is assured. That sociological point is the wisdom of community (sociologos). Ramana's love for children and families is assured in his continuing gaze and the memorials which are held in his honour.

While the grandness of renunciation is seen everywhere, it seems curious to me that it is, however viewed as a 'curse'. Veena Das' significant work on Renunciation, in her book *Structure and Cognition* (1977), shows that the power of the renouncer actually comes from the stabilizing of structures intrinsic to society, that is, kingship and householders. By moving away, the renouncer reiterates the power of these, while accruing status in another mode. In Ramana's family too, asceticism is seen as the consequence of a 'curse'. An ascetic who was not fed by the ancestors of the family 'left them with the curse that in each generation one member of the family would turn ascetic and live on alms begged for sustaining the body' (Natarajan 2006: 8). Ramana's father's uncle and father's brother had left home. So did Ramana. So did Ganesh, the present president's brother. It is a form of divine autism which few understand in the secular domain. Perhaps, Par Lagerkvist came close to it in his Nobel Prize winning novel, *The Sibyl.*

It is understood that the asramam is a site for the celebration of renunciation, but it is the house-holder as manager who is the administrator and power-centre. The wives of the two grand-nephews of Ramana Maharshi have a substantial part to play in the domain of rituals and they are on easy conversational terms with the old and young priests. They also accompany their husbands at prayer time, and their conjugal solidarity is very visible. They are true ritual partners to their husbands.

Conformity to customs and norms is an integral part of life at the asramam. Visitors often come out of curiosity, some are called by their reading and devotion, while others have been inspired by dreams and revelations. Karl Mannheim writes thus, about membership in a group,

> the derivation of our meanings, whether they be true or false, plays an indispensable role, namely, it socialises events for a group. We belong to a group not only because we are born into it, not merely because we profess to belong to it, not finally because we give it our loyalty and allegiance, but primarily because we see the world and certain things in the world the way it does i.e. in terms of the meanings and the group in question. (Mannheim 1936: 22)

The account of Madame Taleyarkhan, published in 1970, discusses at some length the tensions between individual devotees and administration. Clearly the managers have always had a problem with head strong women in an earlier generation. Madame Taleyarkhan's accounts are particularly interesting because she is very dear to Bhagavan and is able to gather large sums of money by way of donations for various significant construction processes; she constantly asserts that these donations were made to her personally and that she loyally made out cheques to the asramam for specific purposes, she is taxed by the patriarchal and authoritarian functioning of the *sarvadhikari*; yet she feels affection and loyalty. She is blessed by connections in many places, in government and the arts; as a result she is anxious that her renovation work be acknowledged. While she says she did this out of love for Bhagavan, nevertheless Ma Taleyarkhan is pleased to have her name inscribed on the stone plaque outside the 1000-pillar hall of the Patala Lingam in the Arunachala temple. A woman, a Parsi, has ultimately immortalized herself as a devotee of Bhagavan, though today no one really remembers her or knows of her, except for those who have had connections with the asramam for decades. Published by Orient Longman in 1970, her book too is hard to find. After a search of three years, I have finally found it in the archives of Ramanasram, and with the permission of the asramam president, I have been allowed to read it.

It was the French sociologist Catherine Clementin Ojha's former husband, an artist, who had told me about the book. We had met at a café in Delhi called Triveni, in 2003, where artists gather. She was collecting data on missionary histories, a field in which I have some published work. I was speaking to them about the Ramanasramam, where I had been recuperating after a cerebral stroke.

Mr Ojha recounted, 'I was there many long years ago. In fact, I experienced a miracle, a kind of miracle anyway!

'I was staying at the asramam, and it was Christmas. I wanted very much to visit some friends in Pondicherry, to greet them at Christmas, and to take them some gifts. But I had no money. I was very sad. I told no one about it. I went for my bath, sadly thinking about my friends whom I could not visit on their festival day. Then there was a loud banging on the door! I yelled, "I am just coming out!" So I hurriedly dried myself. When I came out, there was a man whom I had never seen before or since, who gave me money. He thrust it in my hand, and said, "I think you wanted some money?" and he went away before I could ask how or why! So I did buy fruits and sweets and visit my friends in Pondicherry for Christmas!'

He then told me about Madame Taleyarkhan's book which must have been the cause of much critical discussion when he was a guest at Ramanasramam.

Madame Taleyarkhan explains in this book why she took on the magnificent task of renovation of the 1000-pillar Patala Lingam,

> Although I had seen marks on the person of Bhagavan of insect bites suffered by Him during a period before I came to the asram, my curiosity had been sufficiently excited to enquire how Bhagavan came by these marks for quite a long while. One day in reply to a question put to Him, Bhagavan said that they were the legacy of the days He spent at the Patalinga Srine, very early in His life there. Bhagavan desired me to see the place. I had not seen it before. He asked Naina to take me to the Sri Arunachaleswarar Temple one evening. Naina pointed out to a part of the thousand pillared mantap as the place where the shrine referred to by Bhagavan was. We could hardly approach the place, so dirty it was, having been used as a public lavatory rather than as a shrine. The news saddened Bhagavan and He remarked in a sad, soft and gentle voice, "Oh, they have no other place but this for that purpose. Do you know the place is a very sacred one and is the Samadhi of a very great saint?" I felt that must be the reason for Bhagavan having chosen that spot for his austerities and something impelled me to say, "I will do up the shrine and see that the place is put to its proper purpose." Bhagavan asked me, "Oh will you?" and I reaffirmed my intention, although I did not know then what I had undertaken. I had not been to the South for many

> years and hardly knew any people and had avoided the members of my community for the reason that I was looked down as a renegade, having given up "high life" for the life of a sadhu. (Taleyarkhan 1970: 57)

Nathiakiamma, a devotee who knew Ma Taleyarkhan well, said that the latter spent many years, with the pallav (tasselled end) of her sari outstretched, going from person to person for funds. Ma went on to meet Sri Tarapore, an established architect, with the plans of Sri Patalinga given to her by the *sthapathi* who had been responsible for the building of the exquisite Sri Mathrubutheswara temple in Ramansramam (59). The archivist, Mr Ramani tells me that the craftsmen were called from Mahabalipuram for this work, each figure so evocative and classically sculpted.

> Sri Tarapore took the plans and asked me to meet him at his office the next day when he put some questions and then told me simply to leave the thing to him saying that whatever was required would be done. When I mentioned this to Sri Goenka (who had supported Tarleyakhan's cause) he was not inclined to believe me as he felt that the work was too small for one of the status of Sri Tarapore to undertake and yet he wished me good luck. I wrote to Bhagavan a long letter of my good luck that Sri Tarapore had undertaken the entire responsibility of the construction of the shrine of Sri Patalinga. I told Him also how I felt considerably relieved in that the asram would have little to do in the matter.
>
> Sri Tarapore and his engineers came a week later, inspected the place and set to work on the construction of the temple. Removing the accumulated dirt itself was something of a problem. Bhagavan evinced considerable interest, as was usual with him and I reported daily to him the progress of the scheme. Experts had been engaged by Sri Tarapore on the work and he and his family would often come to Tiruvannamalai to inspect the progress of the work and satisfy them selves thereon. On all these occasions they never failed to pay their respects to Bhagavan. (59, 60)

She goes on to recite the manner in which Bhagavan had sent her to visit the Arunachala temple. She went with other devotees from the asramam.

> We went hardly half the way when a sepoy stopped Naina and started discussing with him. Somehow I felt this was something about me, so I

enquired if there was any enquiry about me. Dear Naina did not want to embarrass me and said they were taking me to be a non-Hindu, as non-Hindus were not at all allowed into the temple. Immediately I went and saw the Executive Officer, who understood me and took us all inside. When I went to Mother Parvathi in the temple, I nearly cried and said – "Oh, Ma, if you are a real Mother, then see that today's insult should give me the chance to serve you in such a way that one day my name would be in this Temple." I was not aware of what I was saying, and lo and behold, five years later, I took up the Patalinga work, which I shall ever cherish as the great Mother's answer to my prayer. (61)

Ma Taleyarkhan had invited Rajaji for the Muhurtham. Consequently he became governor general of India, and while she thought he would be too busy to come, he himself confirmed his interest in being there (60). The auspicious date was fixed for 14 May 1949. She proceeded to get the temple tank cleaned, since they were stinking with moss and dirt. 'I set about it in a big way, rushing pumps from Polur and Vellore and seeing to it that both the tanks received the long overdue spring cleaning.' She had the entire premises of Arunachala temple cleaned with the help of the executive officer. In honour of Rajaji's arrival 'I saw to it personally that all the stations on the railway line from Madras to Tiruvannamali received the long overdue coat of whitewash and that the houses lining the streets of the town of Tiruvannamalai along which Shri Rajaji was to pass were also whitewashed and gaily decorated' (63). It was Rajaji who asked (on entering Patala Lingam) Sri Tarapore, 'to put up a plate in English and Tamil to commemorate the occasion, which was done subsequently' (64).

That evening the A.I.R. broadcast a recording of the function at the temple which Bhagavan heard with rapt attention. When the broadcast was over, Bhagavan said with a sigh of relief that for three or four days, He was moving in dread lest I should pick Him up and take Him to the function. What an opportunity I had missed, I shouted, but Bhagavan motioned me kindly to resume my seat and said He was much relieved.

A little later, someone informed Bhagavan that a fee was being levied for admission into the newly constructed temple. Bhagavan asked me if it was true and pointed out the informant, who affirmed it. Immediately, I wrote a strong letter to the Executive officer to stop that practice. Bhagavan said that no levy ought to be made for entry into the temple. (64)

The *Kumbhaabhishekham* was performed only on 3 November 1968 for various reasons – Bhagavan fell ill and then meteor like his mortal body passed away, leaving his grace as a steadfast reminder to devotees of his constant presence. Quarrels between asramam administration and Ma continued sporadically.

Madame Taleyarkhan's fund collecting drives were such that previous to the Patala Lingam, she had organized through the generosity of friends, the purchase of Ramana's birthplace, the house at Tiruchuli and at Madurai, where He had achieved liberation while he was still a boy (56). Taleyarkhan always communicates in her book that she was close to the British, the freedom fighters, and the nawabs and royalty of pre-independence India. It allowed her to be one of the most powerful fund collectors for the asramam, and the book is an interesting momento to feminism, suppressed histories, and what the asramam would call the Ego. Nameless as devotees wish to be in their service of Bhagavan, for the sociologist, personal biographies and official histories are interesting juxtapositions to the telling of a story.

Madame Taleyarkhan states in her book that she had found ten thousand rupees for building the samadhi to the mother (70). She was also responsible for beginning the construction of the visitor's bungalows. She asserted her will over the placement of the samadhi. Differences arose between the *sarvadhikari* and her at almost every point (70). She says:

> The manager was freely giving it out that the building would be completed only by his grandson or great grandson, and not before.
>
> When, however, the Board of Trustees came to be appointed under the scheme framed for the management of the asram by the sub-court at Vellore, Dr T.N. Krishnan and I were on it and with the co-operation of Shri K. Srinivaschari, a member appointed as the representative of the Government on the Board, the Board at it's meeting on 17 September 1965 passed a resolution reading "The mantapam construction work is entrusted to Mrs Taleyarkhan who is requested to take charge immediately and choose and co-opt men to help her to execute the work as quickly as possible." I am glad to say that if ever there was any resolution of the Board of Trustees that was put into effect against the opposition of the manager, this was one and that too because of the grace of Bhagavan. (71)

She immediately advertised for assistants, hired one, and was with 'the stone masons, morning and evening urging them to get the work done efficiently and quickly. The close personal watch thus kept did expedite the work although several obstacles came in the way such as personal animosities (71) lack of finance, etc. (72). She says that,

> On August 22, 1966, the gopuram went up and on Dec 26, in that same year, the Samadhi was almost completed except for fencing around the Samadhi. Thus work kept pending for 17 years long, got completed in 17 months, thanks to the Grace of Bhagavan. (72)

Grand though her scheme was, some amount of renovation continues with the passing of time. T.N. Venkataraman has placed a new grille at the sanctum over the samadhi, which present-day devotees see as much more elegant than the previous one which was removed.

Much of the analyses of mysticism has centred around the idea of the dissolution of the world through mechanistic categories which are typical of industrial and consumerist societies as explained to us by Mahatma Gandhi, Romain Rolland, Simone Weil. Whether it is the varieties of colonialism or forms of fascism, or war as a constant symbol of industrial society, the need for detachment is a fundamental response.

Bharati Mirchandani, a well-known designer who has crafted some very memorable art work for Ramanasramam (calendars, also a best-selling picture and text collation), spoke at an international conference on Indic religions in CSDS in Delhi in January 2006. I quote from her paper:

> Today feelings of isolation are common despite people being connected across the earth via satellites: TV, Internet. Social support systems are faceless. The individual is given prime importance while existence itself is dehumanised. This paradox seeks resolving through a philosophy that is inclusive.
>
> Ramana Maharshi's philosophy seems to apply to most situations and personality types. Those who have no place for god in their world view, no time for rituals and religious exercises, find answer to the inner primordial urge; while those who need a god and sacred routines find his guidance increases efficacy in their chosen form of worship. However, any who seek religion as a means of belonging to a clique can find it satisfying only by

> misinterpretation, denying that spirituality is an intensely personal, inward-looking and not an outward-looking activity.

She continues:

> Many of us receive summons from our truest inner self, but lack of courage to recognise or heed the call, to let go the familiar and leap into the timeless mystery. A rare brave one was Ramana Maharshi. In material terms he accomplished nothing major in his life built no empires, wore almost no clothes, and seldom spoke. He performed no miracles, though innumerable remarkable "coincidences" occurred around him. His special feat was his silent energy that could quieten minds of those who came to him, giving them a taste of the exalted state he lived in. Power over people's minds is perhaps the only real power. I think he wore a cloak of ordinariness so that those who met him were not awestruck by the immensity of his being.

Karl Mannheim believes that knowledge is a shared process in group life, that all members co-operate in the making and dissemination of knowledge, 'within the framework of a common fate, a common activity, and the overcoming of common difficulties (in which however each has a different share)' (29).

Traditions operate in such a way that certain habits are carefully passed down, and in their significance become accepted as almost *forms* of genetic coding. Morris Carstairs many decades ago, showed that caste customs presumed that biological drives such as food, the need for shelter and recreation would be practiced differentially by Brahmins and Kshatriyas. Cooling the passions and heating the passions would be differential modes of encounter with the natural world which is thus experienced through food and drink and concomitant forms of leisure and occupation.

In her classic work, *Patterns of Culture*, published in 1934, Ruth Benedict writes of cultural patterns, which have a local and sometimes internationalizing character, if we accept the impact of a local symbolic frame in a globalized world. In the case of the Ramanasramam, rituals and customs have been duplicated in *kendras* all over the world. There is a belief in a theology and a way of life associated with Ramana's devotees. Writing on the integration of culture, Benedict asserts that,

> A culture, like an individual, is a more or less consistent pattern of thought and action. Within each culture there come into being characteristic

> purposes not necessarily shared by other types of society. In obedience to these purposes, each people further and further consolidates its experience, and in proportion to the urgency of these drives the heterogeneous items of behaviour take more and more congruous shape. (Benedict 1959: 47)

She uses a linguistic metaphor to understand the variability of culture and the limits to our understanding of probabilities.

> The numbers of sounds that can be produced by our vocal cords and our oral and nasal cavities are practically unlimited ... The total that are used in different languages of the world no one has even dared to estimate. But each language must make its selection and abide by it on pain of not being intelligible at all. A language that used even a few hundreds of the possible – and actually recorded – phonetic elements could not be used for communication. (23)

The point so sharply made here is the significance of cultural selection. Yet she also makes a plea for the acceptance of diversity.

> In culture we must imagine a great arc on which are ranged the possible interest provided either by the human age-cycle or by the environment or by man's various activities. (24)

Further, she says that,

> ... the possible human institutions and motives are legion, on every plane of cultural simplicity or complexity, and that wisdom consists in a greatly increased tolerance toward their divergencies. No man can thoroughly participate in any culture unless he has been brought up and has lived according to its forms, but he can grant to other cultures the same significance to their participants which he recognizes in his own.

My argument has been, following Mahatma Gandhi, Simone Weil and Romain Rolland, that the need to escape from war, consumerism, extravagance, wholesale anomie or normlessness, makes individuals in the modern world seek alternatives, where mystical experience is a palpable and observable phenomenon (Visvanathan 2007).

However, it has been made evident, that mystical experience is located within a site of power, where a routinization has already taken place. Utopias (No place) or Eu-topias (Good place) are structured by rules. Here characteristically, mystical experiences will follow those mechanisms where order and conformity will be asserted. Barbara Goodwin in her classic book *Social Science and Utopia*, lists these as coercion, terror, legal punishment, education or rational instruction, morality, inducements, indoctrination, psychological conditioning and total conditioning (Goodwin 1978: 86). This list is a theoretical construct and it is not necessary that all the aspects of control in Utopia should be found in any one given place. However, the need for conformity is the highest index of success of the routinization of charisma, because it is not the magnetism of the cult's founder, but the ability of the responsible caretakers of the cult to carry forward the impetus of ideas.

The differences between then and now are apparent, and often discussed. Most frequently, two examples are given: the quiet of a small monastic asramam then, and the density of the crowds now; Ramana's love for the monkeys and the predatory and problematic nature of them now. However, the presence of a loving spirit, immortalized by legend and reminiscence, and the continuity of the rituals and prayers to Shiva in Ardhanareeshwara form, is constant.

The Ramanasramam is often criticized for its Brahmin imprint, as the influence of the Brahmins is seen to be very apparent in the rituals and customs. Chadwick, (or more familiarly known as Sadhu Arunachala) writes,

> People often complained that caste was observed in the Ashram dining room, and why did Bhagavan permit when he himself was beyond caste? The dining room was divided into two by a screen which extended almost the whole breadth of the room. Bhagavan sat in the opening at right angles to the screen and so was visible on both sides. On one side of the screen sat the Brahmins and on the other side the rest. Many people used to complain about this and especially at Bhagavan for allowing such thing, for was he not beyond all caste? Yes, certainly he was, and that was why he took his meal with both sides.
>
> "But why does he allow it?" people asked. Not only did he allow it but he insisted on it. Brahmins would come to the asram, say that with Bhagavan all were equal and sat down on the non-Brahmin side of the screen. But Bhagavan would object.
>
> "Do you eat with non-Brahmins in your own home?" he would ask.
>
> "No, but with Bhagavan it is different," they would answer.

> "So you want to use Bhagavan as an excuse for breaking your caste rules?" Bhagavan would ask. "If you do not observe caste outside, there is no objection to your doing the same here. But you are not going to use as an excuse for doing something which you consider at home to be wrong."
>
> (Sadhu Arunachala 1994: 34, 35)

In his analysis of custom, Carl Gustav Diehl writes in an essay entitled 'Human Reaction to Divine Identity in Tamil Nadu' that there is a division of religious practice into worshipping the deity in form, worshipping according to fixed rituals and the practice of yoga, and the quest for spiritual knowledge. He takes the case of the Arunachala temple, and describes customary practice:

> A complete guide for temple visitors is given in Arunachala Puranam of Tiruvannamalai (Maturai Mutaliyar 1967) Directives for the worshipper are given in 35 sections .... A summary is attempted as follows. A Saivite should go to the temple everyday and perform civataricamum with devotional faith (sraddha) according to the rules. He should take a bath in a sacred tank (tirtha) and put on dry clothes, and after finishing the religious rites (amasthanam) and prayer, go to the temple. He should not come empty handed but carry a pot lifted up high with coconut, fruit and areca nut or some flowers with a view to placing it in the sanctuary. Approaching the temple he must salute the tower, "the pillar linga" folding both his hands over his head.
>
> A man can pay homage by letting eight parts of his body touch the ground, a woman by five parts. For both, tryanga-namaskara is possible, that is, touching the head with both hands. It should be done three times, five, seven, nine or twelve times, stretching the legs in a westerly or southerly direction, but not towards the east or the north. Then slowly, looking down, one should walk around, with the sanctuary on one's right (pradikshanam) Vinayakar one time, the sun two times, Parvati three times, and Vishnu four times. One must also walk around the altar and the bull Nandi, praying the latter for permission to enter and for success. Having reached the sanctuary one must meditate and touching the right ear with the left hand and the left ear with the right hand, bow down three times in salutation. Thereafter one must hold both hands on one's head, salute with meditation and with devoted heart, sing praise .... (Diehl in Parapola 1986: 112-14)

These traditions are evident in pilgrims' activities at Ramanasramam, but for Christians, Buddhist, Muslims (hereafter people of other faiths) the custom is to pay obeisance at the samadhi, to visit the mother's shrine, where the deities are beautifully sculpted, to visit the other shrines of Bhagavan's friends and helpers and the last habitat of Bhagavan (a single room which is set in an exquisite garden) where they pray, meditate and prostrate.

Not all of them who come here in search of Bhagavan are knowledgeable about Hinduism, and they either ask others, as I did, or they imitate, or they feel free to do what they are comfortable doing.

Yet, Ramana rather than demeaning other ways of life or being, always celebrated diversity by comfortingly resolving the issue with his counsel to be 'As you are.' That tradition is still vivid in asramam practice. For western pilgrims the meeting point of cultural symbols, as in the eagle and the snake, are familiar icons. They see the local people standing under the banyan tree near the water tank hoping to sight the eagle which will comfort them in the tussles of the day ahead, and they see that the snake appearing means that Shiva is near. Rudolf Wittkower in his *Allegory and the Migration of Symbols* (1977) argues that it is not difficult to understand the importance of the eagle and the snake in Greco-roman civilization, both pagan and Christian. In the pagan world, the eagle stood for kingship and power over darkness, 'equivalent to the king vanquishing enemies' (Wittkower 1977: 31). The snake in Christianity has stood for both knowledge and for wisdom. The two principles (knowledge and wisdom) can be in contradiction with one another, hence represents what has been defined by Ruth Benedict as the Spenglerian problem of the tussle between an Apollonian viewpoint in paganism, and a Faustian viewpoint in established forms of Christianity.

'Apollonian men conceived of his soul as a cosmos ordered in a group of excellent parts.' There was no place in his universe for will, and conflict was an evil which his philosophy decried. The idea of an inward development of the personality was alien to him, and he saw life as under the shadow of catastrophe always brutally threatening from the outside (Benedict 1959: 52). ... On the other hand, the Faustian's picture of himself is as a force endlessly combating obstacles. His version of the course of individual life is that of an inner development, and the catastrophes of existence come as the inevitable culmination of his past choices and experiences. Conflict is the essence of existence. Without it personal life has no meaning, and only the more superficial values of existence. Faustian man longs for the infinite and his art attempts to reach out toward it (55-56).

Ramana Maharshi understood the dialectic between these two world views, and thus engaged with his devotees each according to his or her need, using the gift of his great imagination to bridge the gap between two world views, which were for him fundamentally real and subject to experience. It is for this reason, belief in *prarabda* (past actions), destiny and the understanding of modern rational technological symbols were so important for him.

In his guidebook *Beyond Ecumenism: A Journey into Light*, the theologian Mathai Zachariah provides a simple format for those who come from different faiths encountering the space of Advaita or that which overcomes dualism. He draws inspiration from Abhishiktananda, to say that we are rooted in our categories, rooted in our individual psyches, education and so on. How can we then engage in dialogue?

He prescribes acceptance of the sacred books of the other, as well as contemplative meditation. Prayer and gathering with people of other faiths in silence and prayer, the living together in asrams with people of other faiths, avoiding what he calls 'triumphalism' and further, the acceptance that religious experiences of others can happen in us (Zachariah 2002: 55, 56).

The questions of body and spirit, history and cosmos often figure when attempting to understand the nature of divinity. They are central to christological debates. For believers, Ramana Maharshi's agony in the time of cancer, was a representation of his detachment, although 'pain was there,' palpably there.

Chadwick, known at the Ramanasramam as Sadhu Arunachala, writes of his first meeting with Bhagavan,

> The first question I asked Bhagavan was why Christ called out from the cross, if he was a perfect jnani, then surely he would have been indifferent to all suffering. Bhagavan explained that though a jnani has attained Liberation already and for him there can be no such thing as suffering, some may appear to feel pain, but his is only a reaction of the body. For the body continues to have its reactions. It still eats and carries out all its natural working. All its suffering is apparent only to the onlooker and does not affect the jnani, for he no longer identifies the self with the body, he lives in a transcendent state above all such. (Sadhu Arunachala 1994: 21)

Madame Taleyarkhan writes that at the end of his life, at his death-bed, Chadwick had a vision of Jesus Christ,

From the description he gave of the figure in white that he saw we inferred that it was Christ come to receive him in his last moments. He was greatly devoted to Bhagavan, yet Jesus Christ came forward to receive him at the moment of leaving the mortal coil. May he be at peace! (Taleyarkhan 1970: 216)

In Arthur Osborne's poem *Ramana Sat-Guru*, published in *the Mountain Path* of January 1966, we see the same identification of Ramana with Christ.

To feel, to know, to be the Christ within –
Can there then be love for Christ on earth,
Walking like men, seen as a man is seen?
Seek not to argue; love has greater worth.
Love makes man kin
With the Beloved. Such have I known,
Him of the lustrous eyes, Him whose sole look
Pierced to the heart, wherein the seed was sown
Of wisdom deeper than in holy book,
Of truth alone
Not to be learned but lived, Truth in its hour
To sprout within the heart's dark wintry earth
And grow a vibrant thing, then, come to power
To slay the seeming self that gave it birth,
Or to devour. (Osborne 1966: 9)

All Ramana devotees constantly accept the blessings of grace, but affirm that they are in Bhagavan's power.

Sadhu Arunachala, had further questions to ask Bhagavan.

I had always wondered how it was that St Paul, who was a most orthodox Jew, hated Christ and persecuted the Christians, interpreted his great experience on the Damascus road in terms of Christ and afterwards became an ardent Christian himself. So one day I asked Bhagavan.

He said that St Paul was always thinking about Christ and the Christians, they were never out of his mind, so when he returned to self-consciousness after his experience he identified his realization with this predominant thought. And he referred to Ravana as an example. Ravana hated Rama, never ceased to think of him and dying, Rama was the uppermost thought in

> his mind and so he realised God. It is not a question of love or hate, it is just the question of what is in the mind at the time. People judge the deeds of others as good or bad, but it is the doing itself that matters and not the complexion of the deed. The whole secret lies in whether we are attached to our actions or not. A person who spends his time in good deeds can be much more attached to them than the so-called bad man to his. And it is the one who drops off all attachments first who will be self-realized soonest. (Sadhu Arunachala 1994: 24)

At the asramam, it is understood that Ramana's teaching participated in the sense of the experience of the godhead, that ignorance is removed because the mountain Arunachala liberates, that one would not be there but that one is a seeker. Because it is a congregation of seekers, the experience of bliss is commonly understood among those who gather here. Those who know of this describe it as a calmness of the heart and mind, a tranquility that forces them to return or hope to return. Failing that, there is a continual remembrance of pleasure. K. Swaminathan a biographer of Ramana, described wanting to return to the asramam to see Bhagawan, as so strong a desire that he wished he could be tied down by elephants.

In the summer of 2003, one of the trustees introduced me to another writer, 'a very interesting woman', as he described her. She was Ranga's granddaughter. Her grandfather was always leaving home to be with Ramana, he was so desperate to be with Bhagavan that he was unable to carry out his obligations to his family and his wife and children suffered because of this. Bhagavan was continually advising Ranga to return to his family but to no avail. Ranga's own account has been presented by David Godman (who as the most ardent of devotees has been described as the incomparable David Godman!), in the *Power of the Presence*.

> In June 1907 I went with my wife, mother and daughter to see Bhagavan. It was the first time I had seen him since we were at school together.
>
> "Do you recognize me?" I asked Bhagavan.
>
> With great difficulty he muttered the name "Rangan" in guttural tones. In those days, because Bhagavan spoke little, he found it very difficult to use his voice.
>
> ... At the time of my departure, after this first visit, I told Bhagavan, "You have reached great heights."
>
> Bhagavan replied, "The far-off mountains look even and smooth." (Godman 2000: 2)

Rangan visited him after many years, and Bhagavan said to him on this visit, 'Darshan (seeing or being seen by) of holy people is not readily attainable. It is better to visit them often. They get the cloth woven and keep it ready for wear' (3).

On this visit, Rangan asked Alagamma, 'Mother, do you know whether I have a share in your son's earnings?'

> I thought we were alone but mother called out to Bhagavan, "Did you hear what Rangan said?"
>
> Bhagavan appeared, smiled and replied, "Yes, yes! Is he also not one of us? Certainly he has a share."

Rangan apparently took this very literally. He returned to Bhagavan.

> My financial circumstances were not in a good state at that time. Bhagavan seemed to know this even though I never mentioned the subject.
>
> As soon as I prostrated at his feet he said to me, "Look here Rangan. A man, by himself, can go anywhere in the world and get by somehow. But women and children are different. Have you provided enough for the maintenance of your wife and children at home?"

Bhagavan kept very close watch over Rangan and his family, and always knew when there was trouble. Indeed there were many miserable days for the family, but Rangan was on a short leash, wherever he went, he always found his way back to his childhood friend.

> On one of my visits I missed the connecting train in Villipuram. I was very disappointed because the next train was not due for many hours. I told the stationmaster, who was a friend of mine about my problem and he very kindly arranged for me to travel in a goods train that was going through Tiruvannamalai. The train was not due to stop in Tiruvannamalai, but the driver slowed down so I could jump off. Unfortunately, as I was alighting from the train, I fell over and wounded myself. I started to limp towards the asram, but the path was not clearly visible. I ended up scrambling through some bushes and thorn trees that added to my injuries. I arrived in the asram in a very disreputable state.
>
> When Bhagavan asked me where all my cuts and scratches had come from? I told him what had happened. "Why all this haste?" he asked.
>
> "In order to see you," I replied.

> Bhagavan made all my troubles worthwhile by saying, "The yearning for darshan matters more than darshan itself."

Rangan's granddaughter was also a devotee, by custom and by personal experience. She had suffered the loss of her husband. Before he died, he had woken her up in the morning, and said, 'Come with me.' She had dressed and accompanied him, but while on the morning walk, he suddenly said, 'I want to take up *sanyasa*, and I want you to be my companion. Let us go now!'

She had pleaded with him, and then flatly refused, since she had responsibilities to her growing sons (now employed in America, with families of their own) and to her ailing father-in-law. Her husband was deeply disappointed with her for not agreeing to his plan of renunciation, they returned home, but he died soon after.

Is there a presentiment of death before the desire for renunciation? Some announcement perhaps, that before life ceases, one should carry out one's spiritual if not ritual desires and obligations? It does not always seem to be the case. Vijaya Ramaswamy in her compelling work, *Walking Naked* wrote of Kanakamma, one of Bhagavan's most endearing and well-known devotees, who asserted that though she had been compelled to marry, she told her husband that she was an ascetic, and could not consummate the marriage.

In *Cherished Memories*, Kanakamma tells this story, and then goes on like a faithful witness to describe her adoration for Bhagavan. She was also the friend of Murgunar, and managed in her book to describe some truly amusing stories about Murgunar's devotion to Ramana Maharshi and some of their exchanges which she has immortalized in her lucid and careful style. Kanakamma still visits the asramam everyday, and she is always available to seekers for advice and counselling, including explanation of *jnana marga* to those who want elucidation from a teacher.

II

In April there is a great white heat that settles on everything, but it is cool and breezy under the trees. Since the asramam gets hundreds of people every day, routine and discipline are integral to the scheme. Personal love cannot threaten this structure. Abstract love is permissible, everyone knows when there is a chord of attachment between partners, but even in marriage this is sublimated to responsibility and care, while devotion to the Sadguru is paramount. The need for discipline at the asramam is very great, and so at all times decorum is to be maintained. The greatness of Ramana's teaching is expressed in the ability to tolerate deviance, but it's a virtue of the most exalted. The trustees keep a strict eye on order, watch carefully over everything. The majority of the residents are essentially concerned that their own jobs be done perfectly, and that devotees keep the harmony of the asramam.

I climbed the hill for five minutes. My swollen insect-bitten foot does not allow me to proceed in this heat. Ramana loved the heat and climbed the mountain everyday; before that time when he got so famous that crowds followed him; there was not a path that he did not know. I sat on a very hot stone, and saw an eagle, a parrot and a squirrel. There is a new rule which says one must get a pass to climb the hill. I had gone to the office which is in the heart of town, on 8 April 2006, and though it was twenty minutes to closing time, the staff was charming and co-operative. This is the forest office, and it fills out a ledger on the number of visitors and the number of days they intend to climb Arunachala. The ASI is in charge of Ramana's former abodes, each of which is now protected from day-trippers and cigarette butts. Forest office workers guard and monitor the hill, and their gardeners go every morning to plant young trees and watch over the saplings.

When I climbed down, making the pigs and chickens flee with grunts and squeals and terrified flapping ('if cabbages were kings and pigs had wings!' as Lewis Caroll would say) there was a promise of rain, and the sky hung grey and deliciously cool and low over my head. There were a few drops of rain, so I returned to the asramam compound. The forest guards asked the former alcoholic slum dweller, who always begs to be a guide (for the cost of a cup of tea), 'Is it true that the Mountain gives you whatever you ask for?' he replied, 'Whatever you want, Vayar or Vallu!' (belly or sword – which might mean a full stomach or power, but I'm not sure). My only wish in 1996 was to write a book about the asramam, and that did come true.

The day continues to be hot, and I stay in the cool verandahs watching people coming, enjoying the gardens, and leaving. I like them, these picnic minded droves, though older residents are irritable, since they feel that Ramana's quietitude is destroyed. But Ramana understood the love people had for him, he was completely sensitive to them, and that aura of protection 'be as you are' continues.

In the *Mountain Path* of January 1966, N.N. Rajan writes, under the title 'Suffer Little Children' (which is the phrase Jesus used when his disciples tried to turn away small children for fear of disturbing the master, 'to come unto me'.)

> Being a householder, I felt that it was not right for me to follow a spiritual path alone, so I began taking my wife and children also to Bhagavan's Ashram. Within a few months I found, to my astonishment, quite a conspicuous change in my wife and noticed that she had outstripped me in her understanding of Bhagavan. She had become a greater devotee and was imbibing more peace from him. My children also enjoyed his presence and he used to laugh and joke with them. Indeed he had a special fondness for children and often used to joke with them and touch or caress them. He scrupulously avoided touching adults or being touched by them. The children themselves derived a certain peace and joy from his presence and would sometimes sit motionless before him, as though under a spell, free from childish wriggling. (Rajan 1966: 10)

The meditation hall is always cool and quiet, with the khus-khus, hiding the glare of sunlight. Inside on the couch rests Ramana's portrait, so vivid and intensely creative, he seems to be there, smiling back at you, is always garlanded with fresh flowers, usually hibiscus or jasmines. And one immediately feels tranquil. Ganesh, the youngest of Ramana's grand nephews, was editor of the *Mountain Path*, for many years, but is now a recluse. His collection of editorials has been published by the asramam and is delightful reading, since there are vivid images of Maharshi as well as his devotees. One of these descriptions is about the imitation of Ramana (rather in the manner of the imitation of Christ), only it is a practical exercise in daily life provided by a scholar from Madurai, about being loving, generous and disciplined.

The asramam is crowded because these early days in April are festival days. Ram Navami is just over and it coincided with Bhagavan's mother's liberation day. Alagamma is Ramana's mother. She was a loyal, steadfast woman, wife of a successful and hospitable lawyer, who was suddenly left widowed. Niranjananda Swami, who was her youngest son and became the *sarvadhikari* of the asramam, brought the asramam to this state of grandeur by managing the details of everyday events. This was institutionalized further by his son Swami Ramananda (who is the father of the present president, Mr Sundar,) and at ninety-three a very visible presence and known by many as the man who saw the asramam through the years of depleted resources and structural changes.

Today the festive celebrations around Alagamma are myriad, because she represents the Mother Goddess. Her deification has probably been the most visible in these decades, when she has become identified with the Earth Goddess. It is 14 April 2006. It coincides with Good Friday, and with Tamil New Year. The asramam follows a lunar cycle, so it will celebrate Aradhana or Bhagavans's liberation day on 25 April. The thing with the secular anthropologist is that they always bungle on the small details, and as with law, ignorance is no excuse! I discovered on my arrival that my decision to go to Kerala for five days, was a breach in more ways than one. But it was only four hundred years ago that Tamils and Malayalis found they were not one people, and when in Tamil Nadu, the Chera country always beckons! I did not know how to cope with my distress at finding out that the central ritual of Aradhna was to happen while I was away. Dr Murthy, who is in charge of the keys, and who always has a complex job handling hundreds of visitors, all of whom want to return over and over again, said irascibly, 'Stay till Aradhna is over and then go to Kerala after that.'

'But my tickets were booked two months ago, and my sister is travelling from Bangalore to meet me at my mother's home!'

The president, who is a gentle soul, looked troubled at my distress, and Dr Murthy went back to his work. I went to the railway station, stood in a queue and rebooked my tickets, so that I would be back on 25 April. The railway station is charming, having an exterior which is like any post-independence station, but the narrow meter gauge still exists, though in 2007, plans are in place to modernize it. The clerk who sells the tickets is an amazingly calm young man, who is tri-lingual, very cerebrally connected and interrogative and helpful. There are ten of us in line, it is lunch time, the electricity and the computer keeps going off, but the ticket sales clerk is clearly capable of rising above everything.

11 April 2006 is *Pradoshan puja*. The temple has been decorated and in the Mother's sanctum, lamps have been lit before all the gods. The hibiscus flowers are large and pink. *Pradoshan* is celebrated before every full moon and every new moon. It also symbolizes the moment when the gods and demons churn the sea, and receive poison. Shiva helps them by drinking the poison. Then they churn the ocean again, and receive nectar. They drink this and dance, and then remember that they forgot Shiva. They invite him, he dances with them and from 4.30 to 6.30 in the evening, if people have fasted at that time they get to see all the gods. Every year, Mr Mehta who is a long-time resident of Tiruvannamalai

with his wife, tells me ritual stories. He always says that if one is ashamed of one's ignorance, one can never learn.

I'm re-reading Paul Ricoer's *Freud and Philosophy* (The Terry Lectures). Ricoeur suggests that the ideas around Thanatos, Eros and Ananke are the central principles of analyses in the unravelling of symbols. In the analyses of faith, we are not skeptics, we are observers and there is dialectic to our observation, born from our empathy and our suspended disbelief. Therefore we (as analysts) 'cannot and must not avoid the question of the absolute validity' of the object of our study. We must believe that they believe.

The people flock on Sundays and holidays, on other days the routine goes along quietly. When I first visited the asramam in 1996, there were about thirty people at dinner time; now about 200 people routinely appear on an ordinary day. Residents say that since the mid '90s there has been a surge in the number of visitors. I get an email from Bharati Mirchandani. She has written that in the week prior to my arrival she had been at the asramam, and it was so hot that the snake had crept out to eat the toads, and winged creatures were numerous. However, the passion flower (it's associated with Good Friday, like the lily for Easter) is out. It grows in beautiful clusters on the wooden frame near Bhagavan's last darshan site, and I have never seen them before, beautiful exotic red flowers. There is a yellow flower too, near the other gate, just behind the temple and the meditation hall. It is called Manoranjana. It has a strong sweet scent. The small children play in the gardens and in the hall, unmindful of sanctity and with a real pleasure in the largeness of the hall. Today it has been cleaned with a large vacuum cleaner which makes a loud roaring noise. The younger priests hose down the samadhi with large swathes of water, the women servants and some of the devotees wipe out the water. In the morning Doc scrubs the garden outside Bhagavan's little room and Niranjanananda's sanctuary. The sound of the hose on the palm trees is like rain.

I speak to two women. One is a lady, very erudite and simple who in one breath tells me lots of things, which I know from books, but in her telling Bhagavan's life unfolds in the kindness of things, the order he provides, the nuances of the ordinary. There is an immense vitality these women who, like me, prop up the walls of temples in our awe and loneliness at the greatness of god. They're available to their families and yet are drawn to the hushed calm of asramam life.

Neeraj, my companion with the French visitor Marie, on the mountain perambulation at night, has accepted an invitation to go to the Skanda asramam, but as they set out, she remembers that she has not taken her slippers. 'When we returned at 10.45, the rocks were so hot that I felt I had paid for the sins of my past life. Half of those sins had been paid the previous night when we did *giripradikshana*. Now only a few of my sins require atonement.'

It is Good Friday, Bhagavan's Samadhi and New Year. I find the confluence puzzling, but almost every one is wearing new clothes. Since my illness and the hallucinations accompanying it (probably the consequence of treatment with L-dopa – described so well in Oliver Sack's Awakenings – and later, heavy doses of cortisones) the suffering of Christ is very vivid to me. I don't practice in a ritualistic fashion, but I understand hunger, thirst and the hammering of nails.

On Samadhi day, the priests had a complex ritual of adorning Bhagavan's *sthala*. Mama, the head priest, first washed the lingam in milk, then water, then scrubbed it with ashes and curds, and then put a hibiscus on it. Then he put a silver cobra snake's hood on the lingam itself. He decorated it with flowers – yellow chrysanthemums and white jasmines. He then went to the devotees with a basket of hibiscus and jasmines and accepted their prayers. Then he and the other priests went on to intone, jasmine by jasmine and presented it to Bhagavan.

The heat is mind-blowing, and I don't even try to deal with it. I keep the same timings of work that I do in Delhi, but here I follow the routines of the residents. I'm not one of them, but I share what they have, and the unintended consequence is an overpowering sense of grace. It's like a warm sense of being loved, an almost tactile sense of the greatness of divine consummation whose joy fulfills human beings, it is about being one of the earth's children. I respond with gratitude that I can only put in words. For others, it is a different kind of work, and for yet others, it is the gift of tears and of silence and solitude, none of these are exclusive, and devotees apparently oscillate between many states. Tears are seen in mysticism as divine space, and often appear in conversation as descriptions of trance or mutual recognition between devotees.

Since Samadhi day is also Tamil New Year and Malayali Vishu (a harvest feast) people wish one another with real delight. In the afternoon lunch is elaborate, with *pal payasam* and *aviyal*, and in the night there is a recital of the 'Marital Garland of Letters'. This is my favourite text, and it has the sensuality of androgynous love, where Maharshi takes on the voice of eroticism and divinity (Visvanathan 2007).

The singing and chanting take place outside the small antechamber where Bhagavan breathed his last. It is a beautiful little room, with the loveliest garden, where thunder ball flowers and harsinghar and anthuriums grow side by side in a fecund and orderly way. We sit cross-legged for forty-five minutes and everyone sings. It is physically agonizing for me because I can only sit cross-legged for about five minutes or so but I do it, with Mrs Mani, who has a much worse spinal condition, keeping me company! The passion flower creeper is luxuriant over the little room (it blooms with lovely red flowers in the morning) and the garden looks very green and tropical. After the chanting is over, at 8.40 p.m., everyone is silent, and then we file past the room one by one, like those who have had a final darshan.

There is a bomb blast in Delhi and I am worried about my children. But luckily I am able to speak to them everyday.

I go to the shop opposite the asramam to get a newspaper. The proprietor is always brusque, but he keeps the *Hindu* and the *Deccan Herald* and the *Indian Express*. And by mid morning it's all sold out. I normally visit his shop to get *bindis*. He only keeps garish ones for foreigners, so we always quarrel. I can't possibly wear tinsel stuff on my brow like a Christmas tree decoration. This time I have to go to town to buy red stick-on bindis. Here you cannot be seen without one, and if you do appear with a blank undecorated forehead, every one superstitiously turns away. It is a mark of widowhood, not to wear a *bindi*, which apparently causes collective distress. In some ways the Tamils are a very superstitious people. However, all the old, single, abandoned and widowed are on the whole very much part of asramam life. Here most of them have found happiness, doing work, or congregating or praying or chatting together. There is a sense of joy in having Ramana as a patron – life can now be never unhappy for them. The devotees spill in by the hundreds every day. It is rather like passengers in a bus. One never knows who one will sit next to at meal times. Everyone maintains decorum. I often watch the rapport people strike up by asking one another various things. I watch three young travellers, one is Far Eastern, two are Americans. The American woman asks the man from the Far East,

'What were your most interesting travelling experiences?'

'Hamma.'

'Hamma?'

'Hamma in Turkey.'

'Oh, Hammam in Turkey.'

'Yes, and Port Rush.'

'Port Rush?'

'Port Rush!'

'But it's cold there.'

'Yes, but I liked it.'

And sitting with them, visible to them, and yet not in their vision somehow, I thought Port Rush was one of my favourite places. I made a trip to this place in 1997, quite by touristy chance, in Northern Ireland, and on those windy cliffs I happened to coincidentally meet, an old lady who knew Abhishiktananda, one of the French devotees of Henry Le Saux. I do not know many people who have been to The Gaint's Causeway (Visvanathan 1998).

It's a 'floating population', as Mahalakshmi Suryanandan says, of the crowds in Tiruvannamalai. She and her husband have been living here for a decade. They are one of the first families, since Mahalakshmi's father was K. Swaminathan, the Gandhian, who was one of the most renowned of the devotees. They stay in a lovely house overlooking the mountain, and very often Mahalakshmi comes to sing at the asramam. She has composed 108 songs in praise of Bhagavan which have also been sung and recorded. The songs composed by Maggie, as she is known to friends, have been published as a book designed by one of Chennai's most well-known illustrators. On 3 May 2006, Mahalakshmi and a dozen women, including the president's wife Sushila sang the songs dedicated to Ramana. There was something beautiful about them, simple and exquisite in their melody. Mahalakshmi's husband was present, as was Captain Narayanan, but it was essentially a women's gathering. One of the singers has composed a song in honour of Shankaracharya. It is about the grandness of the Kanchipuram mutt, which the song says will outlast the threat of scandal. She says she prays everyday for the Shankaracharya who have been facing court cases for crimes ranging from allegations to scandal to murder. The singer is a gentle old woman who spends a lot of time composing songs sitting in her room while sewing or listening to the radio.

My friend Kanaka, whom I met at tea time, has been visiting the asramam for some years now, her husband is a devotee at Thirupati, but this time he accompanied her to Ramanasramam. Previously, she had been coming alone to Tiruvannamalai since 1996. I did not ask her why, since she was asking me all the questions. Later in the evening, her husband spoke to me. He is in his late seventies and very badly crippled. He stays in the room most of the time – a man with a majestic face. He tells me that he is a retired squadron leader from the Indian Air Force, and that he has been a Himalayan Mountain Climber. He narrates a riveting incident about an expedition which he led during which he and seven others were climbing. They hung from a rope for two hours; the seven men, connected to him by rope hung over a ravine. He said Vishnu appeared and opened a little ledge. 'But I survived all that. In the end the bathroom got me! I fell once, broke my hip. Then some years later, I fell in the bathroom and broke my other hip. I have implants in both my thighs.' Worse was to follow. In 1996, his son who was also in the Air Force took a posting close to his parents in order to help them after the fractures. But returning from his sister's wedding he was killed. For the first few years his wife fainted a lot, then slowly, she began to recover. He begged me not to tell her that he had told me, and asked me to go to Skandasramam with her, since he was unable to move. She was so devoted to his well being, that she had declined both Neeraj's offer and mine made previously to circumambulate the hill with her, saying that she preferred to accompany her husband by auto.

So she and I go up the hill to Skandasramam. There is something robust and child-like and vulnerable about her, and everything pleases her, the fragrance of the grass and blueness of the sky. She plucks some grass for me and says, 'Smell it and see!' It has a wonderful fragrance. 'This is what they put in Liril soap,' she says. It is very early and the climb is pleasant. Skandasramam is always peaceful – a gentle easy peace – difficult to describe, a harmoniousness of mother and son. The jackfruit on the trees hang heavy, and it's always very green and beautiful. The swami who looks after it has planted a lot more trees at the entrance, since I last visited. The mountain water gushes through a tap and can be collected for drinking. Shravana, my young guide from several years ago is waiting to take new visitors to the Virupaksha cave. He looks much healthier and is taller now. He has pulled out a water lily from somewhere, and after slitting the long stalk, had made a complicated pattern with it. He then offers it to the swami to gift to Ramana, and the swami hangs it carefully over a large smiling portrait.

On the way, the stone carver sells me a little round ornamented carved stone box. When I open it, there is a spider. I throw it out, and it flings a single line of silk, which the carver laughs and catches.

We go down to Virupaksha. This is a very still place. Ramana lived there for seventeen years. It has a male sense about it, which is completely muted in Skandasramam. I have sat in the meditation cave, which is circular, pitch dark and hot, for exactly three minutes during each visit, while practiced meditators sit there for long hours. I leap up, I knock my head, as I have so often, since the roof of the cave is so low, and then sit in the room where Ramana often sat while speaking to his visitors, which often included children. That room is bright and sunny and the floor is painted with wonderful geometric designs.

In the afternoon, the sun catches me as we are descending, I developed an ear splitting headache. During tea-time people sit in circles and chat desultorily or singly and in silence. Queues are formed during all times, and the workers are most visible at tea-time. Like in any other institution, gossip and ridicule are the most potent weapons against the assertion of self-willed behaviour. The tea, however, is hot and sweet boiled tea, railway station tea, but very satisfying – the goodness of the asramam cows milk is always a mnemonic to Ramana's love for them.

My headache is no better. I have to accept this as a symptom of my condition, heat metabolises the agents of multiple sclerosis. I might as well accept this and get on with life. On days which are hot and dangerous, I hide behind Swami Niranajana's memorial. It is in Bhagavan's garden.

Swami Niranjandasa was the brother of Maharshi. Ma Taleyarkhan writes of him,

> Swami Niranjandasa, Sarvadhikari was a great devotee of his Mother. I was told that while dying she requested Bhagavan to look after him and be with him. Later on devotees made him the Manager. Though not at all educated or refined, he was very kindhearted and very hard working. His great pleasure was to feed people. When any visitors came to the asram, the first thing he would do, was give them something to eat and drink. His favourite plantains were hilly three-cornered ones. If he was pleased with you, then he would offer you three corner. If he gave you a round one, then you must know that he was not very pleased with you
>
> Many a time, I used to make his secretary Mouni laugh, when he would offer the round plantain. I would refuse saying, "Why, Swamiji, why? Are you angry with me?" After the Mahasamadhi of Bhagavan this poor man had very hard times. Many devotees were against him and were ready to put the whole family out. Many unpleasant happenings took place. But I had love

> for him, so always stood by him. Anxiety and fright made him very ill. So we removed him to the asram dispensary. First he was very annoyed with me for removing him there. But later on he knew that I was nursing him day and night. Vishwanathswamy and Kittu who is now doing Pooja, we three were attending him. He was so afraid of his life that he would not take medicine or food unless I tasted it. (74)

Ma Taleyarkhan goes on to say that he was nervous whenever she left his side, and he told Taleyarkhan's sister and Chadwick, 'I have looked after hundreds of people. Where are they now? No one is even enquiring about me, except Taleyarkhan – alone.'

She continues:

> Thereupon my sister Mrs Capadia said, "You must bless her", and took me near him. He put his hand on my head and said, "I feel Bhagavan's hand is on your head. Bless you. Forgive me if I have any time hurt you. I never knew that you have a heart of gold. You are proving it in your service to me." I could not control tears pouring down my cheek. I said to Swamiji, "It is better to have one sincere loving friend than many without true feelings. Have no fear, I shall be always near you." His last wish was that I should close his eyes at the last moment. Mr Cohen and I sat by his side till the last, and I am glad I fulfilled my promise to a man who has served the asram with the greatest devotion, love and service. (75)

I have had a headache all afternoon. I could not read, but it was fun watching a clever untamed brown cat (very tiny and not at all sociable) playing marauder among the thick foliage of the lilies. Then there were two squirrels chasing one another in the coconut grove. One went all the way up to the crest of coconuts and the tangle of twigs at the very top. The other suddenly changed the rules of the game, and went hurtling down. Then they tangoed all the way across the wire mesh.

A lone peacock walked a branch of trees. And there was something dramatic and blue that lit up the dark foliage – its long neck, and the other peacocks flashed their circle of feathers over and over again for who ever was watching.

It rained. Fabulous rain. The mountain was misty. I was watching the bubbles float like boats in the puddles. I realize that I'm always happy here. Sometimes hot and bothered, sometimes resistant to the crowds and the routines, so implacable! But always I feel happy and grateful to be among those who are children of Ardhanareeshwara, the conjoined body of *prakriti* and *purusha*, the children of Nature. It was one of the sisters of the asramam president, who had said this to me, 'We are but the children of Nature.'

CONCLUSION

When I first visited 'Thiru', as it is called by frequent visitors to the town, it was a 'small' town. Now it has burgeoned by the influx of pilgrims (5000 visit the temple every day, according to the local chemist who has a shop next to the Arunachala temple) and the numbers multiply geometrically as the years pass. It seems to have become the hub of priestly and commercial activities. Television has contributed much to the missionary appeal of Shaivism. The descriptions of market, temple and pilgrims remain fairly constant in the anthropological literature whether it is Christian, Muslim or Hindu. Religion and commerce, with the possible yeast of politics, makes a town what it is. In Tiruvannamalai, there is faith, but fortunately no communalism.

To me, as a theoretician of dialogue between religions, non-dualism is the answer to varieties of discord which we see as everyday occurrences in a globalized world. Non-dualism is the space in which everyday pluralism surfaces. It is an existential quality, which allows the myriad nature of the world to be ever present. As individuals we enter a space of communitas and this involves both respect and sharing.

On the other hand, technological imperatives (such as the megaphone) can be very rude interruptions in the quiet and sacred spaces that Nature allots us, and which is confirmed by cultural or theological formulae. Tiruvannamalai, eleven years after my first visit in 1996, provides such a sense of shock and rupture. Trucks bringing agricultural produce and other merchandise, buses bringing pilgrims by the hundreds veer through a traditional street with enormous noise in its wake. The gods during carnival time are taken around in tractors which spew the most horrible smoke. The pollution levels, because of diesel and firecrackers during festival occasions have to be seen to be believed. In December 2006, the sound of firecrackers and megaphones disturbed asramites so much, that being present in that hallowed spot seemed to be a mistake. The woman in the room next to mine was a publisher's wife from Germany, who had come to visit Ramanasramam in memory of her husband who had been a devotee of Ramana and whose works on Ramana were well known to the librarian. Yet within three days, in spite of commitment to theology and her nostalgia for her first visit decades before, she left looking for a quieter room. The previous nights neither of us had slept, having been kept awake by a megaphone, where a piping child's voice yelled continuously for hours '*Pathu rua Pathu rua pathu rua!!*' a cry which never stopped. 'What are they saying?' she asked me the next morning, looking haggard. She wanted to know if it was a political speech.

'Ten rupees,' I said. 'It's the cost of a packet of puffed rice and dates which the merchant wanted pilgrims to buy before setting off on the *pradikshanam*'.

On the third night, my patience having worn thin, and fearing a nervous breakdown, I went downstairs at 11 o'clock. The asramam compound was dark and silent, only one pilgrim was returning from the circling of the hill.

'That noise! Can't anyone do anything?'

'What to do?'

I went and accosted the merchant.

'Put that off!'

He nodded smilingly. He had not heard a word of what I had said. His ear was next to the megaphone.

'Is money the only mantra you have?' I yelled.

He still could not hear, and smilingly, serenely pointed me to his assistant who was packing the dates and puffed rice.

'It's illegal to have a megaphone in a residential street. I'll call the police tomorrow.'

The word 'police' seemed to penetrate, and he lowered the volume, so that he could hear me.

'I'm from Delhi, and megaphones are illegal, and you must switch it off!'

He smiled and nodded and agreed. It went off that night, and Beatrice was relieved, 'I was praying and praying that you would go, since you know the language, and could speak to him!' she said in the morning. For her it was a miracle wrought by Ramana Maharshi, that I had gone, coincidentally, just then to bellow at the merchant.

However, the megaphone was on again the next day, and consequently Beatrice found a room far away from the main commercial road on which Ramansramam is now located. From being part of a jungle to a road lined with gem shops, hippy clothes, junk and fast food joints, foreign currency-changing shops, ticket offices, internet cafés; it's a very great change. The rustic road with its local shops of bananas and tea and newspapers has now been replaced by the kitsch and mélange of the post modern and the traditional.

And every day is a festival in this ancient town, because every day is a holy day. Every day brings to pilgrims, honours and rewards, both material and spiritual. And who can be excluded? The numbers only increase. As a result there are problems of discipline and order. Residents of the Ramanasramam are forced to become aggressive bouncers who keep the crowds at bay, using only their eyes, linked arms or speech to keep the crowds from hurting each other or damaging the shrines. Women, who visit Ramanasramam to meditate, say that young men in the crowds swirling outside, during Deepam, the annual core festival of Tiruvannamali, are lascivious and eager, and hands reach out to touch women's bodies. The swirling river of people is charged with emotions which are very mortal.

A great deal of Durkheimian sociology is about the size, density and violence of the city, and how this affects social interaction. At the Ramanasramam, residents are able to cope with the greatness of numbers by coping with their needs pragmatically. 5000 guests a year stay in asramam rooms, according to Dr Murthy who is the keeper of ledgers and keys; he shows me by adding serial numbers in the visitor's book. During festivals and Sundays, day-trippers constantly float in and out, for a brief view of Maharshi's Samadhi and garden. The bookshop remains open all night, and the monks and householders looking after it never sleep, it seems, for the throngs of people are so continuous. The cooks are kept busy without a day's break, and seemingly without any holidays, in the service of Bhagavan. Pilgrims have now started celebrating their personal functions and commemorations of their own birthdays and anniversaries by coming to the asramam and asking for special favourite foods to be cooked. It has the appurtenances now of an industrial kitchen, and in order to cope with the crowds, sometimes the priests help the servers. They have to run with heavy buckets of rice, *sambhar*, vegetables, *rasam*, buttermilk, *payasam*; and an entire convoy of pilgrims, 300-500 people on festival days and on weekends, are fed in twenty minutes, before the 'second batch' is called in. The 'second batch' consists of Ramana office staff and workers, and the atmosphere is easier and colloquial. There is a general camaraderie, food is sometimes short, and buttermilk watery, but the workers eat heartily with conversation and laughter and an unself conscious joy in the everydayness of their routine obligations and duties. While asramam guests are fed on washed banana leaves, workers and residents have stainless steel plates ('ever silver' is the local name for these plates) and only if they are not entirely integrated as wage workers, are they given banana leaf or stitched leaf plates. Service vs. wage work is a very sharp divider. Those who serve in the asramam often come from wealthy households, bringing their capital with them as donations to the asramam.

To have given everything to the asramam is a sign of one's privileged standing. They have left their homes because of being called by Ramana (revelation, dream, prayer, indescribable longing to be near his samadhi) or requested to serve by the trustees. To join the Ramanasramam as a devoted server, one must show a predilection for silence, hard work and self-abnegation. Men, who have families, foreground their asramam duties before conjugal, filial or parental loyalties. Ramana made no distinction between householders and renunciates and the tradition of friendship and solidarity continues. Lay monks may sometimes change orientation and marry, husbands and wives may on the other hand, turn celibate and so on. Tradition and time are interlinked in traditional ways. If a renunciant still feels passion, inflamed by glance or gesture, if a mutual lust still burns between path finders, these are 'skins to be shed'.

Ramana is well known for having said that inhibitions by themselves were hypocritical and he once said, 'It's better to do it, than think about it too much.' Therefore even if passion blows a person apart for a while, 'these are just *vasanas*, fleeting emotions, which should be disregarded while remaining constant to the chosen path.'

C.S. Lewis talks of the common fantasies of the human minds, where god and nature meet.

> That spearhead of the Supernatural which I call my reason links up with all my natural contents – my sensations, emotion and the like – so completely that I call the mixture by the single word "me". Again, there is what I have called the unsymmetrical character of the frontier relationship. Where the physical state of the brain dominated my thinking, it produces only disorder. (Lewis 1984: 35)

What Lewis means is that it is perfectly natural to want, to aspire to cosmic fullness, to say with the psalmist 'In thy presence is the Fullness of God.' Spontaneity, originality and action is what Lewis associates with Nature, Space and Time which lie beyond the individual, everything is interconnected, thus the denial of free will is a corollary because 'a total series of events' provide symmetry to the Universe. We are thus only part and parcel of Nature. Even our atomization is part of a myriad of such episodes. Naturalism thus, for Lewis is democratic in its aspect. '... for the naturalist one thing is as good as another, in the sense that they are all equally dependent on the total system of things. Indeed each of them is only the way in which the character of the total system exhibits itself at a particular point in space and time' (Lewis 1984: 11). Non-dualism has place for the super-naturalists who believe in a point of origin, of departure, of existence from which all things proceed. For the super-naturalist who is monarchical in his disposition, 'The one basic Thing has caused all the other things to be. It exists on its own – they exist because it exists. They will cease to exist if it ever ceases to maintain them in existence; they will be altered if it ever alters them' (11). The paradox of hierarchy between the mountain and the manifestations is a literary one. In non-dualism there are no good or bad thoughts, only thoughts. There are no good or terrible events, only events. The *sadhaka* attempts to attain the light which is beyond all thoughts, all events. These are people who are permitted to renounce the world and so become its ornaments. Some find it as *karma-yogis* transcending therefore the dualism of thought and action.

For a sociologist, what is not difficult to imagine are the routines and the symmetry arising from these. The everyday tasks are set out and are immediately comprehensible. Times of meditation, community prayer, chanting, meals, work, social interaction and silence, all of these are exact. Yet the clock time of the factory does not approximate the rhythm of asramam life. As numbers increase, there is a strain to conform to the ethos of service and the velocity of demands. Each visitor feels he or she is unique, looks forward to comfort, quiet and aesthetic pleasure. Learning the roots of detachment is linked to various other tasks which include conformity to the values of the asramam – the penultimate rules are silence, meditation and work. Ramana Maharshi never believed that idleness was the path to spiritual experience. Meditation was a part of everyday life, and while some were set apart for this, the risks were always elaborated. 'Discount all visions as distractions' was Maharshi's primary advice to novitiates to continued meditation. These were in fact seen to be 'disturbances'. There is no reason for those of us who have particularly stress full lives, in war torn cities, to believe that meditation will not lead to calm lives, and the ability to carry out our duties whatever these are.

Those who are familiar with the annual ritual of Arunachala, the lighting of the *deepam*, will find in C.S. Lewis' poem published as frontispiece in his book *Miracles* (1984) some archetypical allusions.

Among the hills a meteorite
Lies huge, and moss has overgrown
And wind and rain with touches light
Made soft, the contours of the stone…

Nor is it strange these wanderers
Find in her lap their fitting place…

All that is Earth has once been sky
Down from the sun of old she came,
Or from some star that travelled by
Too close to his entangling flame…

Maharshi always said of Nature that manifested or unmanifested, we as human beings, shared in the essence of the largeness of its existence. Much of how we read Nature is in the animistic terms of poetry and love. Durkheim read this in the metaphors of power magnetism, current, force, all of which he saw as common to religion, magic and science. In the post-modern world, the boundaries between these are again blurred.

To understand Nature in terms of the mystery is part of the quest for solitude whether it is in religion or science. Love is part of this quest. Thomas Merton writes, 'Identification by love leads to knowledge, recognition, intimate and obscure but vested with an inexpressible certainty known only in contemplation' (Merton 1975: 68).

This search for solitude is represented in the unity of the self.

> To love solitude and to seek it does not mean constantly travelling from one geographical possibility to another. A man becomes a solitary at the moment when, no matter what may be his external surrounding, he is suddenly aware of his own inalienable solitude, and sees that he will never be anything but solitary. From that moment, solitude is not potential – it is actual. (79)

He goes on to say that a 'merely subjective and inward solitude, the fruit of an effort at interiorization' would not be enough. It has to be a 'communion in something greater than the world as great as Being itself, in order that in its deep peace we may find God' (83).

While writing his many books, Thomas Merton recognizes, as asramites do, that words are an obstacle. 'We put words between ourselves and things' (83):

> The solitary life, being silent, clears away the smoke screen of words that man has laid down between his mind and things. In solitude we remain face to face with the naked being of things. And yet we find that the nakedness of reality which we have feared is neither a matter for terror nor for shame. It is clothed in the friendly communion of silence, and this silence is related to love. The world our words have attempted to classify to control and even to despise (because they could not contain it) comes close to us, for silence teaches us to know reality by respecting it where words have defiled it. (83, 84)

In silence, it is a larger reality that confronts us, which words cannot encompass. For Merton, work and creation is unity, bringing about a total peace.

> Now contemplation no longer needs to be a special "state" that removes one from the ordinary things going around for God penetrates all. One does not have to think of giving an account of oneself to anyone but Him. (85)

This silence is not absolute or final. It requires 'a continual crying in the night, a repeated bending over the abyss.' It is according to Merton a continual searching for god.

Merton cautions against the loudness or our entreaties which is 'an emotional noise.' Pride he says counterfeits god, for,

> Pride imitates the silence of God, it is a forced immobility. The silence of pride is the silence of death. Pride is afraid to go out of itself, for fear of losing what it has produced with itself. (87)

Sometimes the egoism of the self imposes silences on everyone, so that the sole voice may be heard. When there is no focus on being alone, but solitude is seen as a continuous state, it does not interrupt work.

'The solitary is necessarily a man who does what he wants to do. In fact he has nothing else to do. That is why his vocation is both dangerous and despised' (104). He compares the two predominant and oppositional loves that exist, the carnal and the spiritual, by saying that the first is the 'darkness and peace of the flesh' (112), while the other is found only by the path of our spiritual activity. For Ramana Maharshi, the holy sage of Tiruvannamalai, this opposition is dualism, and that is why the Ardhanareeshwara form as Arunachala becomes the site of abstract and mystical poetry.

But Merton recognizes that the true solitary is one who seeks, and would presume any attempt to distract him or her from this path as futile.

And yet, when we create the material conditions of that solitude, we stand the chance of losing it.

One of the problems of populism is the ability of people to believe that the space they occupy belongs to them. Much of the questions raised by social anthropology is about how we look at trusteeship. The definitive nature of the organization of space is a legal question, which is in the purview of the forest department, the archaeological survey, municipal offices and so on.

How the increased number of pilgrims affects the town has already been mentioned. In the asramam, monastic life is continually under threat. Dr Murthy tells me he keeps out people with money who want to use the asramam as a holiday resort, people who are eager to meet friends and relatives for festive occasions like New Year. This is complicated by the fact that each language group has a New Year quite different from others, complicating festive and ritual life ... 30 per cent of asramam visitors are, for instance, Telugus who have now built their own imposing guest house, just across the road, facing Arunachala, since asramam cannot accommodate their number and the frequency of their visits and their desire for a long duration.

Thomas Merton writes that we must be careful not to reduce monasteries to a 'purely common-sense machinery of rules and official decisions in which there are only token sacrifices and formal worship, and in which there is no longer anything predictable except the day-to-day detail of trivial and absolutely necessary frustration.' While being concerned with every one's problems, the trustees are careful to keep at bay those sentiments which destroy discipline, specifically adulation and other forms of gluttony.

There is the excerpt in Merton's work from the writing of Barry McLaughlin,

> Yet one of the surest signs of the resolution of the identity crisis is an increased capacity for being alive, for being responsible for oneself. The gradual process that will end in perfect identity involves an awareness of the fact that there are decisions in life and aspects of life's struggle that a person must face alone ... And as a person in this formative isolation becomes more able to appreciate the moods and feelings of others, he also becomes more able to have meaningful relationships with them. (Mclaughlin cited in Merton 1980: 42)

'Togetherness' and 'Herdism', according to Merton is not what community is about. To love, one must respect the other; one must comprehend the need for solitude. To incorporate, to merge, to present the ideas of 'family' 'brethren' or 'community' as ways to integrate the solitary who has his/her own path, is a common method.

Yet Merton has a fear of those who take to monasteries the 'emptiness and angst' of depersonalization and angst. There can be politics, tension, marginalization. He says,

> I would like to suggest one area where we can hope for good results and that is monastic's work. Work that is productive, purely organized, and remains in contact with nature, work that is truly physical and manual, out door work, work that is properly learned and well done, work that is managed and taught on a human and monastic level, and not carried out like factory type drudgery or office routines – such work can do much to help.

Merton contrasts what he calls normal life with the life of solitude. 'Normal' life is about comfort, reassurance and diversion.

> If we fulfill the role imposed on us by others, we will be rewarded by approval. These roles impose definite limitations, but in return for accepting the limitations we enjoy the consolations of companionship, of understanding support and so on. We are made to feel that 'we belong' and are therefore 'all right.' What the seeker of solitude does is to renounce these; the monk is some one who wanted to look for something else. (Merton 1982: 100)

The comfort and joy of married life, conversations and friendship with others, a place in the city and commerce all these are given up.

> The monk is a man who in one way or other pushes to the very frontier of human experience and strives to go beyond, to find out what transcends the ordinary life of existence. (101)

Aware that man is somehow sustained by a deep mystery of silence, of incomprehensibility of god's will and god's love – the monk feels that he is personally called to live in more intimate communication with that mystery. And he also feels that if he does not respond to this summons, he cannot be happy, because he cannot be fully happy with himself (101). It is this, which Ramana Maharshi called *sahaja*, whether for the monastic or the householder, and where I would conclude with Merton that detachment is the lot of the social scientist as much as the mystic, and that we must be careful that our techniques do not lock us in (103).

The world is a complex web of loves, hates, joys, greed and hope and we traverse it in our different ways, always hoping for that reconciliation which will allow the earth to prosper. It is in this context that I raise the problem of the court case which pertains to the greening of Arunachala. I place it in the conclusion, for purpose of record, for the battle to protect the holy hill has been in the forefront of many devotees lives.

Environmental Concerns and the Courts

The case is known in the Supreme Court of India, as the '*Civil Appellate Jurisdiction, Nos. 12443-47*' and it arose out of the final judgement and order, dated 11.5.2001, passed by the High Court of Judicature at Madras in writ petition no. 17109/97, 7396, 7397, 7398 and 7400 of 1998.

The petitioner was the commissioner, Tiruvannamalai municipality and the respondents were Arunachala Giri Pradaksina Samithi and others.

The case in the Madras High Court centres around the fact that the government of Tamil Nadu had provided guidelines for the preservation and maintenance and development of 38 temple towns, by G.O. Ms No. 163, Rural Development and Local Administration dated 6.7.93.

In 1997, writ petitions under Article 226 of the Constitution of India were filed before the High Court of Judicature at Madras, by the respondents as a public interest litigation (PIL). 'It was alleged that the public in general and the followers of Lord Arunachala and innumerable persons who go around the hill found that there are encroachments, unauthorized constructions, deviations, illegal felling of trees, destruction and devastation of water tanks. Caves, temples, asrams and other religious places in the Hill Arunachala, and in the holy town of Tiruvannamalai, and the monuments have to be protected, by removing the encroachment, by restricting and regulating the constructions. It is submitted that the entire Holy Pathway and Holy Hill be protected, and requests various reliefs/directions against the petitioner and various public authorities'.

In March 1999, the municipal commissioner argued that there was a bias in the manner of description. 'It was submitted that the first respondent has invented the Holy Pathway and the Holy Hill Arunachala afresh without any basis or record. It was submitted that the petitioner as a civic body is taking action to control development.' The petitioner argued that there were no temple encroachments at Arunachaleswara temple except the shops which were permitted by the temple authorities. The other petitioners against the Arunachala Giri Pradikshina society and others were the Aathaiandal Village Panchayat, Adi Annamalai Panchayat, and Adaiyur Village Panchayat; the Hindu Religious and Charitable Endowment also filed its oppositions against the respondent.

In May 1999, the High Court appointed an expert body to provide a report to the court, with suggestions regarding maintenance, and preservation, of the heritage town of Tiruvannamalai specific attention on the pathway around the hill. T.S. Arunachalam, acting chief justice of the High Court Judicature at Madras, was appointed as chairman of the body. Justice Arunachalam was to be assisted by the district collector, who was to be the secretary of the expert body, and also by an architect, an IAS officer, an archaeologist, by conservator of forests, by secretary to government, municipal administration and water supply department, by the PA to the district collector, by the director of town and country planning, by the director of municipal administration, by the executive officer and joint commissioner of Annamalaiar temple, the municipal commissioner, the executive officers, presidents of village panchayats of Anapuandan, Aathaiandal, Adi Annamalai, Vengikul and Adaiyur. Also by the executive engineer, Tiruvannamalai, Annamalai Reforestation Society, executive engineer State Agricultural Engineering Department, district revenue officer, revenue divisional officer, deputy commissioner, HR and CE, engineers with highways and rural works having jurisdiction along the Srepradakshina Salai and the surrounding regional transport officer.

There were in the expert committee representatives of important asramams, such as one representative each of Yogi Ramsurat Kumar, Ramana Maharshi, Seshadri Swamigal and Gowthana Ashram. Three prominent public persons, who had an interest in conservation and maintenance, would be nominated by the expert body.

The records of the case describe the consequence of setting up the expert body thus:

> 8.12.1999. The expert body exceeded its scope and gave its report to the High Court and suggested that a single authority should be created, which should have power to implement the plan not only in Thiruvannamalai town, but in all other Panchayats falling within the limits of the master plan on the lines of the Chennai Metropolitan Development Authority. A District Heritage Conservation Act (Bill) to ensure protection and restoration of all heritage buildings, precincts and areas, until the Bill becomes an Act. The Town Planning Authority will act on the basis of recommendations of the District Heritage Conservation Committee, in all matters relating to heritage. A Heritage Conservation Fund for financing projects identified by the District Heritage Conservating Committee has to be set up and the Committee can decide what will be the sources of this inflow for this fund. The Expert Body suggested in all 29 suggestions. In all it suggested changes in existing building rules, provision of some basic infrastructure.
>
> 29.2.2000. The Report of the Expert Body was placed before the petitioner Council pursuant to the order passed by the Hon'ble High Court.
>
> 2.5. 2001. The Government of Tamil Nadu filed its objection to the draft scheme stating that the present scheme is against the Constitution of India. It tries to set up an executive authority endowed with enormous powers and which encroaches into the powers and responsibilities of the Constitutional Body. On the whole, the scheme appears to allocate all land use, water and sanitation functions to the committee. As per the XII schedule of the Constitution of India, these are functions of Municipalities and they cannot be transferred to a Committee, which has nominated members only. The scheme is both impractical and unnecessary to expect all Departments of Government to function under the directions of this Committee. The Committee cannot be allowed to function as an organisation which is beyond existing legislation and deemed to function like a super power.

Clearly, there is a substantial shift in this note, from a position reached in the Madras High Court where respondent and petitioners accepted that they had interests in common, which was the protection and maintenance of a holy town. Here questions of authority and hierarchy are being raised, and while the expert body consisted of members who were specialists in their field, belonging to the government, both state and central, along with townspeople, and asramam delegates, the actual praxis of power is the problem now. Can the offices of government be supervised and directed by a committee proposed by the judiciary? The opposition to the committee is put forward very sharply in the court record:

> 30.3.2001. The petitioner Municipality filed an affidavit stating that the proposed scheme authorizing so much power to such committees will make serious inroads into the powers of the Municipal Council and the local authorities. The Committees proposed are contrary to the provisions of the Tamil Nadu District Municipalities Act, 1920 and these Committees will run parallel to the Municipal Council and the same is against the provision of Article 243 of the Constitution of India.

The assumption that the municipality makes as petitioner is that the High Court has exceeded its jurisdictions and taken on a privilege that is associated with executive, legislature and judiciary.

Interestingly, the court proceedings in the High Court of Judicature at Madras, on Friday, 11 May 2001, has a preface: Order passed by Justice Jagadeesan, Hon. Justice E. Padmanabhan states,

> The Law in the past was directed unconsciously and it should now be directed consciously, to the same end as custom, manners, religion and other types of social control, namely with the preservation, furtherance and transmission of civilization.

It is this conflict between governance by judiciary and governance by state institution that sets up dialectic. Public interest litigation, according to one of the lawyers who fought the case for Arunachala Pradakshina Samiti, is always vulnerable at a time when individuals may have honourable intentions, but not the staying power to keep with a case till the end.

Since it was a matter of encroachment and over-build, all those who had a commercial interest in construction became offensive, and

Ramanasramam was visited by a large number of individuals, saying they were townspeople, and if asramam did not withdraw its case, there would be trouble. According to Apeetha Arunagiri it was very frightening for residents. I quote from one of her letters to me:

> A recent move on the part of devotees to the mountain to seek legal protection for the sacred mountain has recently failed entirely in the Supreme Court, paving the way for the building of hotels and tourist facilities on private lands adjacent to the mountains. Someone said the opposition of the town was so tremendous, that the ASI did a deal with them: they would stand back if the Municipal Council started to keep the town clean.

The real question was of livelihood, and if the pristine quality of conservation was to be put into institutional space and it's guardianship assured, then a great deal of how people actually made a living from the merchandise of objects, for sale to pilgrims would decline. On one of my visits to Tiruvannamalai, in April 2007, I visited the house of a child who wished to try out her English language skills with me. She excitedly called out to her friends that I was a teacher, and the whole platoon followed me. She filled my water bottle from the *koddam*, kept in a very clean kitchen. The whole house had been renovated, for it was previously a hovel. It was now tiled and cemented and whitewashed. I asked her ancient grandmother where they got the money from.

'Bank loan!'

'How do you earn?' She said, 'From selling things to visitors.' Curiously, the petitioner in the Supreme Court, the municipal commissioner, argues that pilgrimage cannot be confused with tourism, and that Tiruvannamalai is a sacred town, where the livelihood of people is at stake. He describes archaeological survey operatives, or tourism development 'intrusion', as having to do with visitors who are not pilgrims. That is not his concern. He also provides the Supreme Court with photographs of a Tiruvannamalai at the time of day, when there are few people on the street, and the roads cleared of garbage, to show how well the municipality deals with crowds and refuse!

In the Madras High Court, the municipality had stated that,

> It was bound to grant permission for the construction under the provisions of the Tamil Nadu District Municipalities Act, 1920 and the rules framed

> thereunder. There is no authority whatsoever to prevent the construction on private lands adjoining the Giripradakshina pathway and beyond the 50 metres of Giripradakshina pathway and also there is no authority to limit the height of construction not exceeding 6 metres either adjoining the Giripradakshina pathway or in the remaining portion of the path and up to 50 metres beyond the Giripradakshina pathway against the principles contained in the Heritage Act and the guidelines issued thereunder in G. O.Ms no 22. MAWS Department dated 30.1.1997.

The municipality argued that the shops are permitted by temple authorities, and that the municipality is discharging its duties.

The honourable judges wrote,

> Admitted Facts and stand of petitioners and respondents.
>
> On the facts of the case it is clear that there is no controversy; besides it is almost admitted by every one, including the respondents, about the existence of the Holy Hill Arunachala, which has been personified as Lord Shiva, and the existence of Giripradakshina Path, over which millions go around the Holy Hill, commencing from sixteen pillar mandapam of the eastern entrance of the temple, and ending with the very same sixteen pillar mandapam. Every one concerned whole heartedly supported and expressed that either the State or Central Authorities should step in to regulate the entire area, remove the encroachments, regulate the construction of buildings so that visibility of the Holy Hill is not affected, when it is viewed from any corner of the Giripradakshina path, besides the requirement of the necessary basic amenities or facilities to pilgrims and the villages and the residents who reside on either side of the Giripradakshina path as well as the Tiruvannamalai Municipal limits. Every one anxiously expressed that the entire pathway should be maintained free from all encroachments whatsoever, and all the obstructions and encroachments between the pathway and the Holy Hill have to be removed, and regulations have to be brought in with respect to the height of the building or location of the buildings, and as to the using of the space and leaving of vacant place abutting the Giripradakshina path on both sides, and with respect to various measures to be taken in this respect to preserve the Holiness and sanctity of the Holy Hill Arunachala.

The honourable judges asked the state government to follow up the consensus reached by both parties that the holy hill needed protection.

During the entire hearing, everyone has supported the move, but only had different views as to the steps to be taken, or extent to which restrictions are to be imposed, and with respect to the details of restriction to be imposed and the regulations to be followed. In fact we called upon the learned Additional Advocate General, to get instructions as to whether the State Government is in a position to take up immediate legislation for the area in question which would give quietus to all the issues. But the learned Additional Advocate General on instructions expressed the State government's inability to bring forth a comprehensive legislation and the response of the State government, so to say, is not only lukewarm but it has failed to comprehend the problem and it had failed to respond.

(From file titled, Supreme Court Of India, Civil Appellate Jurisdiction, Nos. 12443-47 Commissioner Tiruvannamalai vs Arunachal Giri Pradakshina Samithi and ORS)

The judgement continues,

However in principle though the state govt. agrees they are not willing to take up the appropriate legislation, and time granted in this respect also had not elicited any response. In the light of the said background this Court on 4.5.1999 passed a detailed order with the consent of the petitioners as well as all the respondents and every one concerned. The said direction is a consent direct as everyone agreed that Giripradakshina running to the length of 16 kms. or thereabout from Anmanalaiyur Temple proceeding along with Tiruvoodal Street, Sengam Road, Pei Gopura Street, and Soma Vara Kula Street etc, and ending at the same starting point of Annamalayar Temple has to be cleared from all encroachments and unauthorized constructions and a comprehensive scheme has to be framed for the area and Giripradakshina Salai in the larger interest of the public as well as in the interest of residents of Tiruvannamalai Town as well as Villages in and around the Hill. (42)

The judges reiterate that both parties are agreed on the sanctity of the hill. This very sanctity will be disrupted by unregulated construction, haphazard and a health risk to all. They note that,

Mr Sriram Panchu, Senior Counsel appearing for one of the writ petitioners persuaded this Court to frame a scheme so that the entire locality could be protected not only from encroachment, unauthorized construction,

> deviations, but also the cleanness of the town and environment could be saved from further deterioration. (42)

In furtherance of the objectives resolved in consensus, the honourable judges, requested a study of Tiruvannamalai which would be presented by the expert body. One of the recommendations was certainly forbidding megaphones in public places! The judges did see that the townspeople would have to make sacrifices for the greater good (78).

The Arunachalam Committee gave an extremely detailed report, and as a momento to town planning, it is a valuable record for urban historians and sociologists. The Tiruvannamalai municipality reacted sharply. The court records state:

> In fact the counsel on record for Tiruvannamalai Municipality attended all the hearings but did not object to the proposal to frame a scheme. The counsel for Municipality, the State, the Centre were called upon to get instruction from the respective authorities, whether they are willing to take comprehensive measures, but all of them despite opportunity failed to avail the opportunity, which would exhibit their failure to discharge the public and statutory functions. Further, all of them also represented that this court may frame appropriate scheme. In the light of the above, we are unable to appreciate or sustain the belated objection raised on behalf of their municipality as if their power or jurisdiction is being reduced. Factually, it is not so as none of the powers of the Municipality as conferred by the District Municipalities Act or the Constitutional provision are being interfered since the provisions of the Scheme is in addition to the statutory provisions. We overrule the objections and herby frame the Scheme appended herewith which shall be implemented by everyone. (79)

When it went to the Supreme Court the municipal commissioner basically communicated that it was not his place to take orders from a parallel body, the expert committee, which presented itself as a super power. The municipality's jurisdiction had been replaced. When the suggestion that the Central government believed that heritage and tourism were important issues, the commissioner made a distinction between tourists and devotees, saying that their needs were different. The violence of the agitators who wished to build guest houses and adjuncts for commercial reasons at Ramanasramam was such that the PIL was withdrawn.

One resident of Ramanasramam told Apeetha Arunagiri and me that, 'At least the municipality did not get to build their offices on the Chengam road, otherwise imagine the bottleneck that would have been created with people from all over the hinterland appearing with their papers, for audience with the commissioner, and jostling with pilgrims on this narrow road!'

What is interesting for me, as a reader of these court records, is how much of faith is captured even with in the secular jurisdiction of the Indian courts. The litigants, lawyers and judges also accept the sacred manifestation of the divine, and the right of the people to worship and live in a territory which is infused by the heady sense of both love and Maya. But the debates around globalization, modernization, small town ethos and urban resilience in the face of dramatic changes have to be negotiated with. World Heritage status, for one of the most ancient pilgrim centres, where nature and culture are intertwined inseparably, is the only possible way of escaping an untrammeled situation of crowds and encroachments. Tourism, pilgrimage and globalization are the keywords for understanding many such centres, and we need to focus on the problems that they set up for town and country relations, for landscaping, merchandise, town control and the loss of ecologically sustainable lands and forests.

INDEX

1000-pillar hall of Patala lingam, 200, 201
  muhurtham of, 203-204
  renovation of, 201-202
Abbott, Andrew, 42, 47, 49
  Time Matters: On Theory and Method, 42, 47
Aesthetics of silence, 117-118
Aiyer, N.R. Krishnamurti, 173, 174
Aiyer, Ranga, 173, 174
Alagamma, 23, 33-35, 97, 143, 144, 181, 214, 217, 218
  death of, 33, 34, 149
  as Mother Goddess, 218
  return to Tiruvannamalai, 34
  shrine of, 180, 181
  spirit of cooking, 143, 144
Ammal, Meenakshi, 130, 131
Andreas-Salome, Lou, 81
Anuradha, 15
Arunagiri, Apeetha, 176-179, 186, 187, 240, 244
Apology to Hornets, 168
Appachi Mama, 185
Aradhana Day, 83, 218
Archaelogical Survey of India, 54
Arendt, Hannah, 85
Aron, Raymond, 43
Arunachala, 15, 16, 19, 21, 23, 26, 27, 37, 40, 44, 46, 54, 55, 58, 62, 64, 67, 78, 79, 84, 88, 91, 95, 97, 101, 103, 104, 108, 111, 116, 121, 128, 136, 141, 146, 149, 166, 167, 176-179, 181, 186, 188, 195, 200-203, 209, 213, 216, 227, 232, 234, 236, 237, 240-243
  epitome of Shiva and Parvati, 22, 54, 108, 143, 177, 241
  greening of, 178, 179, 236
  court case against, 236-238
  lighting of fire at, 54-55
  pradikshanam of, 56-57, 192-195, 220, 228
  problem of encroachment at, 238-244
  visit to, 13
Arunachala Giri Pradakshina Samithi, 236, 237
Arunachal Kadu Siva Plantation, 177-179
  social ecological import of, 178-179
Arunachala Puranam of Tiruvannamalai
  Directives for worshipper, 209
Arunachalam, T.S., 237
Arundale, George, 133
Auden, W.H., 38
  A Certain World, 38
Aurelius, Marcus, 42
Ayyar, Sundaram, 23, 24

Bachelard, Gaston, 142-145
Baeumer, Bettina, 12, 68
Bakhtin, Mikhail, 37, 57, 195
Barthes, Roland, 44, 67
  Image Music Text, 67
Bateson, Gregory, 122
  Steps to an Ecology of Mind, 122
Bell, Daniel, 37
Benedict, Ruth, 206, 207, 210
  Patterns of Culture, 206
Blackburn, Stuart, 128
Blacking, John, 85
  Towards an Anthropology of the Body, 85
Blanchot, Marc, 41
Bonaparte, Marie, 81
Bosco, Henri, 143, 144

Le jardin d'Hyacinthe, 143
Bose, Chandan, 108
Bose, Monica, 132, 136, 137
The Hill of Fire, 133, 134
Bresson, Cartier, 95, 97
Brodsky, Joseph, 42, 142
Brunton, Paul, 19, 62, 170
description of Maharshi's darshan, 62-63
A Search In Secret India, 62

Captain Narayanan, 33, 54, 65, 176, 186, 187, 222
Carrol, Noel, 39-40
Carstairs, Morris, 206
Chadwick (Sadhu Arunachala), 20, 101, 106, 180-182, 185, 191, 194, 208, 211, 212, 225
first meeting with Bhagavan, 211-212
A Sadhu Reminiscences of Ramana Maharshi, 180
vision of Jesus Christ, 181, 212
Chandramouli (Dr), 193
Chatterjee, Dharma, 138
Chellam, 182-183
Chinnaswami, 60, 61, 193
The Christians of Kerala, 19, 67, 132, 168
Civil Appellate Jurisdiction, Nos. 12443-47, 236, 242
Clifford, James, 42, 44
Code, Lorraine, 22
What Can She Know?, 22
Cohen, 77, 189, 225
Comparative religions, 159
Concept of Eros, Thanatos and Ananke, 78, 81, 219

Dakshinamurthy, 58
Davis, Natalie Zemon, 128
Davis, Richard, 40
Death instinct, 78-80
Deepam festival, 58, 65, 160, 229, 232
Devi, Rukmini, 133
Diehl, Carl Gustav, 209
Dube, Leela, 13, 14
Dube, S.C., 13, 14
Duncan, Robert, 88
Roots and Branches, 88
Durkheim, Emile, 26, 36, 37, 41, 48, 65, 132, 232
Elementary Forms of the Religious Life, 26
Durkheimian sociologist, 87, 158, 161, 229

Echammal, 34, 35
Eck, Diana, 37

Fanon, Frantz, 195
Wretched of the Earth, 195
Fitzgerald, Paula, 107
Frake, Charles, 86, 87
Freud, Sigmund, 77-80
Friendship, Interiority and Mysticism, 21, 39

Ganapati Muni, 34, 174
Gandhi, Indira, 90
Gandhi, Indu, 90
Gandhi, Mahatma, 73, 121, 137, 138, 205, 207, 222
Geertz, Clifford, 159
Godman, David, 31, 98, 164, 173, 176, 213
The Power of the Presence: Transforming Encounters with Ramana Maharshi, 173, 213
Goodwin, Barbara, 63, 208
Social Science and Utopia, 208
Grover, Chandrika, 170

Hampshire, Stuart, 157-158
Havel, Vaclav, 89
Heyrdahl, Thor, 55
Kon Tiki, 55
Hocking, William, 41

Indian Institute of Advanced Study, 12, 68
Iyer, Rajagopala, 61
Iyer, T.K. Sundaresa, 181, 182

Jacob, Karen, 41
The Eye's Mind, 41
Jagadeesan (Justice), 239
Jayaraman, J., 55, 103, 104, 169
Jhoola, Laxman, 69, 70
Jinwansaswami, 133
Jung, Carl, 90, 114

Kanaka, 222
Kanakamma, 58, 98, 100, 107, 131, 132, 146, 215
Kanakammal, T.R., 128, 129
Cherished Memories, 128, 215
Kanchipuram mutt, 181, 222
Kandaswami, 35, 128
Kavayakantha Ganapati Muni, 174

Keralaputri, 11
Kosinsky, Jersy, 40
  Being There, 40
Krishnamurti, Jiddu, 133
Krishnan, T.N. (Dr), 204
Krishnaswami, T.N., 77, 164
Kumar, Sarla (Dr), 69
Kunze, Agnes, 68, 69
Kurukshetra Kendra, 68, 69

Lagerkvist, Par, 199
  The Sibyl, 199
Le Saux, Henri (Abhishiktananda), 14, 18, 19, 20, 23, 36, 40, 41, 49, 68, 69, 125, 198, 204, 211, 222
Leclerq, Jean, 40
Lessing, Doris, 69, 70
Letters from Sri Ramanasramam, 60
Levi, Primo, 164
Levi-Strauss, Claude, 52-53, 70, 175
  Tristes Tropiques, 51, 52, 70, 175
Lewis, C.S., 230-232
  Miracles, 232
Low, Barbara, 79

Mackey, Nathaniel, 50, 88
  Discrepant Engagement, 50
Madame Taleyarkhan, 171, 172, 181, 182, 200-202, 204, 211, 212, 224-25
  Sages, Saints and Arunachala Raman, 181
Maffesoli, Michel, 154, 156
Magic Carpet, Crowds and Markets, 52
Mani, V.S., 15-17, 18, 19, 56, 91, 94, 104, 159, 195, 196, 198, 221
Mann, Thomas, 45, 127
  Magic Mountain, 44, 127
Mannheim, Karl, 200, 206
Marin, Louis, 88, 89
Matthiesen, Peter, 100
Maugham, Somerset, 106-107
  Razor's Edge, 107
  visit to Ashram, 106
Mauss, Marcel, 34, 46, 52, 117
  Sociology and Psychology, 117
Mayo, Katharine, 51, 108
Mazet, Joelle, 98, 137, 148, 153
McFarlane, Shailja, 119, 120
McLaughlin, Barry, 235
Merton, Thomas, 232-236
Mill, C. Wright, 50
Mirchandani, Bharati, 21, 95, 105, 205, 219
Modern rights theory, 89
Mouni Sadhu, 28, 162, 163, 170, 172
  In *Days of Great Peace*, 172
Mudaliar, Devaraja, 24, 35, 60, 77, 128, 171, 172, 193
  Day by Day with Bhagavan, 35, 168, 172
  Gems from Bhagavan and Recollections of Bhagavan, 172
Mudaliar, Guruswami (Dr), 74
Murgunar, 74, 129-132, 141, 167, 215
  friendship with Ramana, 129
  Sri Ramana Sannidhi Murai, 130
Murthy (Dr), 94, 95, 107, 111, 112, 150, 151, 198, 218, 229, 234

Nagamma, Suri, 46, 50, 58-61, 72-76, 163, 164, 167, 169, 193
  My Life at Ramanasramam, 59
Nambiar, K.K., 104
Natarajan, A.R., 112, 113, 168, 171
  Timeless in Time, 113
Natesan, K, 138
  Kavya Ganapathi, 138
Nathakiamma, 182-184, 201
Navalar, Saiva Ellapa, 16
Niranjanananda (Swami), 218, 224
Nirvana principle, 79-80
Non-dualism, 23, 79, 89, 129, 132, 158, 172, 227, 231
Noye, Eleanor, 171

Obligatory mutualism, 159
Ojha, Catherine Clementin, 200
Orpheus' Gaze, 41
Osborne, Arthur, 20, 24, 26-29, 30-35, 64, 148, 149, 212
  Ramana Maharshi and the Path of Self Knowledge, 24
  Ramana Sat-Guru, 212
Osho 120, 166
  merchandise of spirituality, 166

Padmanabhan, E. (Justice), 239
Pannikar, Raimundo, 68
  Mantramanjari, 68
Paranjape, Makarand, 63
  Pilgrims and Other Travellers, 63
Pillai, Thanigaimani Sengalvaraaya, 129
Pinney, Christopher, 115
Pleasure principle, 79-80, 176
Pradoshan Puja, 218

Quammen, David, 159-160
Quasim, Mohammad (Prof), 92

Quilkey, Christopher, 76, 148
  The Maha Nirvana, 76

Rainforest Information Centre, Australia, 178
Rajan, N.N., 217
  Suffer Little Children, 217
Ramana Maharshi,
  birth of, 23
  as Brahmana Swami, 28-29
  death experience of, 23, 34
  death by a fatal cancer, 149, 211
  journey to Tiruvannamalai, 25
  last days of, 76-77
  life as Venkatraman, 24-25, 27-28, 30-32
  Mahasamadhi of, 181, 218, 225
  Nakshatram birthday of, 84
  relationship with mother, 149
  struggle with cancer, 70, 72-74
Ramana's Arunachala, 15
Ramanasramam, 15-38, 43, 45, 53, 58, 59, 71, 75, 81, 83, 86, 92, 90, 100, 104, 105, 111, 117, 125, 128, 130, 136-138, 141-143, 146, 152, 158, 161, 168, 170, 175-178, 181, 191, 194, 201, 205, 206, 208, 210, 211, 213, 228-230, 240, 244
  Brahmin imprints of, 208-209
  condition of, 53-54
  crowd in, 222
  decorations at, 154
  history of, 14
  increase in number of devotees at, 227-244
  life at, 115-117
  a metaphor of nature, 142
  Navrathri puja at, 96, 97, 107, 155-156, 174, 186
  publishing history of, 128
  structure of, 14
  visits to, 11-34
Ramanujan, A.K., 56
Ramaswamy, Sethu, 10, 27, 31
  They spoke with God: Saints of Tamilaham, 27
Ramaswamy, Vijaya, 215
  Walking Naked, 215
Rangan, 29, 213-215
Rao, Anantanarayana (Dr), 73
Rao, Prasada (Dr), 91, 92
Rao, Shankar, 72
Rao, Srinivasa, 72
Resnik, Salomon, 71
  The Theatre of the Dream, 71
Ricoer, Paul, 42, 49, 78, 79, 219
  Freud and Philosophy, 219
  History and Truth, 42
  Terry Lectures, 77
Rilke, 145
Rogers, Mary , 67
Rolland, Romain, 80, 205, 207
Rosaldo, Michelle, 153, 197
Rosaldo, Renato, 86, 87, 153, 197
  Culture and Truth, 197

Sack, Oliver, 220
Sadhu Om, 25, 71, 72
  In the Path of Sri Ramana, 25
Said, Edward, 155
Samadhi Day, 81, 196, 220, 221
Samuel, Raphael, 50, 113-114
  Theatres of Memory, 50
Sangam Era, 129
Saran, Shalini, 168, 169
Sastri, Ganapati, 149
Schur, Max (Dr), 79-81
Schusterman, Richard, 39
Search for solitude, 232-234
Sen, Suzanne Curtil (Sujatha), 132-137, 187-189
  life of, 132-136
  in Ramanashramam, 187-189
Serres, Michel, 121-124
  Hermes, 121
Seshadhri Asram, 28, 104
Seshadhri Swami, 28, 29
Seyhan, Azade, 114-115, 117
Shakespeare, 79
Shankaracharya, 222
Shastri, Ajay, 92
Shastri, D.S., 59
Simmel, 156
Skandasram, 33, 101, 102, 119, 124, 128, 151-153, 168, 220, 223, 224
  building of, 128
Snyder, Gary, 63-64, 191
  Passage Through India, 64
Something Barely Remembered, 90, 92
Sontag, Susan, 70, 117-118
  Styles of Radical Will, 117
Soper, Kate, 86
  What is Nature: Culture, Politics and the Non-Human, 86
Sri Chakra Puja, 181-182, 191

Sri Ramana Gita, 174
Srinivasamurthy (Dr), 17, 55, 56, 91, 110, 112, 116, 175
Srinivasan, Ashok, 198
Stills, Judith, 86
Feminine Economics, 86
Stuart, James, 14, 36, 125
Suri, Vinit, 91
Suryanandan, Mahalakshmi (Maggie), 72, 83, 137-141, 222
The Story of Ramana, 138-141
Swaminathan, K., 73, 84, 137-138, 213, 222

Tamil New Year, 77, 196, 218, 220
Tarapore, Sri, 202, 203
The Mountain Path, 54, 56, 77, 88, 102, 104, 120, 168, 191, 195, 212, 216, 217
Theory and Society in India, 21
Theosophical Society, 133, 135, 136
Theravada Buddhism, 133, 134
Tiruchuzhi, 30-31, 138
Tiruvannamalai Greening Society, 179
Tomkins, Silvan, 85
Trikha Inter-Religious Asram, 69

Uhland, 82

Varalakshmi Amma, 96, 102, 103, 185
Vediyappan shrines, 178
Venkataraman, T.N., 205
Virupaksha Cave, 34, 35, 140, 141, 146, 167, 169, 223
Visvanathan, Shiv, 89, 91
Unravelling Rights, 89
Viswanathan, Rajam, 97

Waddel, Helen, 38
The Desert Fathers, 38
Wax civilization, 144
Weber, Max, 43, 85, 86
Weil, Simone, 20, 41, 42, 43, 48-49, 205, 207
Williams, Raymond, 87
Marxism and Literature, 87
Wittkower, Rudolf, 210
Allegory and the Migration of Symbols, 210
Woolf, Virginia, 198

Zachariah, Mathai, 198, 211
Beyond Ecumenism: A Journey into Light, 211
Zimmer, Heinrich, 37

REFERENCES

Abbott, Andrew. *Time Matters: On Theory and Method.* Chicago: University of Chicago Press, 2001.

Aiyer, N.R. Krishamurty, *The Mountain Path*. Vol. 34.

Alder, Monica. 'Suri Nagamma', *The Mountain Path*. Vol. 44, No.2, Aradhana, 2007.

Arunachalam, K. 'The Maharshi and the Mahatma', *The Mountain Path*, Vol. 6, July 1969.

Arunachala, Sadhu (A.W. Chadwick). *Reminiscences of Ramana Maharshi*. Tiruvannamalai: Sri Ramanasramam Trust, 1994.

Auden, W.H. *A Certain World: A Commonplace Book*. London: Faber and Faber, 1971.

Bachelard, Gaston. *The Poetics of Space*. Toronto: The Beacon Press, 1969.

Bateson, Gregory. *Mind and Nature: A Necessary Unity*. Toronto: Bantam Books, 1979.

Bateson, Gregory. *Steps to an Ecology of Mind*. Chicago: University of Chicago Press, 1972.

Bakhtin, Mikhail. *Rabelais and his World*. Cambridge: Massachusetts Institute of Technology Press, 1968.

Barthes, Roland. *Image, Music, Text*. London: Fontana, 1977.

Bauemer, Bettina and John R. Dupuche. *Void and Fullness in the Buddhist, Hindu and Christian Traditions*. Delhi: D.K. Printworld, 2005.

Bauman, Zygmunt. *Liquid Life*. Cambridge: Polity, 2006.

Bell, Daniel. *The Coming of Post-Industrial Society*. New York: Basic Books, 2001.

Blackburn, Stuart. *Print Folklore and Nationalism*. Delhi: Permanent Black, 2003.

Blacking, John. *The Anthropology of the Body*. London: Academic Press, 1976.

Blonsky, Marshall. *On Signs*. Oxford: Basil Blackwell, 1986.

Bourdieu, Pierre. *The Logic of Practice*. Stanford: Stanford University Press, 1990.

– *Photography*. Oxford: Basil Blackwell, 1990.

Bose, Monica. *The Hill of Fire*. Bangkok: Orchid Press, 2002.

Brodsky, Joseph. 'Homage to Marcus Aurelius,' *Artes*. Stockholm and New York, 1994.

Brunton, Paul. *A Search in Secret India*, London: Random House, 2003.

Caldwell, Sarah. *Oh Terrifying Mother*. Delhi: Oxford University Press, 1999.

Carrol, Noel. 'Art, Invention, Conversation', in Gary Iseminger (ed.) *Intention and Interpretation*. Philadelphia: Temple University Press, 1992.

Castenada, Carlos. *A Separate Reality*. Washington: Washington Square Press, 1991.

Cederlof, Gunnel and K. Sivaramakrishnan. *Ecological Nationalisms*. New Delhi: Permanent Black, 2005.

Clifford, James. *The Predicament of Culture*. Cambridge: Harvard University Press, 1988.

Code, Lorraine. *What Can She Know? Feminist Theory and the Construction of Knowledge*. Ithaca: Cornell University Press, 1991.

Dalrymple, William. *From the Holy Mountain*. London: Flamingo, 1998.

Das, Veena. *Structure and Cognition*. Delhi: Oxford University Press, 1977.

Davis, Richard H. 'Writing as if Icons are Really Alive,' in Michael Meister (ed.) *Ethnography and Personhood*. Jaipur: Rawat Publications, 2000. Pp 87-100.

Diehl, Carl Gustav. 'Human Reaction to Divine identity in Tamil Nadu,' in Asko Parapola (ed.) *South Asian Religion and Society*. Copenhagen and London: Bent Smidt Hanson Curzon Press/ The Riverdale Company, 1986.

Dube, S.C. *Indian Village*. Ithaca: Cornell University Press, 1955.

Duncan, Robert. 'Roots and Branches,' in (ed.) Nathaniel Mackey *Discrepant Engagement*. Cambridge: Cambridge University Press, 1993.

Durkheim, Emile. *The Division of Labour in Society*. New York and London: The Free Press, 1964.

– *The Rules of Sociological Method*. New York: The Free Press, 1966.

– *Moral Education*. New York: The Free Press, 1973.

– *Sociology and Philosophy*. New York: The Free Press, 1974.

– *Elementary Forms of the Religious Life*. New York: The Free Press, 1979.

Eck, Diana L. *Encountering God: A Spiritual Journey from Bozeman to Benares*. Boston: Beacon Press, 1993.

Forest, Kristal. 'All Commotion Eclipsed by Mighty Tsunami of Silence,' *The Mountain Path*, Vol. 42, No., 2005.

Freud, Sigmund. *The Basic Writings* (tr. and ed. A.A. Brill). New York: Random House, 1938.

Gandhi, Ramchandra. *I am Thou*. Delhi: Indian Philosophical Quarterly Publications, 1984.

Geertz, Clifford. *The Interpretation of Cultures*. New York: Basic Books, 1973.

Ginzburg, Carlo. *Wooden Eyes: Nine Reflections on Distance*. New York: Columbia University Press, 2001.

Godman, David. *The Power of the Presence*. Boulder and Pondicherry: Avadhuta Foundation, 2000.

Goodwin, Barbara. *Social Science as Utopia*. Sussex: Harvester Press, 1978.

Hagger, Nicholas. *The Fire and the Stones*. Dorset: Element Books, 1991.

Hampshire, Stuart. *Public and Private Morality*. Cambridge: University of Cambridge, 1978.

Hayden, White. *Tropics of Discourse: Essays in Cultural Criticism*. London and Baltimore: The Johns Hopkins University Press, 1990.

Heller, Agnes. *The Power of Shame*. London: Routledge and Kegan Paul, 1985.

Heyerdahl, Thor. *The Kon Tiki Expedition by Raft Across the South Seas*. London: Allen and Unwin, 1960.

Highburger, Michael. 'Sri Ramana: Friend of Animals,' *The Mountain Path*, Jayanti issue, 2005.

Hillman, James. *Revisioning Psychology*. New York: Harper Perennial, 1976.

Hocking, William Ernest. 'The Mystical Spirit and Protestantism,' in Richard Woods (ed.) *Understanding Mysticism*, New York: Doubleday, 1980.

Holden, Pat (ed). *Women's Religious Experience*. London: Croom and Helms, Barnes and Noble, 1982.

Isemenger, Gary. *Intention and Interpretation*. Philadelphia: Temple University Press, 1992.

Ivan, Illich. *Gender*. New York: Pantheon, 1982.

Iyer, Pico. *The Lady and the Monk*. New York: Vintage, 1991.

Jacobs, Karen. *The Eye's Mind, Literary Modernism and Visual Culture*. Ithaca and London: Cornell University Press, 2001.

Kanakammal, T.R. *Cherished Memories*. Tiruvannamalai: Sri Ramanasramam, 2002.

Kriemild, Saunders. *Feminist Post Development Thought: Rethinking Modernity, Post-Colonialism and Representation*. London: Zubaan and Zed Books, 2004.

Kosinski, Jerzy. *Being There*. UK: Black Swan Publishers, 1999.

Leclercq, Jean. *The Love of Learning and the Desire for God: A Study of Monastic Culture*, New York: Fordham University Press, 1961.

Levi, Primo. *Other People's Trades*. University of Michigan: Summit Books, 1989.

Levi-Strauss, Claude. *Tristes Tropiques*. Harmondsworth: Penguin, 1976.

Lewis, C.S. *Miracles*. Glasgow: Fontana, 1984.

Merton, Thomas. *Thoughts in Solitude*. Trowbridge: Redwood Burn Ltd., 1975.

– *Contemplation in a World of Action*. London: Mandala Unwin, 1980.

Mackey, Nathaniel. *Discrepant Engagement: Dissonance, Cross-Culturality, and Experimental Writing*. Cambridge: Cambridge University Press, 1993.

Maharshi, Sri Ramana, *Collected Works*. Tiruvannamalai: Sri Ramanasrmam, 1996.

Maharshi, Sri Ramana and Murgunar, *Ramana Puranam*. Tiruvannamalai: Sri Ramanasramam Trust, 2006.

Mauss, Marcel. *The Gift*. London: Routledge and Kegan Paul, 1969.

McLellan, David. *Utopian Pessimist: The Life and Thought of Simone Weil*. New York: Poseidon, 1990.

Meister, Michael W. (Ed.) *Ethnography and Personhood*. Jaipur: Rawat Publishers, 2000.

Melvin, J. Lasky. *Utopia and Revolution*. London: Macmillan, 1976.

Menxal, Maria Rosa. *Ornament of the World*. New York: Little Brown and Company, 2002.

Merston, Ethel. 'A Yantra for Scorpion Stings', *The Mountain Path*, Vol. 11, No. 2, April 1965.

Merton, Thomas. 'The Contemplative Life in the Modern World,' *The Mountain Path*, Vol. 11, No. 4, October 1965.

– *Thoughts in Solitude*. Trowbridge: Redwood Burn Ltd., 1975.

– *Contemplation in a World of Action*. London: Mandala Unwin, 1980.

Michel, Maffesoli. *The Time of the Tribes*. London: Sage, 1996.

Mudaliar, Devaraja. *Day by Day with Bhagavan*. Tiruvannamalai: Sri Ramanasramam, 2002.

Myerhoff, Barbara. *Number Our Days*. New York: Touchstone, 1980.

Nagamma, Suri. *Letters and Recollections of Sri Ramanasramam*. Tiruvannamalai: Sri Ramanasramam, 1992.

– *My Life at Sri Ramanasramam*. Sri Ramanasramam, Tiruvannamalai, 1993.

– *Letters from Sri Ramanasramam*. Volumes I and II. Tiruvannamalai: Sri Ramanasramam, 1995.

Natrajan, A.R. 'The Hound of Heaven,' *The Mountain Path*, Vol. 23, No. 4, October 1986.

Om, Sri Sadhu. *The Path of Sri Ramana*. Tiruvannamalai: Sri Ramana Kshetra, 1997.

Osborne, Arthur. *Buddhism and Christianity in the Light of Hinduism*. Tiruvannamalai: Sriramanasramam, 1996.

– *Be Still, It is the Wind that Sings*. Tiruvannamalai: Sri Ramanasramam, 2000.

– *My Life and Quest*.Tiruvannamalai: Sri Ramanasramam, 2001.

– *The Teachings of Ramana Maharshi in his own Words*. Tiruvannamalai:Sri Ramanasramam, 2002.

– *Ramana Maharshi and the Path of Self-Knowledge*. Tiruvannamalai: Sri Ramanasramam, 2004.

Osborne, Katya. 'Images,' *The Mountain Path*. Advent, 2004.

– 'The Hill,' *The Mountain Path*, Aradhana Issue, 2005.

Otto, Rudolf. *The Idea of the Holy*. London: Oxford University Press, 1981.

Pamuk, Orhan. *Istanbul*. London: Faber and Faber, 2005.

Pandian, M.S.S. *Brahmin and Non-Brahmin*, Delhi/Ranikhet: Permanent Black, 2007.
Panikkar, Raimundo. *Mantramanjari: The Vedic Experience*. London: Longman and Todd, 1979.
Paranjape, Makarand, 'Pilgrims and Other Travellers,' *The IIC Quarterly*, Spring, 1999.
Petrement, Simone. *Simone Weil: A Life*. New York: Pantheon, 1976.
Pinney, Christopher. *Photos of the Gods*. Delhi: Oxford University Press, 2004.
Quammen, David. *The Song of the Dodo: Island Biogeography in an age of Extinctions*. New York: Scribner, 2004.
Quilkey, Christopher. 'The Maha Nirvana,' *The Mountain Path*, Aradhna Issue, 2004.
Ramaswamy, Sethu. *They Spoke with God: Saints of Tamilaham*. Delhi: D.K. Printworld, 2009.
Ramaswamy, Vijaya. *Walking Naked: Women, Society, Spirituality in South India*. Shimla: Indian Institute of Advanced Study, 1997.
Ramamurthy, T.V. 'Henri Cartier Bresson, Photographer,' *The Mountain Path*, Jayanti Issue, 2005.
Rajan, N.N. 'Suffer Little Children,' *The Mountain Path*, Vol. 111, No. 1, Tiruvannamalai: Sri Ramanasramam, 1966.
Resnic, Saloman. *Theatre of the Dream*. Tavistock, London, 1987.
Rhys, Jean. *Wide Sargasso Sea*. New York: W.W. Norton, 1992.
Ricoeur, Paul. *History and Truth*. Toronto: University of Toronto Press, 1977.
– *Freud and Philosophy*. New Haven and London: Yale University Press, 1978.
Rosaldo, Renato. *Culture and Truth*. Boston: Beacon Press, 1989.
Sacks, Oliver. *Awakenings*. London: Vintage, 1993.
Sadhu, Om. *The Path of Sri Ramana*, Sri Ramana Kshetra, Kanvashrama Trust, Pondicherry, 1997.
Sadhu, Mouni. *In Days of Great Peace*. Tiruvannamalai: Sri Ramanasramam, 2001.
Said, Edward. *The World, the Text and the Critic*. Cambridge: Harvard University Press, 1983.
Sivakumar, M. 'First Photograph of Sri Bhagavan,' *The Mountain Path*, Deepam Issue, 2004.
Samuel, Raphael. *Theatres of Memory*. London: Verso, 1994.
Schur, Max. *Freud: Living and Dying*. Hogarth Press, London, 1972.
Serres, Michel. *Hermes, Literature, Science, Philosophy*. Baltimore: The Johns Hopkins University Press, 1982.
Seyhan, Azade. *Writing Outside the Nation*. New Jersey: Princeton University Press, 2001.
Sharma, Arvind. *Ramana Maharshi: The Sage of Arunachala*. Delhi: Penguin Viking, 2006.
Singer, June. *Androgyny: Towards a New Theory of Sexuality*. New York: Anchor Books, 1977.
Snyder, Gary. 'The Voice of the Dharma,' *The Mountain Path*, Vol. V, No 2, 1968.
– *Passage Through India*. San Fransisco: Grey Fox Press, 1983.
Sontag, Susan. *Styles of Radical Will*, Anchor, 1969.
– *Illness as Metaphor*. New York: Random House, 1979.
Soper, Kate. *What is Nature? Culture, Politics and the Non-Human*. Oxford: Blackwell, 1995.
Sri Bhagavan's Devotees. *Ramana's Arunachala*. Tiruvannamalai: Sri Ramanasramam, 2004.
Sri Ramana Maharshi and Sri Murgunar, *Ramana Puranam*. Tiruvannamalai: Sri Ramanasramam, 2006.
Stills, Judith. *Feminine Economies*. Manchester: Manchester University Press, 1997.
Stocking, George. W. *Observers Observed*. Wisconsin: University of Wisconsin Press, 1983.
Stuart, J.D.M. *Swami Abhishiktananda: His life told through his letters*. Delhi: ISPCK, 1989.

– *Abhishiktananda: Ascent to the Depth of the Heart*. (selections from the Spiritual diary by Raimon Panikkar, and translated by David Fleming and James Stuart.) Delhi: ISPCK, 1998.

– 'Swami Abhishiktananda: The Awakening,' *The Mountain Path*, Aradhana Issue, 1993.

Suryanandan, Mahalakshmi, *Ramana Glory Be To You*. Chennai, 1997.

Swami, Narsimha B.V. *Self-Realization*. Tiruvannamalai: Sriramanasramam, 1931.

Taleyarkhan, Firoza. 'How I came to the Maharshi,' *The Mountain Path*, Vol 11, No 2, 1965.

– *Sages, Saints and Arunachala Ramana*. Delhi and Madras: Orient Longmans, 1970.

Supreme Court of India Civil Appellate Jurisdiction: Commissioner Tiruvannamalai vs. Arunachal Giri Pradikhina Samiti.

Turner, Victor. *Process, Performance and Pilgrimage*. New Delhi: Concept Publishing House, 1979.

Visvanathan, Shiv. 'Unravelling Rights' in *Sacred Mountains Everywhere* (ed.) Corinne Kumar, Streelekha Bangalore, 1995.

Visvanathan, Susan. *The Christians of Kerala*. Chennai: Oxford University Press, 1993.

– *Missionary Styles and the Problem of Dialogue*. Shimla: Indian Institute of Advanced Study, 1995.

– *An Ethnography of Mysticism*, Shimla: Indian Institute of Advanced Study, 1998.

– *Something Barely Remembered*. Delhi: Roli Books/IndiaInk, 2000.

– 'Through Death to Devotion,' *Heroes, Pilgrims, Explorers*, The IIC Quarterly Winter 2003-Spring 2004.

– 'Activism and Detachment,' *Trajectory of French Thought*. Vol. 2. Delhi: French Information Resource Centre in association with Rupa, 2006.

– 'Travellers and Pilgrims,' *Think India Quarterly*. Vol. 9, No 4 October-December 2006.

– *Friendship, Interiority and Mysticism*. Delhi: Orient Longman, 2007.

Weil, Simone, *Oppression and Liberty*. Amherst: University of Massachussets, 1973a.

– *Waiting on God*. London and Glasgow: Collins, 1973b.

– *Gravity and Grace*. London: Routledgae and Kegan Paul, 1987a.

– *The Need for Roots*. London: Routledge and Kegan Paul (Ark), 1987b.

– *Formative Writings 1924-1941*. London: Routledge and Kegan Paul, 1987c.

White, George Abbott (Ed.). *Simone Weil: Interpretations of a Life*. Amherst: University of Massachusetts Press, 1981.

Wilden, Anthony. *System and Structure: Essays in Communication and Exchange*. New York: Tavistock and Methuen, 1980.

Wittkower, Rudolf. *Allegory and the Migration of Symbols*. Hampshire: Thames and Hudson, 1987.

Susan Visvanathan is Chairperson, Centre for the Study of Social Systems, School of Social Sciences at Jawaharlal Nehru University, New Delhi. From 1983 till 1997 she was Lecturer in Sociology, Hindu College, University of Delhi.

She was Fellow Nehru Memorial Museum and Library, New Delhi, from 1989 to 1992; Honorary Fellow at Indian Institute of Advanced Studies, Shimla, from 1990 to 1995; Charles Wallace Fellow to Queen's University, Belfast, in 1997; Visiting Professor to Maison des Sciences de L' Hommes, Paris, in 2004, and is consultant editor, *Contributions to Indian Society*.

She is the author of *The Christians of Kerala*, *An Ethnography of Mysticism*, *Structure and Transformation* and *Friendship, Interiority and Mysticism*. Her works of fiction include *Something Barely Remembered*, *The Visiting Moon*, *Phosphorous and Stone* and *The Seine at Noon*.

